HOW TO
BEAT THE
SALARY TRAP

HOW TO BEAT THE SALARY TRAP

8 Steps to Financial Independence

RICHARD KING RIFENBARK
WITH
DAVID JOHNSON

McGRAW-HILL BOOK COMPANY

New York   St. Louis   San Francisco
Düsseldorf   London   Mexico   Sydney   Toronto

Book design by Stanley Drate.

4 5 6 7 8 9 0   B P B P   7 8 3 2 1 0 9 8

Library of Congress Cataloging in Publication Data

Rifenbark, Richard King.
How to beat the salary trap.
Includes index.
1. Finance, Personal.   2. Investments.   3. Real
estate investment.   I.   Johnson, Dave, 1931–
II. Title.
HG179.R53   332'.024   77-16118
ISBN 0-07-052810-1

It is important t
affection my late
Rifenbark, D.D.,
attention and lov
her patience with
her father and m
encouragement.

For professio
experts:

William J. A
Robert S. Ba
Gordon Betz
Theodore Ch
George Elkir
Edward John
Robert W. G
Guy H. Hay
Douglas Hill
Burt Hughes
Joseph H. Jo
Franklin Lar
Richard Mac
Robert M. N
Cleve Traug

Contents

HOW TO
BEAT THE
SALARY TRAP

Introduction

Freedom from Salary

By bourgeoisie is meant the class of modern capitalists, owners of the means of social production and employers of wage labor. By proletariat, the class of modern wage laborers, who, having no means of production of their own, are reduced to selling their labor-power in order to live.

> FRIEDRICH ENGELS (1820–1895)
> Footnote to Manifesto of the Communist Party

Please, sir, I want some more.

> CHARLES DICKENS (1812–1870) *Oliver Twist*

Some people are born rich. Most of us are not. Some nine months before our first breath of life, the die was cast—and we lost out on that free ride to fortune.

Some people marry rich. Most of us do not. The parent tells the child, "It's as easy to marry rich as it is to marry poor." But that's not the case at all. Besides there being a chronic shortage of eligible rich of the proper gender, the peculiar chemistry that attracts one man and one woman to each other does not depend on a fat bank account as a necessary ingredient. And marrying for money alone may be one of the less successful social contracts.

So we have had two chances at easy riches—and lost out on both. Have we used up our lifetime allotment of possibilities?

1

Consider this: behind every family fortune is one ancestor of modest means (not unlike you or me) who set aside an amount from his earnings, put it into something he thought would increase in value, and was successful at it.

If we are *not* rich and we *want to be* rich, the conclusion must be: we shall have to accomplish this for ourselves. And it is probably more attainable than you think—no matter how sourly you view your current condition. Especially if you are a salaried worker.

In fact, if you now enjoy a regular, dependable source of income—salary, hourly wage, or fees—you have a powerful tool for the creation of wealth. Too few people understand the true power of it.

The regular income from a job gives you a number of very real advantages. A job presents you with specific amounts of cold cash at predetermined time intervals. It has a history and a future, and therefore is reasonably predictable. It does not occupy all your waking hours—you have surplus time which is yours to use at your discretion for your own advantage.

These are tremendous assets.

But your life as a salaried employee is not all wine and roses. On the debit side of the ledger, you have traded away part of your soul—your independence—for cash. You are no longer a completely free man or woman. Your work is not at *your* will, it is at *management's*. If spring beckons through your window, you can't go; you are chained to the obligations of your job. You are trapped by your need for regular income.

With a job, your future is fenced in. Your pay is reckoned at the going rate. Other than annual salary increases (which are soon devoured by the rising cost of living and taxes) you have few ways of getting more spendable dollars —unless you moonlight a second job or put your spouse to work. If you have reached the top of your trade or profession, the future may be even bleaker. Upward movement is halted.

If you enjoy your job, you are blessed. The majority of American workers do not. For many, the job is a box, a cage, a treadmill to oblivion. They are forced to live a grey half-life of economic necessity.

What about this apparent conflict between the financial security of salaried employment and independence? And which is more important to you?

If it is a hard decision, don't worry about it. You can take the salary earned from your present occupation and put it to work obtaining your financial freedom. You can have both.

That is what this book is about: the alternative to being born rich or wed rich, the alternative of self-gained wealth— how to take the assets you have today and build them into something of far greater value. These are lessons in how to become richer by the paycheck, in discovering how to beat the salary trap.

I know it works: I've been there and I've done it.

I was not born rich.

My father was an Episcopal clergyman in San Jose, California, who spent a disproportionate amount of his life fighting the battle of the budget on a minister's salary. When my sisters and I wanted to go to college, it was a struggle for my mother and father.

Although I don't believe my father was unhappy with his lot—he was dedicated to his calling—living would have been easier if there had been more money. In the end, his comfortable retirement was financed less by his church pension than by a number of small, shrewd investments he had made in the stock market over the years.

As I write this, I sit in the study of my home, surrounded by the trappings of wealth. Around me are files and records of three decades of wealth-building. How well have I done? Better than I imagined I would do when I began. And I have no great yearnings for more. I'll give you a partial list of my financial assets—not out of egotism or pride, but to illustrate a point.

This house and land are today worth over $200,000. I own these free and clear. My home is decorated with art and antiques valued at nearly $100,000—although, because they were lovingly collected, I have no wish to sell them. The garage below houses two cars, a Jaguar and a Mercedes, for which I paid cash. My safe deposit boxes and brokerage accounts hold close to $300,000 in stocks and bonds. I own two apartment houses which could be sold tomorrow for upwards of $2,000,000.

I belong to several of Los Angeles' most expensive clubs, where, if I wished, I could play golf or tennis or swim with fellow members whose names you might recognize. If I wanted to take a trip around the world or buy a jet or a yacht, I could do so without financial inconvenience. If I wanted to do absolutely nothing useful for the rest of my life, I could do it and still leave a substantial estate for my children.

My point is this: nothing that I own came to me by inheritance or windfall or a great stroke of luck. For thirty years I was a salaried employee—and all that I have today grew from the simple manipulation of that income.

When I was a very young man, fresh out of the Navy following World War II, I took a job with a large Los Angeles department store. I started low on the corporate ladder, as a salesman in the men's clothing department. My salary was $43.50 a week.

This was barely enough for a man and wife to live on, much less provide us with all the glorious toys the world has to offer—for those who have money enough. I wanted *things* —a lot of *things*. A better car, a home of my own, dining out in expensive restaurants, more freedom to maneuver about the world. I was very impatient. I wanted to get on with it.

Caught between my need for a regular income and my ambition to be financially independent, I decided I would take matters into my own hands. With a small amount of money saved from military service, I would invest.

To my surprise and chagrin, I generally made a botch of it. I committed most of the classic errors of the novice investor: I was ignorant about the ways money works; in too great a hurry to get it fast; with no comprehensive plan; without the know-how to ration time.

Dumb about Money

Money knowledge is a critical gap in our educations. We do not learn it at our parent's knees nor in our classrooms. There is literally no one to teach us. The theoreticians have too little practical experience—and the rich keep their secrets. As a result, few ordinary citizens know much more than bare basics about money—especially when it comes to the effective management of personal financial affairs. This applies even to bright, talented, sophisticated people who are money-motivated. I have found, for example, many fine executives who are brilliant at handling their companies' monies yet dismal failures at managing their own.

As it ended up, I had to teach myself about money and investing—slow work, trial and error (more errors than I care to recall). I became financially sophisticated only through practice—developing an investment mentality, and learning the rules of the game.

Rushing for the Gold

When ambition is the spur, many of us will dash off after the first rabbit that looks like opportunity, ignoring any dangers in the pursuit.

The quickest gains are promised generally in investments with higher risks. With only a limited amount of capital, the tendency is to concentrate on a few high-opportunity, high-risk investments. While one can be lucky from time to time, the odds against an unbroken string of successes in high-risk investments are against you. I have known smart investors who have lost several years' progress in their wealth-building through a single stroke of bad judgment.

The salaried person managing risk investment with limited means is like a cat on a hot tin roof. Between the immediate demands of the job and the chancy nature of your private enterprise, it is hard to do justice to either: one or the other is bound to suffer. Most important, the wild, "crapshooting" type of investment precludes sensible controls. You have thrown your destiny up in the air to see where it bounces. It is the Las Vegas syndrome. Historically, the most successful investors are those who develop a methodical attitude. They plan to shape events rather than allowing events to shape them.

Early on, I learned to curb my impulsive instincts to a degree. Certainly, thousands of winning investers have been more cautious than I, and as many have been more courageous.

I have chosen the middle role, somewhere between the tiger and the chicken. And, to date, I have avoided being either shot as big game, or plucked.

Planning to Get Rich

Accumulating wealth is not a random affair—a few dollars invested here and there, now and then, willy-nilly. It is a planned endeavor, orchestrated like a symphonic work rising to a grand finale.

Once I had accepted planning as an essential ingredient

of my financial success, my wealth-building moved ahead at a much quicker pace. Not everything in life is plannable—the world has a quixotic way of presenting you with surprises, pleasant and otherwise. But with a set of goals in mind and a realistic plan about how you expect to achieve them, you have both a blueprint for success and a measure against which to mark progress. You can even plan to expect the unexpected.

Time to Get Rich

For the salaried person, free time to indulge in personal pursuits—especially during the business day—is a precious commodity. It took me a while to get a handle on time.

Retail is a demanding occupation requiring endless attention to detail, long hours, weekend and holiday work, and constantly changing patterns of endeavor. The hours I spent with my investments were largely caught on the fly—captured and accumulated in fragments from lunchtimes, evenings and weekends—a few minutes here, a few there; time that I might have spent in relaxation or busy work, or dreamed away.

As I moved up through the organization, time became even more dear. As my salary increased, so did my responsibilities. Free time rarely presented itself; it had to be sought. I was forced to learn to use time as a tool, grasping and manipulating it to suit my objectives.

I regret none of these snatched bits of time. I enjoyed them. I felt I was applying them to build my ultimate financial independence. It proved to be time well spent.

By the time I had gone through my financial growing pains, I had developed a strategy for the methodical building of wealth, refining and shaping my program to suit the tenor of the times.

It was a program ideally suited to my needs as a salaried person, starting with tiny capital, little free time, and no wish to jeopardize my family's future with risky enterprise. Most people would call it a conservative money plan—not a way to get rich quickly, but a way to get rich surely and safely.

These are some of its advantages:

1. *It does not take a lot of money to get started.* You can begin it today, whether you are saving only a little, barely breaking even, or going into debt.

2. *It is relatively hassle-free.* It won't interfere with your job. A few hours a week are all that are needed to manage your personal wealth-building program.

3. *It is safe.* You do not have to take big chances. And wherever risk is assumed, there is a secure spot to fall back to.

4. *It is structured.* Many of the most difficult decisions have already been tested, evaluated and judged. Where practical, it is firm in spelling out opportunities to take and hazards to avoid.

5. *It is flexible.* As economic patterns change, so do your wealth-building strategies. You can learn how to manage recession and inflation, rising and falling interest rates, and the penalties of taxation—the factors that can hinder or destroy many ambitious financial programs.

However you regard it, as conservative or visionary, chicken or tiger, I will tell you that it worked for me (as it has since worked for others). Over the years, I watched my net worth grow from paycheck to paycheck, through good times and bad.

When I turned fifty-five, I retired from the retail world. Thanks to the success of my financial plan, my net worth had grown to over a million dollars. I earned more from my investments than from my salary.

As I look back over my salaried years, I do not recall my wealth-building efforts as being particularly difficult. It was more like a hobby, a sport played with money. While there were times when I wished I had somewhat more discretionary cash to spend on one or another of life's pleasures, I never really deprived my family or myself of life's necessities. Actually, the process was relatively painless.

In point of fact, for the past fifteen years or so I have lived like a millionaire—without actually being one. Someone, I forget who, defined living like a millionaire as having as much cash to spend each year as would be generated from a million dollars conservatively invested. If, for example, a person invested a million dollars in 5 percent tax-free municipal bonds, the annual income derived would be $50,000. From my combined salary and investments, I have been able to spend this with surplus left over for quite a number of years.

I bring this up only to illustrate that I did not pursue wealth with the accelerator flat to the floor. If I had, I might have been far wealthier than I am today. But what would be the purpose of it? I preferred to dally along the path, enjoying some of the wild berries of my success rather than rushing them off to market.

That, for the moment, is enough about me. This is not an autobiography—I am to appear for brief moments, as a case in point, in profile, with my good side showing. This book is intended to be about you—your money and your life —and what you hope to gain from them.

If you are a salaried worker and are dissatisfied with the way your days and dreams are going, perhaps there is something in my experience that can help you change your life around to the way you want it.

I have been where you are. I will tell you the things I have learned about money and wealth-building—from the point of view of the salaried employee. I will lay out the hard facts of where your opportunities lie and what you should beware of. These are practical facts: many you can put to use right away.

I think you will find this book useful . . .

- if you are on a salary treadmill and want to get off
- if you are losing too much income to taxes
- if you wish to retire at an age young enough to enjoy it
- if you want to build an estate for your children and grandchildren
- if you want freedom from financial worries for the rest of your life
- if you want to start a business of your own some day
- if you want to put spare income to work and not have to worry about it
- if you want to safeguard yourself against inflation and recession
- if you are intrigued by the secrets of wealth-building and want to start something on your own
- if you have been a financial loser up to now and want to get on the right track
- if you find happiness in material possessions
- if you enjoy the fun of seeing your wealth grow day by day
- if you are serious in any way about money—making it, spending it, saving it, investing it.

If you are interested in any of these, I have some things to tell you.

LEARNING THE STEPS

One able career woman I knew who had always lived to the limit of her income came upon an unplanned emergency and was suddenly inundated with bills she could not pay.

When she came to me for counsel, I outlined a step-by-step financial recovery plan for her, which she promised to follow. First she retrenched, cut her expenses in order to work herself out of her immediate problem. When the bills had finally been paid off, she decided to continue to live within her reduced budget, saving some money each month. She invested prudently in a bullish stock market and with part of her profits bought a piece of income real estate. With the depreciation she earned from the real estate sheltering a portion of her income, she continued to save and enlarge her investments.

Today she is financially secure and independent. Although she started her program late in life, she will be able to retire at least five years ahead of normal company retirement with no money worries.

This woman's story is not exceptional—it is the rule. I have seen it played out many times over. *Any person* with a regular source of income, a little knowledge, a little discipline, a little judgment, *and a plan* can find financial security.

Following is an outline of the personal financial plan that I gradually assembled and shaped in the course of my salaried career.

The Steps to Financial Independence.
1. Know your net worth.
2. Budget your expenses.
3. Define your goals.
4. Choose your team.
5. Create a cash equivalent reserve.
6. Build a liquidity reserve.
7. Establish an optional investment fund.
8. Invest in residential income real estate.

Eight steps—they are all you need virtually to assure the financial rewards you seek. You will find some easy, some hard, but all attainable. I will flesh out these bare bone rules for you, show you how they work and why they are important. You will discover the techniques and strategies that have helped build a fortune for me. I'll show you formulas to live by, temptations to avoid.

Once you develop a taste for wealth-building you will find it becomes a life-long interest. As your net worth grows, as you achieve success, you will discover within yourself an eagerness to reach out, to do more, to try more.

If you have the will, and fortune is on your side, I would not be at all surprised if you don't do better than I have.

You can beat the salary trap. All that is required is that you decide that you *want* to do it.

The decision is yours. Make it. The clock is ticking.

1

The Rules
of the Game

*There is nothing about money that cannot be understood by the person
of reasonable curiosity, diligence and intelligence.*
—JOHN KENNETH GALBRAITH (1908–   ) *Money*

> *The rich man has his motor car,*
>   *His country and his town estate.*
> *He smokes a fifty-cent cigar,*
>   *And jeers at fate . . .*
> *Yet though my lamp burn low and dim,*
>   *Though I must slave for livelihood,*
> *Think you that I would change with him?*
>   *You bet I would!*
> —FRANKLIN PIERCE ADAMS (1881–1960)
>   "The Rich Man"

This book is a scenario for the methodical development of
wealth. It is a thumbnail sketch, a plot outline, a road map,
a blueprint, for the regular, orderly creation of wealth from
ordinary income. It is designed specifically for the man or
woman who is gainfully employed and earns a reasonably
dependable income (large or small) from salary, hourly wage
or fees—and who will continue working through most of the
course of the program. It is a step-by-step program, de-
scribing the kinds of wealth-building opportunities and liabilities that lie along your route. It shows you the factors that

are wealth-enhancing (i.e., have the potential to increase your wealth), and those that are wealth-inhibiting (have the potential to stifle or decrease your wealth). Before you take your first step, however, there is some preparation involved.

If you want to climb a mountain and prefer to accomplish it with life and limbs intact, you embark on two prudent procedures before you even approach the base. First, you will want to assure that you are personally prepared—that your training is sufficient; that your physical conditioning is adequate; and that your climbing equipment is complete and in good order. Then when you are required to cross a sheer rock face or climb an ice fall, you will know what to do, be ready with the proper gear, and have the stamina to carry it out. Second, you will want to become thoroughly knowledgeable about the mountain's terrain—where the easy ascents are located and where the hazards lie.

These are the first two rules of mountain climbing. They will considerably improve your chances of reaching the peak, and of descending at a speed less than the acceleration of gravity in free fall.

Building wealth requires similar preconditions. The first is personal—the development of a wealth-building mentality, an investment mentality. The second is learning the terrain —the facts of life about money and money marketplaces. These are the first two rules of wealth-building.

Profile of a Wealth-Builder

I assume you are already an achiever—that you want more from life than life is willing to lay in your lap. And that is a very good beginning. But it is only a beginning. The critical factor that separates the wealth-*winner* from the wealth-*loser* is your wealth-building mentality—the ways you think about your money and its use. Let me give you some examples of the influence of the wealth-building mentality on our ambitions for wealth.

According to an Associated Press article emanating from Detroit, the typical U.S. wage earner in 1976 made $13,847 a year but ended the year $500 in debt.

B. James Theodoroff, executive vice president of trusts at Detroit Bank & Trust Company, describes the typical wage earner as a thirty-eight-year-old father of two who lives in a comfortable home, drives a fairly new car, never has more than $50 lying around the house, and whose checking account usually drops below zero before his next paycheck rolls around.

He hasn't saved enough money either for his retirement or for his children's education. He typically has a small estate with a net worth of $38,000. Says Theodoroff: "If he dies, he's going to leave it all to his wife, and she's going to have to go to work right after the funeral." His financial affairs are in such a mess, he can't afford to die.

"He's living hand-to-mouth," says Theodoroff, "and it's because he refuses to change his lifestyle.

"Back when we had the big layoffs in 1974, when things were very bleak around here, you could go out to Woodward Avenue, Detroit's main street, and all of the restaurants had cars lined up with people going to dinner on Friday night.

"Now if the economy was so bleak, why in the world were all these people having dinner out, rather than buying hamburger at the store and cooking at home?"

The *typical wage earner*—is this a wealth-enhancing mentality? You tell me.

Let's take a step up in income, if not in acumen.

The *Wall Street Journal* quotes Francis W. Keane, vice president for financial counseling for New York's Citibank. Mr. Keane advises mostly senior business executives earning in excess of $50,000 a year, many with estates of a half-million dollars or more.

". . . Most of the successful businessmen (we) advise have made glaring errors or omissions in handling their personal finances. One counselor says fewer than 25% of the executives he sees have systematic savings."

Mr. Keane notes that even among executives who are fifty years or older, fewer than one-third have any plans for financing their retirement. Ninety percent of the executives he advises are overconcentrated in their own company stock. And, of the executives who trade in securities, for every one who trades too often, five are sitting and holding investments which no longer make sense.

Mr. Keane remarks: "And they consider that this year's overspending is harmless because next year's income will be higher. A lot depend on their bonuses to make payments on their boats.

"The fundamental flaw, counselors say, is lack of a coherent plan. Many executives have failed to set financial goals. Consequently, their investments are dictated by what they think they can spare now . . . instead of what they will need in the future."

The *typical high-salaried executive*—is this a wealth-enhancing mentality? I don't think so.

How many citizens from the highest to the lowest income groups end their careers disillusioned, disappointed, living out their retirement years with far fewer of life's pleasures than they have been accustomed to, simply because their life scenarios have betrayed them? The number must be staggering.

The "typical salaried worker" treated himself to his Friday dinner out on the town even as his financial world was crumbling about him. He had worked, he had suffered: he *deserved* a reward—or at least so he told himself. The "high-salaried executive" was buying his boat, relying on a bonus to pay for it. If the bonus never came, he was in trouble. But he had worked, he had suffered: he *deserved* a reward, etc.

Both groups of salaried workers could be extolled as achievers and for their hard work. Remember, at least half the population is not trying so hard or doing so well.

Yet as wealth-builders they are losers. Their life attitudes are wealth-inhibiting. Neither will end up approaching his potential wealth. Different settings, different salary levels—same scenario.

The typical winner in the game of wealth-building is *goal directed*—that is, he can look into the future, see what he wants of it, and then take steps to get it. He has long-range goals—and short-range goals.

Many achievers have short-range goals—a new car, a higher position in the company, a European vacation, or whatever. But when they acquire their limited objectives, their goal direction peters out. They float again in the sea of untranquility, moved by the winds and tides, going who knows where.

Another attribute of the wealth-game winner is what psychologists call "recognition of the delayed reward." In simplest terms this means that he is able to postpone the pleasures of today in return for the expected greater pleasures of tomorrow.

A monkey in a laboratory experiment can be trained to press a lever in return for the immediate reward of a banana or a grape. Gradually he can be educated to perform even more complex tasks with multiple buttons, levers, symbols and flashing lights—so long as he is rewarded at the end of his efforts.

A squirrel, who has acquired his survival mechanisms in far harsher climates, has it built into his genes that at certain seasons of the year he will gather food, not to eat on the spot, but to cache away in anticipation of the need for a midwinter supermarket.

I have no particular preference for one animal over the other, but when the economic climate turns wintery, I think I would rather be a squirrel.

Certain life attitudes are wealth-inhibiting—the hedonist, the passivist, the plunger, the visionary . . . each has a particular life *modus operandi* that discourages the accumulation of wealth. Each of us, to some degree, will exhibit these tendencies from time to time. We will spoil ourselves, we will lie back, we will gamble unwisely, we will dream foolish dreams. It helps make life more interesting. But when any one of these wealth-inhibiting character traits becomes our dominant way of doing business, our futures are in jeopardy.

Developing life attitudes that are wealth-enhancing can make the difference between success and failure. No amount of information or intelligence can survive the lack of an investment mentality.

Following are some life attitudes that I believe are essential for the development of wealth. Since I am directing my attention to you as a salaried worker, I will emphasize those most significant to you.

The Priority of the Job

Your job (and the income you derive from it) is the primary source of your wealth. Without it, you have lost your source of wealth-building power. Therefore it must continue to take precedence over any personal wealth-building efforts. Your job comes first.

This places certain limitations on the scope of your wealth-building activities. They must be relatively low-maintenance and hassle-free. They cannot be a constant concern. Too much attention to your personal program can create job problems which you do not need.

You cannot afford, for example, to become a super-active trader in any of the investment markets. These are fast tracks and call for close supervision. While they have great wealth-enhancing potential, they can be wealth-inhibiting (you can lose your shirt) if the market turns suddenly against you when you are ill-prepared for it.

Of necessity, you must begin as a most conservative investor, conducting your business in safe, slow-moving markets where the safety of your equity is not endangered by a lack of daily attention.

If you are desperately unhappy with your job as it is, you may find it necessary to change it for one you would like better—even to the extent of accepting a lesser salary. If you are only mildly disgruntled with your job, frustrated by your inability to move ahead faster, you may find your personal wealth-building program giving you a whole new, cheerful attitude about it. As the source of your future wealth, it may suddenly be surprisingly attractive.

The Conservation of Capital

Your first effort in wealth-building is the accumulation of discretionary cash from your income. This means accepting the discipline of a methodical savings program. There is no other way.

Even if you have already gathered an investment nut, you must still develop a savings program for yourself. The creation of investment reserves is absolutely essential—without exception.

Your second effort in wealth-building is to keep the capital you have saved. In the beginning, you will take no risks with it. No risks. None. These earliest dollars saved are the most precious dollars in your entire investment life.

Later, you will be able to accept calculated risk as you

reach out for greater appreciation of your capital. But at the start there can be no jeopardizing of the cash you have taken so much time and effort to gather.

The Requirement of Compounding

As you invest your capital savings in safe investment vehicles, you will receive a return on them; that is, they will give you a profit. Most, if not all, of this profit must be returned to the investment vehicle to compound.

Compounding of profits is the simplest way of pyramiding your wealth—profit dollars creating more profit dollars creating more profit dollars, and so on, ad infinitum. If you lived long enough, this simple compounding alone might make your rich.

Let me give you an extravagant and impractical example —just to illustrate the mechanisms involved: Place a chessboard in front of you, and put a penny in the square in the lower lefthand corner. The penny is your initial investment. The game works like this: As you move your penny one square to the right, you are paid a one penny profit. You now have two pennies to invest. Move your two pennies one square to the right and you are paid a profit of two pennies. You now have four pennies to invest. And so forth.

In other words, each time you move your investment to a new square, you receive a profit equal to it—your investment doubles. And you will let your profit ride to compound.

If you continued advancing your investment and compounding your profit along the rows of squares on your chessboard, how much do you suppose you would have by the time you reached the final square? $50? $100? $1000?

Remember that the chessboard has 64 squares, so if you took your profit as you went along, you would have earned 63¢ plus your original investment of the penny—for a total of 64¢ capital and appreciation.

If you let your original penny compound across the chessboard, on the final square it would be worth more than eight hundred *quadrillion* dollars—$801,374,208,000,000,000. (Don't hold me to this precise figure as my calculator and I both got fatigued before the process was over.)

I don't know how you can mentally handle a number this large. Annual retail sales in this country are currently running at about $600 billion (which itself is no easy amount to picture). Our chessboard figure is more than a million three hundred thousand times this.

If you enjoy this sort of fantasy, consider the effects of compounding from another perspective: If you started at the age of twenty setting aside $2.80 a day from your income, and invested it in ways that would give you a compound growth rate of 15%, you would be a millionaire before you were fifty-five. (This does not take into account the melancholy aspects of the IRS, so it is as much a science fiction as the first example.)

In real life you'll have trouble enough getting a 15% return on your investment year after year, much less doubling it. But the effects of compounding can be quite startling when carried forward over long periods of time.

Still, simple compounding is not enough. You have neither the time nor the patience to depend on compounding alone—but it is a sound beginning.

The Necessity of Good Health

Any investment program that starts near ground zero needs time to realize its full potential. This means that you must live a good long life to enjoy its fruits.

Taking proper care of your money-making machine (you) is wealth-enhancing. Burning your candle at both ends is wealth-inhibiting. If you let yourself get sick enough, you

won't give a damn whether you make your million or not—
all you want to do is get well.

The Factor of Planning

To get from where you are today to where you want to
be is a long trip—it will take time. How long it will take
depends on too many unknowable factors to calculate. If
you are lucky and economic conditions are favorable, your
trip could be shortened considerably.

Nearly all things can be accomplished in time (little
drops of water, little grains of sand, etc.), but to control your
financial endeavors over a long period of time necessitates
planning—setting goals for a year from now, for five years
from now, for ten years from now. You have to know where
you are going, else how will you know when you've gotten
there?

Planning, both short- and long-term, is essential to effective wealth-building.

The Importance of Record-keeping

Memory is a frail and capricious device. You cannot depend on it. There are great differences between reports
written in the heat of battle and memoirs of the battle set
down years after.

For some people, record-keeping is a tedium, a drag, a
joyless endeavor. However, for success in wealth-building,
the maintenance of current, accurate records is vital.

If record-keeping repels you, think of it in the same
light as taking out the trash every night: not one of life's
ennobling activities, but the alternatives are even less appetizing. Develop the habit of keeping accurate records of your

financial enterprises—whether you enjoy it or not. As your wealth grows, it becomes more entertaining.

These, then, are your essential personal wealth-enhancing objectives—the start of your investment mentality:

1. Assuring your continuing income by not short-changing your job;
2. Conserving capital from your income through savings and then insuring it is totally protected;
3. Returning your profits back into your investments so that they may compound;
4. Keeping yourself healthy;
5. Developing short- and long-term plans and goals;
6. Keeping records of your financial activities.

MONEY AND MONEY MARKETS

The game of wealth-building is governed (as are all games) by rules. Some are as strict as those of a monastic order. Others are as tenuous as spider webs—the merest suggestions of rules—allowing you opportunity for creative artistry.

Before participating in any game, you'll want to learn the rules that pertain to it—whether the game is Parcheesi, ice hockey or Russian roulette.

These are some of the rules concerning money and money markets.

The United States Government

When the name of the game is wealth-building, the chief rulemaker is our federal government in Washington, D.C. Our government is the world's biggest business establishment—the biggest employer, the biggest moneylender and the biggest money borrower. In these conditions rest the source of its power.

One of government's first responsibilities to its citizens is to create opportunities for the enhancement of their wealth. In view of this end, our lawmakers have decided that the characteristics of the totally free economy—boom and bust, feast and famine, overheated production and recession—are not in the best economic interests of the population as a whole. So we live, like it or not, in a controlled economy.

However, the controls are imperfect and often clumsily managed. As a result, our economy moves forward by ups and downs—like strolling with a yo-yo, and praying the string doesn't break.

The government also has the power to tax. Here's where it starts getting scary.

Federal Income Tax

Certainly one of the most important ways the government influences your financial life is the federal income tax. Its impact is awesome. On a scale of wealth-inhibitors, the income tax ranks high. The order is:

1. Serious illness or death
2. Economic disaster
3. Poverty-level income
4. Money ignorance
5. Lack of investment mentality
6. Income taxes

If you were to apply income tax rules to our earlier chessboard game, the differences in outcomes would appall you.

Our grandfathers, and to some extent our fathers, were brought up without the countless esthetic delights of the W-2 form and the "simplified" tax return. Most of the money they earned was theirs to use. If they earned more money, they kept more money.

This is no longer true.

Today, the more money you earn, the more taxes are applied to it. The all-American achiever is thus penalized for achieving. The Horatio Alger hero is not dead but he is in traction.

Probably it has been true for a long time that few could get rich by salary alone. Today it is almost impossible. No matter what kind of salary you make, even if it runs into the hundreds of thousands of dollars per year, it will rarely make you rich—not unless you take steps to ameliorate the ravages of the IRS.

Let me give you a concrete example of the way the government's graduated income tax effects our day-to-day living:

There is an electric toaster in a department store and the price tag on it is $20. That means that anyone who walks in off the street will pay the same price for that toaster—right?

Wrong.

Although it takes any old $20 to buy the toaster, the values of the $20 bills proffered differ drastically from person to person. If you think of dollars as payment for work performed—as wages, as effort; as reward for talent, energy, brainpower, or whatever—then you come upon a wholly different way to view the buying power of the dollar.

A person on welfare, for example, produces no effort, does no work, earns no wage. For him, the electric toaster is free, a gift from the government, the city, the county, the state.

The person who earns $6,000 a year and pays no taxes

pays a true $20 for the toaster: It cost him $20 worth of work. His $20 bill is worth $20.

The person in the 20% tax bracket must earn $25 in wages to achieve $20 after taxes. That toaster costs him $25.

The person in the 50% tax bracket pays $40 in value for the very same toaster model that everyone else paid less for.

I am not making any kind of social case. Whether this is fair or unfair, just or unjust, is not the point at the moment. This is the current economic fact of life.

Income taxes are wealth-inhibiting. And, sooner or later, if you wish to gain wealth, you will have to soften the blows of the IRS.

Tax Deductions on Interest

The government, in all its beneficence, allows people *not* to pay taxes under certain conditions. If, for example, you borrow money, the interest you pay on that money is tax deductible. (There is also depreciation. And this, under certain circumstances, can be one of the most effective balms of all for a bad case of taxitis. We will explore this subject in a later chapter.)

Shakespeare had one of his characters proclaim, "Neither a borrower nor a lender be." Good advice in Elizabethan England; in this day and age, it makes no sense at all.

Since borrowing must make up an important part of your wealth-building effort, you are concerned with another federal function—that is, the control of interest rates.

The government, as the world's largest borrower, naturally wants interest rates to remain at reasonable levels, low levels. A few points of increase in the interest rates can mean a difference of billions of dollars in the federal budget. Therefore the government makes an effort, within its ability to control events, to keep interest rates within a modest range.

It is a kind of enlightened self-interest. Whenever the economy heats up too quickly so that inflation rates become unacceptable, the government's Federal Reserve Board raises interest rates to cool the economy down. When the economy starts to freeze over and unemployment rates rise, the Federal Reserve heats things up by dropping interest rates. At the moment, this pattern of inflation followed by recession appears to be a permanent fact of economic life.

The government controls our interest rates in several ways, the most immediate being the rate it charges federal reserve banks who wish to borrow. Banks borrow money just as you and I. This enables them to obtain greater leverage—to lend money to more people or institutions and thus derive a greater revenue. So when you want to borrow from a bank, the rate you pay depends more or less directly on the amount of interest the Federal Reserve has set.

Inflation

The government also has the power to print money. This is a very nice power to have. If you run short of money, all you need do is print more of it. However, this is not as good as it sounds, as a number of other governments have discovered.

If a government prints money out of all proportion to the economic production of the country, the value of that paper money declines in world markets. Today, for example, we see in some South American countries governments that have gone crazy with their printing presses. The result is exploding inflation. The paper money begins to mean nothing because it represents no tangible assets.

So, these countries enjoy inflation rates of up to 100%.

In our terms, a dollar today could be worth only 50 cents next year. This is a ridiculous extreme. It's a wonder there are not more revolutions among our southern neighbors.

The United States government has settled on two permanent policies which it believes to be in the best interests of the public it serves—and for itself as the biggest business in the world. Our federal government is devoted to the cause of reasonable interest rates—and to a modest degree of inflation.

If you can accomodate these two ongoing factors in your wealth-building program, you have the first of a number of powerful tools to succeed.

Long-term Capital Gains Tax

One other federally controlled condition should be mentioned at this point. This is the long-term capital gains tax. In one way you can think about it as a government reward for enterprise. If you stick your neck (and your cash) out on some business endeavor—and make a profit on it after a year or more—the government rewards you by charging you at a lower tax rate than you would normally pay on straight income.

If, for example, you make a $20,000 gain on stocks you have held for a year or more, the government permits you to split this gain in two and treat each half differently. Half is taxed as regular income—the same rate you would pay if it were salary. (Note here, for future reference, that if you have accumulated enough tax shelter, such as real estate, to offset your property income as well as other income derived from salary or capital gains, no income tax will be levied on that portion of your capital gains which would be normally taxed as income.) The second half of your long-term capital gains is subject to a preference income tax. The maximum preference income tax is now 15 percent. However, the first $10,000 of preference-taxable capital gains (or one-half regular taxes paid—whichever is greater) is subject to no tax at all. It's tax-free.

This means that if you are in the 32% income tax bracket, you will pay only $3,200 tax on your $20,000 capital gain. If it were all treated as straight income, it could easily push you up into the 42% tax bracket where the tax would be $8,400. It is not quite so simple as I'm making it seem here, but this is enough to illustrate the precious differences.

The long-term capital gains tax—some people fear it because they despise any kind of tax, but in reality, it is one of the best taxes you will ever pay. Because it is a tax on profits you have made. It is a tax on your growing wealth. I personally am very fond of the long-term capital gains tax—and intend to pay it on every occasion that merits it.

Summary of the Rules

1. The straight income tax is severely limiting to your wealth-building program. At some point you must consider devices that shelter your income from these tax hardships. You will need to make use of tax shelters.

2. Since interest payments are tax deductible and so are, in effect, partially sheltered by the government, you should not be afraid to borrow, wherever the leverage offered by borrowing can multiply your wealth without hazarding either your original equity or your ability to repay the loan.

3. Because of inflation's role in reducing the value of your capital, you must consider investment vehicles which appreciate at a rate higher than the inflation rate.

4. Long-term capital gains is an effective way to reduce the tax burden on profits made. Therefore, the one-year holding period which is the requirement for long-term capital gains must be a key consideration in your planning.

These, in general, are the federal government's rules in

the wealth-building game and the strategies they imply. If you wish to see your wealth grow, you had better understand them and understand them well.

WEALTH-ENHANCEMENT VEHICLES

These simply are any places you can put your money to make it grow. The variety of possibilities is practically endless. Which ones you choose depends a lot on your personal tastes. It's something like a fruit stand—yes, I want the bananas . . . no, I don't want the kumquats.

Over the course of your wealth-building career, you will be using an assortment of wealth enhancement investment vehicles—their nature and timing to be governed by a number of conditions.

The amount of investment capital you have accumulated is one. You can't buy a $10,000 bond if you have only $5,000 to invest.

The degree of risk you are prepared to take is another. If you wish to play the wealth-building lamb, you'll choose your investments with an emphasis on "safe." If you are a wealth-building tiger, your investments will be chancier but your returns might be greater.

Your goals and plans and your strategies for accomplishing them will have an overriding effect on your selections.

Current economic conditions will be a critical factor in deciding which investments you choose. If the economy is in a decline, a recession, you will want your capital in the safest money-making places possible, regardless of whether you are a lamb or a tiger. If the economy is booming, you will want your capital invested in vehicles that can ride up with the boom, that can help counteract the effects of inflation, that can accelerate your wealth.

Following is a brief survey, with some of the rules of the kinds of wealth enhancement opportunities available to you.

Your Job

The income you get from your job is, of course, your first source of wealth. The moment you receive your paycheck (or fee) you are wealthier than the moment before. (What happens to your wealth when you get your paycheck home is another matter.)

If your employment supplies you with a lot of spare capital, it is very enhancing. If it contributes only enough for you to break even, it is not so enhancing—you'll have to do something about it. If your salary is not enough to keep you from going into debt, it (or you) must be considered wealth-inhibiting. Something had better change in a hurry.

Cash Equivalents

These are defined as investment vehicles that safeguard your capital, pay a return, and that will be delivered back into your hands on demand (or brief notice) with your original capital plus earnings intact.

They are generally unexciting wealth-enhancers since they pay such a low rate of return. On the other hand, you will never get an ulcer worrying about them. If you have to carry water, better a small bucket than a large bucket with a hole in it.

Regarding their rules, cash equivalents have four useful applications. Use them when you want:

1. **An emergency reserve.** Cash equivalents keep your capital working for you and yet are ready at your call should some unexpected emergency strike.

2. A collection pool. Cash equivalents are good places to gather capital for large investments or expenses.

3. A capital haven. When all the world around you is losing its collective head and its investment capital, you can have your fiscal ship in a safe port.

4. A peaceful old age. When the slings and arrows and outrageous fortunes of risk investment have gotten too much for you, cash equivalents are serene pastures where a retiree can graze with the assurance that the grass will always be green.

Cash equivalents (to be explained in Chapter VI) include:

> Savings in banks or savings and loans
> Liquid asset funds
> 30- to 90-day certificate accounts
> Treasury bills
> Banker's acceptances
> Certificates of deposit
> Commercial paper

Securities

The average citizen approaches the securities markets with characteristically mixed feelings—a blend of fear and fascination.

Is this an overblown slot machine where you put in your money, cross your fingers, and pray that your investment will pay off? Or is it a solid, buttoned-down business establishment where you can be confident of reaping rewards from prudent investment? The truth is, it is a bit of both— sometimes more the former, sometimes more the latter.

Is it an arena for professionals only—for the cognoscenti of the ticker tape, who can devote a lifetime to exploring its arcane and devious ways—or can anyone play? Again, the answer is mixed. Some areas are practical only for the knowledgeable; in others, all but fools can participate.

Anyone who has wealth-building ambitions must in time realize that he must make use of the securities markets to enhance his wealth. Still, securities investing is a form of gambling—a sophisticated form, but nevertheless gambling. There is no other sensible way to look at it.

If I had to choose between the oak-paneled boardrooms of Wall Street and the velveteen casinos of Las Vegas or Reno, I would opt for Wall Street every time. Because in the long pull, despite its temporary vicissitudes and aberrations, Wall Street is a winner.

A massive study of the performance of all common stocks listed on the New York Stock Exchange between January 1926 and December 1969 showed the following facts:

The median (not the average) annual rate of return was 9.8 percent.

An investor in all common stocks would have made a profit over 78% of the time.

Over two-thirds of the time the rate of return would have been better than 5 percent per year compounded annually.

Losses exceeding 50 percent per year happen only about once in fifty times; losses exceeding 20 percent per year, only about once in thirteen times.

Since the period covered includes the disasters of the early thirties, these are not bad playing odds at all. Then too, there are the spectacularly heroic performances that Wall Street is so proud to display.

If, for example, in 1914 a person had bought 100 shares of IBM Corporation (then known as Computing-Tabulating-Recording Company) for $2,750, and kept the stock, today he would own 74,150 shares (through a series of stock splits) worth over $20.5 million. And he would have received over $4 million in stock dividends along the way.

Another, more current example: If an investor had paid

$10,000 for 100 shares of Haloid Company (which has since changed its name to Xerox Corporation) in 1955, he would now own roughly 18,000 shares (again through splits) worth something on the order of $900,000.

Of course not every company is an IBM or a Xerox, but the securities markets are successful wealth-enhancement vehicles over the long range. How are they then in short range situations?

The answer must be, sometimes a lot better and sometimes a lot worse. Since the securities markets are based on actual businesses, they are (as you would suspect) directly affected by economic conditions that are either good for business or bad for business. Well, not quite directly (and this is one of the factors that complicates securities investing considerably). To be more accurate, I should say that the markets are affected by their *anticipation* of economic conditions. Historically, the securities markets make their moves, up or down, quite far *in advance* of the true economic happening. It could be months ahead, and even more than a year ahead.

Thus, you witness the apparently insane conditions of the economy bubbling happily along while the securities markets are beginning to take a nosedive. And the economy can appear to be in all sorts of trouble while the Dow Jones averages are moving up every day. It is the securities markets' business to look into the future and predict healthy or sick business climates. And they act on what they see in their crystal balls far more than on the economic headlines in today's newspapers.

For example, a small article in the *Wall Street Journal* reported that the cost of living is rising into double digits (that is, more than 9 percent per year). This is usually a sign that the economy is booming. However, for Wall Street this is terrible news. Knowing that the federal government, in its dedication to a low level of inflation, cannot tolerate double-digit inflation, the securities markets *anticipate* that the government eventually will raise interest rates to slow inflation. And higher interest rates are bad for business (just as lower interest rates are good for business). So the markets decline on the expectation of what might happen months from now.

Setting aside the factors of timing for the moment, the natural patterns of the security markets are: up, followed by down; rise, followed by fall; advance, followed by decline.

The rising market is called a bull market; the falling market, a bear. On the way up and on the way down there are always some reverse trends: bear cubs and bull calves.

The main reason for entering the securities markets is to achieve a greater increase (appreciation) on your capital than you would normally find with cash equivalents. The ambitious salaried person who wishes to attain wealth therefore should consider the securities markets primarily as appreciation vehicles. That is, he is less interested in interest rates paid or dividends issued (although these are attractive extras) than he is in the growth of his equity in the security.

For the average investor who does not have a lot of time to spend in figuring out the more sophisticated applications of securities buying and selling, the bull (rising) market is the only place to achieve reasonably safe capital appreciation.

While there is money to be made in a bear (declining) market, it usually requires too much attention for the person otherwise occupied with a job.

The ideal objective for the securities investor is to buy near the end of a bear market and to sell near the top of a bull market—and to stay out of the markets entirely on the down slope. But this ideal is difficult to achieve. Who knows when a bear market is about to bottom out? Who knows when a bull market is about to peak?

Nobody.

The bottoms and tops are only recognized in historical perspective—some time after they have happened.

While it is true that the longer a particular market lasts, the greater the pressures created to turn it around, other factors can come into play which can throw the whole rational scheme of things out of kilter.

In the early 1970s, for example, when a bear market should have been turning bull, the Arabs' sharp increase in oil prices, coupled with the catatonic performance of the Nixon Watergate administration, created an abortion which came to be called "stagflation"—a stagnating economy simultaneous with an escalating inflation. Almost unheard of! Shocking! Totally unexpected!

Beyond the gross movements of the securities markets themselves are the separate and unique movements of each individual stock and bond. (No one buys the whole market— you buy a stock or a bond, and these are what you are truly interested in, no matter what the Dow-Jones or the Standard and Poor's 500 stocks are doing.) And in any one day's transactions there are securities that are advancing and securities that are declining like elevators in adjacent shafts.

Different kinds of stocks have their moments of glory. *Defensive issues,* such as those of utilities, banks and food companies, hold up better under recessionary pressures than most of their neighbors. *Cyclical stocks*—these tend to fluctuate sharply with the business cycle—are typified by automobile manufacturers and machine tool makers. *Blue chip* stocks are issues of old and honorable companies with a history of paying their dividends regularly, like gentlemen, and managing their fiscal affairs with prudence. *Growth stocks* are those of companies whose sales and earnings are generally expanding faster than the economy as a whole and other stocks in particular. Since growth is so desirable to the person who wants his capital to appreciate, the mere label "growth" is like an aphrodisiac to the fervid investor whose panting courtship is apt to push the prices of these stocks far beyond their foreseeable worth. Then the first quarter the company fails to meet expected growth standards, the honeymoon is over and the stock price goes over Niagara Falls without a barrel. *Income stocks* are usually purchased because they pay a higher-than-average dividend rate. Often they do not have a large growth potential. Of late, bond interest has risen to such an extent that these stocks have lost some of their shine for the conservative investor.

Bonds are fixed income securities; that is, you buy a bond for $1,000 to pay a 6 percent per year interest, and that is what it will pay you, come good times or bad, unless it goes into default. Bonds also have a value as appreciation vehicles although not so great, usually, as stocks. It works this way: The $1,000 bond is normally sold at a discount. (Occasionally it may be sold at a premium if its safety and yield are gold-plated.) This means you can buy a $1,000 bond for less than $1,000. If it is a low grade bond you might be able to buy it for as little as $600. In this case, your yield on dollars invested not only has increased to 10 percent but you have the chance of a $400 appreciation on your capital when your bond is called.

Bonds have traditionally been considered conservative investments, but lately, with their higher yields and deeper discounts, they are becoming more competitive with common stocks.

Some stocks will defy market trends. Either their management is so adept or their future so rosy (or both) that shrewd investors continue to buy these stocks despite adverse market conditions. These stocks are called "energy motivated" and may be considered, until proved otherwise, as exceptions to general market rules.

Discussion of the aspects of buying and selling securities can occupy whole libraries. For the moment, we can infer these general rules for the wealth-builder/adventurer starting to hack his way through the securities jungle:

1. Do not enter the securities markets until you are prepared to assume the risks involved. You won't want to use rent or food money to take your fling. Forget about the "sure things" and "hot tips" until your fiscal defenses are in place.

2. Because different kinds of securities react in different ways to various market conditions, it is prudent to diversify your investments among a variety of companies, industries and vehicles.

3. The age-old chestnut on Wall Street is "Let your gains run and cut your losses." This is not so obvious as it seems. If you have lost some money on a stock, there is a temptation to hold it until it returns to its original price. Not a good idea. A stock is not worth what you paid for it, it is only worth what you can sell it for at the moment. If you have purchased a losing stock, sell it—cut your losses— chalk it up to experience—and forget it. You have only to look at a duck-billed platypus to know that even God makes mistakes now and then.

4. Lock up your gains. In most cases, where a security shows a profit—especially if you have held it for a year or more to meet long term capital gains requirements—sell it if you feel it is no longer "energy motivated." Then check with your broker or select another likely candidate for an upward move.

5. If a stock is "energy motivated"—that is, if it continues to show upward movement beyond the time you would normally sell it—ride with it until it shows signs of running out of vitamins.

6. "Buy low, sell high—that's the investor's lullaby." Another Wall Street aphorism, so obvious it must be true. Try to buy near the trough of a bear market, try to sell near the crest of the bull market. Not the easiest things in

the world to do. But if you don't try to be too piggish about it by going for the extremes, you may be surprised how well you can do. As for the down slope of the bear market, avoid it. Sell out and go hide.

Other Wealth-enhancement Vehicles

At this point we will identify only a few other wealth-enhancement vehicles. Most are covered elsewhere in the book. Some are of no interest to the salaried wealth-builder.

Real estate. This is such a big and important subject, I want to hold off all discussion of it until later in the book when we can really get our teeth into it.

Mutual funds, real estate investment trusts and other "group-think" investments. I do not wish to be unduly harsh to this communal form of investing. However, in recent years they have not performed up to their public relations.

Commodities and options trading. These are among the more exotic ways to increase or decrease your capital. They are really professionals' arenas.

Oil and gas ventures, cattle breeding, farming, timber, minerals and mining, etc. All of these have suffered under the Tax Reform Act of 1976. Once, they had appeal as tax shelters and possible money-makers, but not so much any more.

Gold, silver, art, antiques, coins, stamps and other collections. Each has its particular romantic appeal and holds the potential for adding to your wealth. More later.

These, plus the infinite possibilities of a business of your own, cover the majority of wealth-enhancement vehicles.

2

Step 1– How Much Are You Worth?

Money is the seed of money, and the first guinea is sometimes more difficult to acquire than the second million.
JEAN JACQUES ROUSSEAU (1712–1778)
A Discourse on Political Economy

Everybody likes and respects self-made men. It is a great deal better to be made that way than not to be made at all.
OLIVER WENDELL HOLMES (1809–1894)
The Autocrat of the Breakfast Table

If you've never calculated your net worth, you may be in for a surprise—possibly even a pleasant one. You could be worth more than you think.

No single step in the plan for investment is more important than this—the annual taking of your assets less your liabilities to arrive at a fairly stated net worth. This is your score card in the game of investment. You can't calculate it alone by the jingle in your pocket or by the balance in your checkbook.

The growth of your net worth is the measure of your success.

The formula is simple:

Total Assets
—Total Liabilities
Net Worth.

Most people only prepare a net worth statement when they borrow from a bank or seek a loan on real estate. Generally the net worth statement given to the lender is rather optimistic. (Of course, you want to get the loan.) It seldom reflects the true evaluation.

The first rule in calculating your net worth is, To thine own self be true. Don't fudge on the figures. You are only deluding yourself. If you calculate your net worth in the way I suggest, you will be as accurate as can be. You will create an ongoing record of changes in your fortune. You will construct the foundation of a solid investment plan.

You can pick any time you want to figure your net worth, even today as you read this book. But it is important for your records that you pick the same day every year— this so that you have the accurate measure of a full investment year.

I chose January 1, New Year's Day, as my "net worth day." Each year, while watching the Rose Parade on television, I gather my account book and records around me and work with the figures. It is kind of ceremonial. And, if it has been a profitable investment year, as it usually has been for me, the ritual is a tremendously uplifting way to get the New Year launched. Better than champagne and party hats.

I have been keeping track of my net worth for most of my working life. Following is a statement of it. I publish it as an encouragement to you, to show that you need not have the big windfall or the inherited fortune to accumulate wealth. I had neither.

I have friends who have made millions by discovering oil, by becoming large real estate subdividers, by developing shopping centers, by becoming presidents of their corporations, or by inheriting large estates from their forebears. I hope it happens to you. Chances are, it won't. If it does, you can be ahead two ways—with a solid investment plan *plus* the fortunate bonanza.

You'll see from my net worth statement that the early years are the tough ones for moving ahead. This is an almost universal truth. The earliest dollars are the hardest dollars.

Recently at a party I bumped into an acquaintance of mine, a brilliant lawyer who through shrewd investing had accumulated a huge fortune, many times greater than mine. He had read an earlier version of this book and commented that he had enjoyed it.

"I see that you had the same kind of problem I did," he said.

I asked what problem he was referring to. (No one has *a* problem, singular.)

"On your net worth statement," he said, "I had the same trouble you did with getting that first hundred thousand dollars. The first hundred thousand is the hardest."

Certainly, the first hundred thousand *is* the hardest. After that the rapid growth of your wealth comes as something of a surprise. But in your early years, your salary has not yet approached its potential. You may well have an expanding family with expanding needs. Venture capital is very tough to accumulate.

In these early, dollar-short years there is a strong temptation to postpone having children. They *are* expensive. They *are* a responsibility. They *do* take up valuable time and energy. They *will* retard your wealth-building efforts. If you still face this decision, you may find it hard or easy depending on your ambitions, your lifestyle, your sense of family.

For me, the choice was without debate. I chose to have children. Their acquisitions are noted along with my less valuable assets in the following statement of my net worth over the past 31 years.

RICHARD K. RIFENBARK
Net Worth Growth During Salaried Years

Age	Net Worth	Comments
27	$ 13,000	Began keeping track of my net worth—consisting mainly of one car and a few securities. Living in an apartment. First child born. Salary $265 per month.
28	14,000	Second child born. Struggling along on $294 per month.
29	14,000	Bought first home for $11,500. Expenses cancelled out other gains.
30	23,000	Home equity increased $3,500. A good year for me in the stock market.
31	28,000	Sold first home, bought larger one. Home equity increased $4,000. Some stock market gains. Third child born.
32	29,000	Struggling.
33	30,000	Cash value of life insurance and securities increased by $1,000.
34	29,000	Bought quite a few home furnishings, which I assigned a net worth of zero—therefore, a loss. This was an error. This figure should actually show a small gain.
35	32,000	Securities profit.
36	51,000	Profit on sale of second home and purchase of third home. Some profit sharing. Increase in value of my first real estate investment—undeveloped land.
37	63,000	Increased value of new home, land, securities and profit sharing.
38	69,000	A nice $5,000 profit from securities helped.

RICHARD K. RIFENBARK
Net Worth Growth During Salaried Years (Continued)

Age	Net Worth	Comments
39	$ 77,000	Bought ⅓ interest in my first apartment house. Began to realize wealth-building power of residential income real estate. Started to formalize a wealth-building program.
40	127,000	Increased value of apartment house, raw land, securities and deferred compensation.
41	206,000	Home value increased $15,000. Increases in value of apartment house and land.
42	240,000	Deferred compensation and common stocks increased by $21,000. Most of remainder from real estate increases.
43	256,000	Fourth child born. Stocks increased in value by $8,000.
44	283,000	Bulk of increase came from higher values of real estate.
45	344,000	Gains in deferred compensation and securities, $30,000. Increase in real estate value, $25,000.
46	365,000	Loss in deferred compensation—gain in real estate.
47	360,000	Loss in securities and deferred compensation. Gain in real estate.
48	394,000	Strong gains in all areas. Probably spent too much redecorating and furnishing our new home. Traded first apartment house for land, upon which I built a 33-unit apartment house.

RICHARD K. RIFENBARK
Net Worth Growth During Salaried Years (Continued)

Age	Net Worth	Comments
49	$ 419,000	Traded first land for other land plus an office building. Cost some pretty stiff commissions. Built a second 33-unit apartment house.
50	548,000	A terrific year! Increases all over the place. Biggest was $77,000 increase in values of apartment houses and home.
51	760,000	Big gains on values of all properties, plus $20,000 from deferred compensation and securities.
52	840,000	Gains came from: real estate, $30,000; deferred compensation and securities, $42,000; profit sharing, $18,000.
53	915,000	$50,000 decrease in value of office building. Everything else went up.
54	1,051,000	Cracked million dollar barrier for the first time—but not without some pain. Lost $68,000 in securities and deferred compensation. However, my real estate values increased by $145,000—which was better than aspirin to assuage the pain.
55	1,056,000	This year I decided to retire. Reduced value of office building by another $50,000 to get it off my hands in a depressed real estate market. Increases in other real estate holdings made up the difference. Securities market went nowhere.
56	1,057,000	Losses in deferred compensation were balanced by gains in real estate. First full year

RICHARD K. RIFENBARK
Net Worth Growth During Salaried Years (Continued)

Age	Net Worth	Comments
	$	of retirement. Decided to take up real estate investment sales as a "retirement" occupation. I just enjoy it.
57	1,273,000	The economy recovered and so did I. Gain in real estate value, $137,000; gain in common stocks, $49,000; gain in bonds, $30,000. Am considering buying another apartment house to shelter increased income.

There, for better or for worse, is a capsule summary of the growth of my net worth, through my salaried years and into retirement. You can see that my growth was by no means a straight line, and was in fact beset by more than a few setbacks. Still, through it all, the overriding strategies and philosophies worked. I never allowed myself to be put in the position where I could not afford the loss. And when there were gains to be made, I was there knocking at the door.

Here is the rough form I use in computing my net worth statement. As with many accounting procedures, it is subject to interpretation. However, I think it offers an accurate appraisal and, used in the same form year after year, supplies a correct evaluation of the changes in your net worth.

Assets

1. *Securities.* List by name; itemize the number of shares multiplied by end-of-year market value to determine the total market value for each security.

2. *Savings accounts* in banks or savings and loans. Itemize each account.

3. *Checking accounts.* Itemize each account.

4. *Club memberships.* Itemize each that has a cash value if you were to sell it.

5. *House furnishings.* At one time, to be conservative, I carried house furnishings at zero. This is not correct. They represent value and should be appraised by an accredited appraiser every three years. This inventory should be kept in a safe deposit box in case of fire or burglary. Exclude personal clothing which has minor resale value.

6. *Home market value.* Ask a respected broker to give you the range in which he thinks your home would sell. Use the lower figure in the range. There should be no charge for this service, as the broker usually is happy to have his foot in the door if-and-when you might decide to sell.

7. *Cash value life insurance.* A phone call to your life insurance agent will give you the answer. Select one agent to review all your policies even though he didn't sell them all to you.

8. *Automobile market value.* Check the end-of-the-year automobile classified ads for the prices asked by individuals offering to sell cars of the same manufacture, year and model as yours. Select a middle price for your use.

9. *Company retirement plan.* Calculate the vested portion of the plan, which you would receive if you left the company tomorrow. With some companies and organizations you may have to give up everything if you leave before a prescribed period of service. Do not include any retirement equity that is not vested.

10. *Valuable collections.* Include the market value of any unusual collections, such as jewelry, stamps, coins, guns, works of art, etc., which are not included in your house furnishings inventory.

11. *Cash on hand.*

12. *Checks not yet deposited.*

13. *Investment real estate.* Obtain a current, reasonably

informed opinion of market value for each property from a reliable broker in your area.

14. *Loans owed you.* Include principal and interest balance due.

15. *Estimated income tax refund due.* Include federal and state, if any.

16. *Prepaid property taxes.* You may have elected to prepay in the prior year property taxes which are actually due in the new year. You can do this, if you wish, to reduce the prior year's income subject to tax. This applies to your home as well as investment property. This flexibility of income shelter is one important reason why your investment portfolio should include real estate.

17. *Miscellaneous assets not otherwise covered.*

18. Add up all the above to get your total asset value.

Liabilities

1. *Balance of loans outstanding on your home.*

2. *Balance of loans outstanding on other real estate.* Itemize each property individually.

3. *Balance of loans outstanding on life insurance.* Itemize separately by policy.

4. *Balance due on loans to individuals, banks or institutions.* Itemize each loan separately.

5. *Security deposits*—paid by tenants of your apartment houses or other commercial properties. This amounts to money held in trust, which becomes a liability against your assets.

6. *Miscellaneous bills incurred in prior year*—bills which you have not yet received or paid, but which should be estimated as obligations against your assets.

7. *Taxes due.* If your payments of estimated taxes are

not enough to cover your prior year obligations, the remaining amounts due become liabilities.

8. *Miscellaneous other liabilities.*

9. Add up all the above to get your total liabilities.

Subtract your total liabilities from your total assets and you get your net worth.

I recommend that you formalize your calculations of your net worth (total assets minus total liabilities and resultant net worth) in a journal which you can refer back to from year to year.

I incorporate these figures in the account book I keep for myself. I use one page for each month, recording all income received from salary, dividends, monthly apartment house distributions, etc. Then I record the disbursements of this income—to a savings account or to a joint or separate checking account. After the December page, I use one leaf (two pages) for my net worth statement. Following this, I reserve one page for recording all loans outstanding. I show the company from which the loan was made, the interest rate, the amount still owed on January 1 of the new year, and the date the loan terminates. I keep this page current during the year, crossing out each loan as it is paid off. I find this a most useful procedure, as it makes me aware of the loans I am responsible for and the dates on which I must be prepared to satisfy their obligations.

For the carefree soul not accustomed to more account keeping than an occasional hieroglyphic scrawl in the register of his checkbook, it may come as a disappointment that I should ask this much effort and organization to achieve a single number of as yet unknown virtue.

But the task is not so arduous as it might appear on the surface. You may learn to enjoy it, and once the habit pattern is set, execution is simple. You benefit by thinking in terms of your net worth enhancement. The picture of your progress should be inspiring.

One more note about net worth before we leave the subject: The concept of net worth serves two useful functions—and that is about its limit. It can be an accurate measure of your financial growth from year to year. It is a necessary item in your briefcase when you go out into the world to seek a loan.

It tells nothing about your cash flow, your wealth-building potential, or even your fiscal health. Your net worth *plus* your annual income together offer a far more revealing picture than either figure applied alone. Let me give two extreme examples.

Bernie B. owns free and clear an inherited $1-million mansion in the Hollywood Hills. His sole source of income is playing a Moog synthesizer at *Star Trek* conventions, for which he receives $6,000 a year. After paying the high property taxes on his home, Bernie is forced to eat organic peanut butter sandwiches on natural oatmeal bread (which he bakes himself) for breakfast, lunch and dinner. And when he wants to park his 1949 De Soto, he will circle the block several times looking for a parking meter with time left on it.

Charlie C. is a successful salesman earning $50,000 a year. He rents a lavishly furnished $1,500-a-month bachelor pad, carries every major credit card and uses them to the limit, leases a Mercedes 280 C, flies to Aspen every weekend during the ski season, spends generously on gifts for friends (all female), travels to Europe twice a year, drinks only Chivas Regal, smokes only smuggled Havana cigars, wears Givenchy suits and bench-crafted brogans, and pays a huge income tax.

Bernie B. has the net worth of a millionaire and lives like a pauper. Charlie C. lives like a millionaire and has the net worth of a gnat. Until Bernie B. dumps that spooky Hollywood palace that has a strangle hold on his assets and rejoins the real world, he will remain a financial casualty. Unless Charlie C. alters his lifestyle to match his means, he is due for a visit to the bankruptcy courts within 18 months.

For more normal people, like us, our net worth statements are accurate and useful indices of our current financial condition. Calculate yours today, and then refigure it at regular yearly intervals. If it comes out higher than you thought, congratulate yourself, you're on your way. If your figure is less than you believed it would be, don't be discouraged by it—you're only beginning. From tomorrow on, its direction will be up.

3

Step 2—
Your Annual Expenses

Nobody was ever meant
To remember or invent,
What he did with every cent.

—ROBERT FROST (1875–1963)
"The Hardship of Accounting"

"The horror of that moment," the King went on,
"I shall never, never forget."
"You will, though," the Queen said, "if you don't make a memorandum
of it.

—LEWIS CARROLL (1832–1898)
Alice in Wonderland

In simpler times, one could keep track of his expenses merely by counting the coins remaining in the sugar bowl. Those days are long since past. Today life is so complex and expenses are so varied, we can leave the house in the morning with $50 in our pockets, return with $8.25, and be hard put to recall where it all went.

This insidious dribbling away of our dollars can mean the abrupt demise of even the best-founded, best-intentioned wealth-building effort. Of the several kinds of record-keeping you will be called upon to perform as a wealth-maker, one of the most useful is the estimated budget of your annual expenses.

Most people have a vague idea of where their money goes each year. Too few have an accurate accounting. There is only one way to get it, and that is an itemized summary of past expenses and future expectancies—a realistic budget that you can draw up and stick to.

No business worth its stockholders' confidence would think of operating without a budget, and you and I are no different. You are in business for yourself. You owe it to your business to budget expenses. It does not have to be a slavish exercise—no record of "every penny spent." The degree of refinement is up to your personal taste.

At its very least, a budget will give you a sense of how your money flows through your "business." At its best, your budget will give you firm control of your resources. It will help prevent unpleasant surprises. (My God, I forgot that insurance premium was due this month!) Most important, it will allow you not only to live within your income but to budget some capital residual (savings) out of your income to be set aside for investment each year. This area of capital residual is so important, I want to spend some time with it.

In his syndicated column "Dollars and sense," appearing in the *San Francisco Examiner* several years ago, Dan Miller discussed the topic of how to get rich. He quoted Fred J. Young, vice president in the trust department at Harris Bank in Chicago, where he had spent twenty-three years "working with rich people helping them get richer."

According to Mr. Young, "[Becoming] rich involves sacrifice: spending less than you earn and investing the rest." In every rich family Young has seen, "somebody at the beginning made that sacrifice to get the money going and that's the way they all got rich.

"There are only two ways to get rich," says Young. "First, you either inherit it or marry it. Second, you spend less than you earn and invest in something that will go up.

"Most people I've seen have gotten rich from real estate."

About budgets, Mr. Young says, "If you're serious about getting rich, start keeping records so you know how much money comes in and goes out and where it goes . . . but don't kid yourself."

While there may be some shortcuts to becoming rich, ignoring a budgeted savings plan is not one of them. The discipline of a savings program is an absolute necessity—everything else follows. A savings program makes all the future for the investor possible.

In the next few pages I will describe a form which might be useful to you in developing an annual budget. It has been suggested to me that I should include some guidelines as to what proportion of your income should be spent for what. I would prefer not to do this. Everyone, by need or taste, has a slightly different lifestyle. For me to declare that *my* way of allocating expenses is better than *your* way would be fatuous. A vital necessity of life for me may be of no consequence for you—and the reverse.

Beyond this, the economic realities of life of late have had a nasty habit of changing dramatically. When food prices suddenly rise, when energy costs leap, they can scramble priorities in any sensible budget. Once, you could declare with confidence that no one should spend more than a quarter of his income on housing. Not true any more. I defy anyone to name a proper fraction which will hold for all areas of the country.

If you feel the need for guidance in developing a budget for yourself, take a trip to your local library or bookstore and browse through the wide selection of books offering budgetary advice. I have no recommendations. Pick the budget you like and you think you can live with. The emphasis here is more on the latter than the former.

You could also use your own good common sense—trust yourself. I have what may be an inordinate respect for plain, home-grown common sense, perhaps because it seems such a scarce commodity.

Whatever course you choose, the first thing you will need is a budget form. If you have no better ideas, try Boorum & Pease's columnar tablet pad #4916, 11 × 17 inches, with 16 columns. Nearly every stationery store carries it.

On a following page, I show you the budget categories I use. You may expand or condense them according to your needs. (See Exhibit 1, page 59.)

Your first concern is how you spent your dollars last year. So gather last year's records around you at a comfortable desk or table (you will be spending some time there) with your budget form before you, its columns and lines neatly titled.

With a soft pencil (there will be more than a little erasing), fill in the boxes month by month. Your check register and your credit card receipts are your best starting place. If you have the habit of spending cash for much of what you buy and keep no records of it, you will be forced to indulge in some creative guesswork. (As an aside, cash purchases are the bane of a budget. Cash disappears without a trace. That's why so many politicians insist on taking bribes only in cold cash. If you want to play straight with a budget, develop the practice of using cash for petty purchases only. For everything else, pay by check or credit card—and save receipts!)

When you have recorded a year's expenses by month, by category, total each month down and each category across. This will show you how your monthly expense varies and how much you spend for each category annually.

If this is the first time you have summarized your annual expenses you may be in for a few shocks. Your supermarket expenses may look like the national debt, or liquor purchases sufficient to stock the local bar, or telephone bills as if Ma Bell were your favorite beneficiary.

But you can't deny it: This is your financial fingerprint. This is how you have chosen, wittingly or unwittingly, to spend your hard-earned money in the preceding year. In the coming year, with your budget as guide, you may well choose to spend your discretionary income quite differently.

Now you are prepared to estimate next year's expenses based on last year's facts and follies. Here again some judgment and imagination are involved. Inflationary factors must be taken into account. Where your expenses require choice, you may wish to raise your estimates or lower them according to your new goals for achieving wealth.

From your past year's recap page, take the numbers in column 14, "This Yr. Total" (this is now last year's total) and transcribe them to your new page for *this year* under column 15, "Last Yr. Total."

To place your bets (estimates) for your annual totals by category for the coming year, move to column 16. Some numbers you can just drop in from the previous year, others you must derive or guess at. There may be some painful decisions. "Where can I cut down to attain my savings goals?"

Some people like to set up a separate budget estimate for each month. For me, this seems to involve more bookkeeping than it is worth. I prefer to develop an *average* monthly budget by dividing a total year's budget by 12. There are advantages and disadvantages to this technique. The main disadvantage is, of course, that many recurrent expenses will vary somewhat with the season. Heating and electrical expenses will be higher-than-budget in winter months and lower-than-budget in summer months. If this bothers or confuses you, take the extra time to set up monthly quotas. On the plus side of my system are simplicity and the considerable advantage of averaging out some of your heavy annual and semiannual expenses, such as insurance premiums, taxes, etc.

Now that the guidelines are established, you have a budget you can work with.

My first budgeted item each month is a deposit to my savings account. This is the first check I write, and to me it is the most important. This check is an installment payment on my ticket to freedom. Unless you can save regularly, methodically, without even thinking about it, each month from your income, you are postponing or even preventing your financial independence.

The least you should set aside is 5% of your gross salary. Ideally, it should be closer to 10%. Because of compounding and because you will get into the action quicker, 10% will move you ahead more than twice as fast as 5%. But whatever percentage you decide on—stick with it. Let no whim deter you from it. Only the direst circumstances are allowable to let you stray from your target. It's *that* important. That's why you should be careful to choose a savings figure that you can realistically live with. Don't give yourself the excuse that you have aimed too high. Once you start your savings discipline, maintain it.

Take a step back from your budget and look at it. Is it moving you forward as fast as you want to go? Is this the year to cut back on expenses and put more into savings? Can you do without that expensive vacation? Would you find as much fun and relaxation somewhere closer to home? Perhaps you should ease up on entertaining or home improvement or department store purchases.

As I said in the first chapter, developing a pattern of wealth-building will probably involve changes in the way you live. Now is the time, when you have a graphic picture of your finances laid out before you, to decide what you may have to curtail or give up to reach your financial goals. Don't make it too painful; but if it doesn't hurt a little, you probably are not trying hard enough.

A word of caution—planning on salary increases to make your budget work is beggaring your plan. It's pure foolishness. If you don't get the increase, however deserved or promised, you're stuck. Your budget is crippled. On the other hand, if you base your budget on your present salary and your increase comes through, you're ahead of the game. The option is yours whether you wish to invest your increase in purpose or pleasure. You are the master, not the slave, of your finances.

Except for your savings pledge, consider your budget flexible enough to adjust to the changing times. If the price of some goods or services goes up, some other item of your budget must bend. Learn to live with your budget. It's a tool, not a jail.

In Robert Frost's poem "Mending Wall" he notes: "Something there is that does not love a wall." Here Frost comments that nature's forces tend to erode man-made structures. Sun, wind, rain, heat and freeze will tumble carefully piled rocks and will rot fenceposts. I'll paraphrase Frost with, "something there is that does not love a budget." Unexpected expenses or sudden spending whims can reduce a perfectly sensible, useful budget to shambles.

What should you do about it? Restack your boulders and begin where you left off. Man—if he has the will—has the capacity to overcome. Even his own vagaries. Good budgets, like good fences, require conscientious maintenance.

Following is a suggested format for your budget, to be used or adapted to your needs.

Exhibit 1: Form for Annual Budget

CATEGORY	1. Monthly Budget	2. Jan.	3. Feb.	M	12. Nov.	13. Dec.	14. This Yr. Total	15. Last Yr. Total	16. This Yr. Est.
			THIS YEAR'S ACTUAL EXPENSES						
Deposits in savings accounts									
Vacation (or other) fund									
State Income Tax									
Federal Income Tax									
F.I.C.A. (Social Security)									
Property tax on home									
Medical insurance									
Life insurance									
Disability insurance									
Home insurance									
Auto insurance									
Home mortgage or rent									
Auto Licenses									
Church contributions									
Other contributions									
Domestic help									
F.I.C.A. for domestic help									
Electricity									
Water									
Gas									
Heating fuel									
Telephone									
Home maintenance & repair									
Gardener									
Garden supplies									
Pest control									
Supermarket									
Pharmacy									
Cleaners & laundry									
Clothing									
Bank credit cards									
Gasoline, etc.									
Auto repairs									
Auto club									
Local transportation & cabs									
Membership clubs									
Education									
Doctors & dentists									
Subscriptions									
Entertainment (est.)									
Liquor									
Safe deposit box									
Tax accountant									
Attorney fees (est.)									
Payments on other loans									
Cash gifts to children for birthdays & Christmas									
TOTALS									

4

Step 3—
Define Your Goals

If you cannot think about the future, you cannot have one.
        —JOHN GALSWORTHY (1867–1933) *Swan Song*

To drift is to be in hell, to be in heaven is to steer.
        —GEORGE BERNARD SHAW (1856–1950)

Do you want to be rich? Why? To what purpose? If you have some shadowy, abstract ideas about what the pleasures of wealth are, I suggest you put them out of your mind—forget them. They are probably inaccurate.

We all know of miserable millionaires. Poor Howard Hughes, dying alone among a coterie of spear carriers. Poor John Paul Getty, five times divorced.

The rich have problems with children, wives, egos and illness—just like you and me. All suicides are not among the poor—it is the most democratic of self-inflicted disasters.

One aphorism is that money can't buy happiness. Well, maybe. If your self-image is linked to a big bank account, if you enjoy material goods and a roll of bills in your pocket —and I can understand that—you could well get a pleasant glow just from the feel of the green.

Another saw is that money can't buy love. Probably

true. But if you're willing to settle for a period of insincere affection, who knows what might happen?

Money doesn't come with any life-back guarantees. Some people are going to be miserable under any circumstances, rich or poor. If you want money to do something for you, spell it out—see if it will hold up under the light of day. This is for certain: Money can buy hard goods. It can buy services. It can buy a freedom to choose. It can buy a degree of power. It can buy protection. If money is important to you, in whatever way, I suggest you eliminate the intangibles that money *might* buy and think in terms of specifics—the things money *can* buy. Set goals for what you want money to do for you. Think it through. Make a list.

This exercise in defining your money goals serves four useful purposes:

1. It forces you to solidify in your mind exactly what is important to you, not only at the moment, but in the future. Many of us live day by day through unthinking habit patterns. We act and react mechanically because that is the way we have always done things. It is easy and comfortable. We may have trouble anticipating beyond the next weekend, much less five, ten, twenty years from now.

The effort of weighing and balancing the various factors that affect your life (or *might* affect it) is a healthy probe—cracking the shell of habit in which you have encapsulated yourself, opening a window to the dynamic, changing world.

2. In the act of thinking, measuring, making lists of the things you value, you are likely to uncover objectives that you have either taken for granted or buried back in the unsettled recesses of your subconscious mind. At one time, for example, you might have thought it would be grand to take a trip around the world. But then your practical, critical faculties informed your visionary faculties that there was no way at the present time that you should consider such a trip.

"Too expensive. You can't get away from your job for that long. You have better ways to spend your money." So the trip idea got plunked into the deep, dark well of your brain's limbo—never really forgotten, but rarely dredged up to be reinspected.

Recall your dreams; breathe life into them. They may be possible.

3. As you assemble the areas that are important to you and line them up in a neat row, tallest to shortest, some solutions may become self-evident. "This is something that I want and there is nothing to prevent me from having it now." If you know exactly what you want, what satisfaction or function you expect from it, no salesman can sell you anything less or job you off on something you don't want at all.

4. The creative process of defining and aligning objectives provides the basis for rational actions to achieve these objectives. We are so much creatures of emotion—the child remains in all of us. While this can add considerably to our charm, if we wish to plot a course of action in the real adult world, reason, not whim, must govern.

So then, what *are* your priorities? What do you want from money?

To start you off, here are some areas of possible importance to you which you may want to consider:

1. *Protection of family and self during salaried years.* Any wealth-building program that does not take into account the possibility of adversity is built on wind-blown sand. What bad could happen to you? You could lose your job, become too ill to work, or die. You could be sued for damage incurred on your property or if your automobile injured or killed another person. Such things happen every day. They could happen to you. High on your list of objectives must be the protection of your assets and the well-being of your family and yourself.

Money can buy you a degree of protection against such

hazards—mainly in the form of insurance. When you are young and your fortune is in its infancy, life insurance is vital in protecting the welfare of your family. As you grow older and as your wealth increases, life insurance assumes the function of softening the blows of death taxes so that the estate you have so carefully assembled is not shattered and blown to the winds (and the lawyers) when you die.

Disability insurance—usually the state or your employer offers something in this line. If they do not provide it, or if what they provide is insufficient to manage your needs, get it yourself.

Cover your property, your car, the members of your family with liability insurance.

Medical insurance—if not supplied by your employer, you must assume its burden. It need not cover every wound or case of chicken pox or broken toe, but it should provide protection in case of serious illness for every member of your family. Doctor and hospital bills have escalated to such a degree that an illness can wipe out a lifetime of effort within a few months. Major medical coverage is a must.

Loss of your job is another trauma you must be prepared for. While most states provide unemployment benefits, these are pegged at subsistence levels. One of your early steps in creating a wealth-building program must be the accumulation of an emergency fund to help carry you over possible short-term loss of income.

Life insurance, disability insurance, major medical insurance, liability insurance, self-developed unemployment emergency fund—not very exciting ways to spend your money. The satisfaction comes only with the peace of mind you get knowing that your "business" can weather most storms. You can have the freedom to put your mind to more positive matters.

2. *Protection for family and self after retirement.* While the bulk of this book is devoted to helping you create prosperity in your old age and freedom from worry about money,

you should consider other devices for assuring sufficient income upon retirement.

Social security offers some assistance, but alone it does not now, and never will, provide for more than survival living. It must be supplemented to obtain any kind of self-rewarding retirement.

Most companies offer some kind of retirement program. Take advantage of it. If your company does not, the government provides that you may establish your own Individual Retirement Account (I.R.A.), or, if you are self-employed, you can apply for the government-approved Keogh Plan. (We will discuss both of these later.)

The point is that when you are involved in any sort of retirement program, it means taking cash out of current earnings and investing it in some future security. In my mind, there is no question that you should opt for an adequate retirement program. While it takes cash away from your wealth-building effort, the risk is too great to be without it.

You should also include in this category the various kinds of trusts that may be set up to provide you with income during your lifetime, but which will revert to your heirs upon your death. If you are estate-minded and wish to leave your heirs with some of the rewards of your lifetime, you may want to consider this. But I would suggest that most trust efforts be initiated only after your wealth-building program is well under way.

3. *Capital accumulation.* However you set your priorities, this must be high on your list. I'll remind you again of the absolute necessity of a disciplined savings program: your entire plan for wealth accumulation hinges on it. While there is a certain pleasure in seeing large numbers in your bank or savings and loan account, the greater satisfactions are yet to come—seeing your numbers put to work earning larger numbers. For the moment, enter capital accumulation on your list of goals somewhere near the top.

4. *Pleasures, profits, freedoms and follies.* Assuming you have assigned a portion of your income to protecting your welfare, to anticipating your retirement, and to the saving of excess capital—how can you apply some of your discretionary money to reward yourself with some pleasure?

Wealth-building should not, need not, be a Spartan exercise in self-denial. Rather, it should be a sensible plan for creating opportunities which offer you the widest possible choice of material pleasures.

Make a list of the concrete things you want, that might make you happy, and jot them down at random. You can assign their relative importance later.

Your list might include:

> A home of your own
> A mink coat for your wife
> A boat or dune buggy
> A second or third car
> Foreign travel
> Owning income property
> Theater tickets once a month
> A vacation home
> Early retirement
> Antiques, art, artifacts
> Private schooling for your children
> Membership in a new country club
> Large bank account
> Financial independence
> New living room furniture
> Tennis lessons

The list is limited only by your capacity to dream.

Now rank these in their order of importance to you. Is foreign travel more important than owning your own home?

Is the possession of beautiful things more important than a portfolio of securities? The decision is yours.

One factor in your decision might be the side benefits that some of your options provide. For example, owning your own home can be not only a pleasure but a profit asset as well. Your interest payments and property taxes are income tax deductible. For roughly the same amount you are paying for apartment rental, you might be able to realize income tax savings that will actually put more free cash at your disposal. And, if you have chosen property wisely, increases in the value of your home can add measurably to your net worth.

Membership in a new country club may give you valuable business connections.

New living room furniture may permit you to do more business entertaining and enhance your value to your company.

Well-chosen art and antiques should, in time, increase in value and so contribute to your net worth.

Whatever your motives in choosing what you want to do with your money, you should ask yourself what you desire in the short-range future and what you are willing to wait awhile to achieve.

Some of the items on your list may be attainable right away—you've checked your budget and seen that you can afford them. Others will only come about as the result of deliberate planning.

Trim your list to the point where you are down to the few key items that mean the most to you. Don't throw the others away—just set them aside for a while. Now, what strategies are required to get the items you want?

Want a boat? Open a separate savings account devoted strictly to boat. Think you can save enough in three years to make the payment? You might want to consider longer-term financial vehicles that return a higher rate of interest.

It may be that the goal of owning your own home within two years will mean cutting down on your entertainment or limiting your department store purchases. Is it worth it? If you want it, do it. You decide, and then stick to it. With a specific goal in mind, it is easier to summon the willpower and courage to obtain it.

If you can manage to define your goals, budget for them, and then freeze your standard of living for a period of time, you will be surprised how much you can attain with relatively little effort or heartache.

With a realistic plan, a little luck, and a modicum of self-discipline, you can attain your dreams.

5

Step 4–
Choose Your Team

To be conscious that you are ignorant is a great step to knowledge.
BENJAMIN DISRAELI (1804–1881)

A wise and an understanding heart.
The King James Bible, 1 Kings III

In your journey toward financial independence, you will need some help along the way. It is a rare person who can absorb the expertise necessary to do it all by himself. Nor should you even try to go it alone. Even if you could grasp the necessary know-how, you haven't the time.

I suggest you collect a personal "brain trust of experts" and concentrate your business with them. The better they get to know you, your thinking, and your investment goals, the more helpful they will be to you. You need not go out immediately on a recruitment drive to select the entire team. Add members to your group as you need them.

These are the kinds of professionals you should consider including on your team:

1. *Tax accountant* to prepare your tax returns, and to be available for consultation by telephone regarding tax and accounting problems during the year.

2. *Attorney* to draw up your will and set up trusts and, when you are buying and selling property, review escrow instructions. (Eventually you'll need more than one. Attorneys, like doctors, tend to specialize.)

3. *Life insurance agent* for life, accident and health policies.

4. *General insurance agent* for auto, casualty and fire policies.

5. *Securities broker.*

6. *Bank manager* for general consultation and for arranging purchases of banker's acceptances, treasury bills, commercial paper, etc.

7. *Savings and loan manager.*

8. *Property manager,* if you choose professional help in the management of your real estate.

You will be paying fees to some of these experts, while you will be getting services from others without payment as part of their overall business.

Selecting the proper people for your team is a knotty problem. You certainly won't want to let your fingers do the walking through the Yellow Pages to locate them. I have chosen the members of my "team" from many sources—and not without error.

My first tax accountant was an older man, highly respected in his profession and a stickler for detail. A visit to him was like having a thorough going-over by an IRS audit squad. I found myself doing three days of intense preparation before every visit just to avoid his frown of disapproval. He was excellent in his work, but I always had the feeling that I was working for him rather than he working for me.

On the occasion of buying my first apartment house, the seller was an aging motion picture actor who had an unrealistic view of what his property was worth. Negotiations went on for several months. His tax accountant was a young man, younger than I, but very correct, professional and help-ful throughout the tedious discussions.

Then the actor had to go into the hospital for stomach surgery and I decided for one last try. I sent my final offer into his hospital room and the actor finally signed it, almost as they wheeled him out on a gurney toward the operating room. The actor recovered. I had my first piece of income real estate.

When my tax accountant decided to retire (he was in his early seventies), I called this young accountant and asked if he would like to handle my business. We have had an excellent relationship ever since.

The characteristics I admire in my accountant are, when I think about it, nearly universal among all the professionals I call on for my team. We are compatible; we talk on the same wavelength; our heads are in the same place. When I need the answer to a question, I get it, accurate and well thought out. When he doesn't know the answer immediately, he does not double talk or do a soft shoe shuffle around it. "I'll get back to you," he says. And he does. He is generous with information so that I soon learn the right questions to ask. There is the spirit of "we" about our dealings, whether "we" good or "we" bad, I feel that he is an interested par-ticipant in my business.

As important to me, he is fun to do business with. He has a wry sense of humor that never falters. Business can be made a dreadfully dull affair if conducted with deadly seri-ousness. Why not get a few kicks out of it?

Unconsciously, I suppose, I have selected all my team on these criteria. It has made doing business a pleasure in-stead of a drag.

The majority of my team members have been gathered by personal acquaintance or reference. One I went to college with. Another is a social friend. Several I was referred to by people I respected. Sometimes this close relationship can cause problems, but with me it rarely has.

If you have need of professional advice and don't know where to go, inquire of your friends, the ones you would trust to know. If not there, seek out one of your company executives for help in locating a prospect. Most will be flattered by your request for advice. As your circle widens, implementing your team becomes easier.

Here are some specific suggestions for the selection of your team.

As a general rule, I prefer dealing with professionals younger than I am. Usually they are more energetic, less fixed in their ways, and more open to creative solutions. There are a few exceptions. For a securities broker, I would rather have a seasoned veteran who has been around the track; who has lived through the triumphs and the traumas of bull and bear markets; who will not peddle blue sky nor panic at the sight of a dropping Dow-Jones. I have not done well with the young go-go securities brokers.

I have one attorney who specializes in wills and trusts and another who is expert at contracts. Real estate transactions require an attorney familiar with its sunny highways and dark alleys. Tenant evictions are difficult (I have had three over the years) and I employ another attorney for this.

A property management firm must not be too loaded with properties, must be interested in your business, and should be very professional in conduct.

A life insurance agent must be sophisticated in the ways of insurance—and not disappear once the policy has been sold. My agent, for example, informed me of the estate advantages of having my life insurance in my wife's name only, and did not earn a penny for the time and thought he gave to it.

General insurance agents should be totally reliable and

competitive with their offerings. I have had mine for thirty years with never a bad piece of advice.

Bank and savings and loan managers tend to come and go. You must cultivate each new one in turn, deciding whether he is someone you can depend on or not.

As a rule, select people from established, reputable firms and concentrate your business with them. This generally results in better service. If one of your team lets you down— if he's slow to respond to telephone calls or fails to come up promptly with the information you need—it is best to warn the culprit once, and then, if the offense continues, make a change. There's no sense letting deadwood complicate your life.

Your accountant and attorney are generally paid by their time. Thus when you are visiting them or telephoning them for counsel it is prudent to remember that the meter is ticking. Get down to business. If you want to socialize, telling of your latest golf scores, your son's or daughter's school grades, or problems at the office, remember you are paying by the minute. Better converse with your friendly bartender, where you are paying only by the drink.

Remember too that some of your experts make their livings by selling. The securities broker or the insurance agent earns his income by selling you a choice stock or a selected policy. While you can always hope that the members of your team have your best interests at heart, this is not necessarily the case. A certain amount of salesmanship is allowable; but if the pitches become too heavy or frequent, I tend to run for cover and start looking for new team talent.

In your earliest period of investing you will be, by most business standards, a "small account." Don't let this give you an inferiority complex in dealing with your experts. You are the biggest account you have. Getting the right answers and efficient service is just as important to you as it is to a multi-million-dollar corporation.

Although you will count on your team for expertise, you cannot depend on them to do all your work for you. You must shoulder a good deal of the responsibility for keeping yourself informed. You can't get the right answers unless you know the right questions to ask.

Familiarize yourself generally with the tax laws so that you have at least a schematic knowledge of their liabilities and opportunities. Your tax accountant will have small success when you call him on December 15 to bail you out of trouble you have created for yourself through the rest of the year.

Learn the kinds of documents you must deal with in handling your legal affairs. Omit the long preambles as to why you need this paper or that.

Read the insurance company brochures and discover the differences between policies so you can match them to your needs. Intelligent people frequently buy too much insurance or the wrong kind merely because they have not done their homework.

Once you decide to embark on a program of investing, whether in securities or real estate or both, it is mandatory for you to read up on the general principles involved in the area you choose. Since investing in any area involves shooting at a moving target—investment opportunities and liabilities being in a constant state of flux—it is well to keep currently informed by subscribing to one or more publications devoted to business and investment interests.

The *Wall Street Journal* is the daily newspaper of business and investment, with its finger on the pulse of the securities markets and general business interests.

Business Week is a weekly magazine directed toward the business executive, and contains valuable insights into various segments of business and the people who influence them.

Forbes is a bimonthly business/investment magazine of interest to the general investor for its current business thought and its anticipation of future business trends.

Two Kiplinger publications are useful: *The Kiplinger Washington Newsletter* and *The Kiplinger Tax Letter.* Since Washington and taxes play such an important role in any financial endeavor, it is handy to get the news quickly and close to the source.

I have at one time or another subscribed to one or another of the newsletters offering expert investment advice, but found each of them wanting. Perhaps I picked the wrong ones.

If you enjoy business reading, and as your sophistication advances, you may want to expand this list. Then too, many valuable books will give you overviews and insights into the mechanics and strategies of investing. Investment reading, if you can sift through all the debris, public relations and vested interests that pervade it, can help provide a kind of insurance—protecting you from being caught in adverse situations, assisting you when you need help. As in the law, ignorance is no excuse.

Training yourself to think in investment terms, gleaning knowledge to help in your decision-making, gathering a team of experts about you to lift you over the hard places—these are all vital steps in the wealth-building process, contributing to your ultimate victory.

6

Step 5—
Create a Cash
Equivalent Reserve

*How little you know of the age you live in if you fancy that honey is
sweeter than cash in hand.*
— OVID (43 B.C.–18 A.D.) *Fasti*

*Can anybody remember when times were not hard and money not
scarce?*
— RALPH WALDO EMERSON (1803–1882)

A hen is only an egg's way of making another egg.
— SAMUEL BUTLER (1600–1680) *Life and Habit*

The first four steps up your wealth-building pyramid involved preparing yourself for investment. These next four
steps concern the opportunities and processes of investment.

The creation of a "Cash Equivalent Reserve" is your first
tentative, ultra-conservative, no-risk dip into sending your
money out to make more money for you.

I have described cash equivalents as investment vehicles
where your capital is safe, a return is paid (however small),
and both capital and return can be converted to cash on
demand (or brief notice).

So these are the salient points about cash equivalents:

1. very safe
2. guarantee a return
3. easily redeemable in cash.

The requirements for your Cash Equivalent Reserve are derived from your estimate of your annual expenses (Chapter III). There are two rules involved.

Rule 1. *You must at all times have the equal of three months of your expenses invested in a regular passbook savings account.*

Rule 2. *Your total Cash Equivalent Reserve should equal six months' expenses.*

Let's go into some of the reasons for these rules. The first principle of investing is not to lose any of the capital invested. Loss of capital is a step backward in wealth accumulation. But it is not always possible as you reach out for greater rewards from your capital to eliminate the risk of capital loss. Greater risk and greater returns are often Siamese twins—organically inseparable. So the second principle of investing is never to risk more than you can afford to lose. Wherever a possible capital loss might endanger your well-being or that of your family, or might seriously hinder your wealth-building ambitions, you can't afford to assume the risk.

These two rules and two principles are the cornerstones of your investment, your wealth-building, program. They will help give you the ability to challenge risk from a position of confidence and security.

Where do you get the capital to begin your Cash Equivalent Reserve? In Chapter III I emphasized the importance of a regular savings program so that you can accumulate investment capital. It is my conviction that this is the one and only way to begin a methodical wealth-building program.

I also cautioned that your savings program might involve sacrifice and self-discipline. In fact, this step—the creation of a Cash Equivalent Reserve—may require more mental toughness and determination than any other step you undertake.

In a bit, I'll show you why. First, let us go back and review your strategies of saving. If I sound like a graybeard or a joy-killer in this, please forgive me. It is not my intent. If I sound like a fanatic, you have it right. I agree with Ralph Waldo Emerson: "There is no strong performance without a little fanaticism in the performer."

You will aim at saving at least 5 percent of your gross income each month. Better yet, if you can manage it, save 10 percent. (I have a friend, very wealthy now, who nevertheless still maintains this savings discipline. His magic number is 15 percent. This practice helped make him rich—and he intends to stay that way.)

The percentages I give you are arbitrary—but there is a method in them. They are round numbers, easy to remember and simple to calculate. As they are based on your gross income, the variables of monthly expense, taxes, etc. can't creep in and befuddle the process. You are also offered a useful degree of prediction. You can look ahead to a year or two years from now and predict that you will have so many dollars available for your investment adventures.

In contrast, if you were to settle with yourself that you would save half of all your discretionary cash after expenses each month, you might be saving a little this month, a lot next month, and nothing the month after that. This is not methodical; it is not regular—it is capricious. And if it follows a normal human route, it will end with dropping the whole program as a bloody nuisance.

Another condition you should consider is exactly how hungry you are to attain wealth. If you now have an income that barely meets your expenses, would you consider moving to a less expensive apartment, eating cheaper meals, buying new clothes less frequently, taking the bus to work rather than driving a car? If you are this eager for wealth, you might choose an even higher savings rate—living poorer now, to live better later.

If you find yourself in the happy condition of spending less than you budgeted—of having more discretionary cash than you expected—then, and only then, do you allow yourself some options. You may choose to sock away all your extra savings in your wealth-building account. You may decide to start a second savings account to accumulate cash for some wanted item—a house, a new car, a boat, a vacation. Or you may feel like blowing the whole excess on yourself as a reward for your thrift. This is the first sweet fruit of your financial planning: the freedom to choose where your surplus money will go.

The main conditions of a successful savings program are that it be regular, predictable and automatic—as mindless as a programmed robot in a science fiction movie. If you subject yourself to the monthly torture of deciding how much to save, if anything, I think you are playing dangerous games with your future. The average human psyche can't stand the stress of it. Set a savings percentage that *you* want and that you think you can live with—and let no demonic spirits or siren's songs deter you from it.

The check for your savings account should be the first you write each month. If you find your salary check insufficient to fulfill your savings goals and pay your monthly bills too, you will have to do something about it. You must reevaluate your budget, your standard of living, your ways of conducting your business.

It may be you are not being paid a high-enough salary for the kind of work you do. Are you working toward an increase? Do you have a strategy for promotion? If it is not possible to persuade your management that you should be earning more, perhaps you should be seeking a job change.

The desirability of job-hopping varies widely from industry to industry, from occupation to occupation. In some industries it seems the only way to move up is to move out. A prophet is without honor in his own company—until he gets a better offer from the competition.

A higher salary is only one consideration in changing jobs. Better working conditions, greater possibilities for advancement, more fringe benefits, a more congenial atmosphere, proximity to home, etc., will also figure in your deliberations. However, you must understand that job changing can be a damper on your wealth-building plans—even if you get a higher salary. You may suffer the loss of your company's contribution to your retirement benefits. The frequent job-hopper may have more trouble borrowing money. Where job change entails movement from your community or state, you as a salaried wealth-builder must collect a new team of experts, establish new connections. Where income real estate is part of your investment portfolio, you face difficult decisions. Selling it could incur large capital gains taxes. Trading it up into a new piece of property in your new locality may be very hard. Leaving its management to others while you are far away could be most disappointing.

I have no specific suggestions for you in this, other than that you should weigh your alternatives very carefully before you make the decision to change. Salary alone is frequently an insufficient motive to move. Better interrogate your expenses before you convict your salary.

You will be drawing from your savings account to make the large periodic outlays (taxes, insurance, etc.) that you have already accounted for in your budget. Seasonal divergences from your budget averages may require drawing additional amounts from time to time. But, unless there is some unexpected emergency, your savings account should continue to grow at the rate you have predetermined. If it drops below your calculated minimum, your plan is in trouble. You are *not* on your way to financial security.

Let us return to Cash Equivalent Reserve Rule 1—three months' expenses in a passbook savings account. Does this seem like a lot to you? It is not. Some investors prefer a 4- to 6-month minimum.

You can see the sense of this. It is to prevent an unforeseen event from putting you in a negative cash situation. It gives you an immediate supply of hard cash to cover monthly expenses. What if a sudden shift in economic conditions should cause you to lose your job? It is not uncommon in our technicologically sensitive society for even highly trained professionals to be left jobless without warning—and with no ready prospects. Some of the skilled technicians and engineers who helped put astronauts on the moon suffered months of living on unemployment. You feel secure in your job, your industry? So did they.

Assess your own situation. Could you be fired from your job tomorrow and immediately walk into another as good or better? Do you have sufficient major medical insurance to handle a sudden illness? How long will your company continue to support you off the job? Will unemployment benefits be enough to cover your expenses?

If you are satisfied with your resources in case of emergencies, let Cash Equivalent Reserve Rule 1 be your minimum safeguard. If you are uncertain, add to it.

Consider the alternatives. How many people do you know who, when they've gotten into a money bind, have been forced to go to a loan company or a "loan shark" to solve their financial problems? Usually these high-interest-rate solutions only compound their plight.

Now we'll look at the purposes of Cash Equivalent Reserve Rule 2—the total equaling six months' expenses. Rule 1 provides for a minimum of three months expenses in a passbook savings account; Rule 2 calls for an additional reserve of three months' expenses, made up not of savings deposits, but of cash equivalents.

There are two reasons for this sectioning of the Cash Equivalent Reserve. In emergency situations you may need extra cash in a hurry. The accessibility of ready cash in a savings account allows for this. But the chances are you won't need all your reserve cash at one time. Three months' worth of expenses should be enough to handle things for a while. A regular passbook savings account pays only 5 to 5½ percent interest. This is not a return calculated to increase your wealth at a rapid rate.

Other kinds of cash equivalents are short-term investments—not as quickly convertible to cash as money in a passbook savings account, but they will pay you higher interest rates. So you are trading a better return on your money for slightly less liquidity.

The philosophy of the Cash Equivalent Reserve (and of this entire book) is to protect your assets while giving you the maximum ride for your investment dollars.

The cash equivalents I suggest all have a high degree of safety, generally earn rates higher than savings accounts, and may be purchased to mature (turn back into cash) in three months or less. Some have high minimum cash requirements ($10,000 for example), and so are not for everyone. Also, they require more maintenance than does a savings account. When one of these cash equivalents matures, you must go out and invest in another to keep your cash active.

Each has its advantages and restrictions. Following is a brief survey of some of the cash equivalents available to you. Your bank manager should be able to give you further information about current opportunities and rates of return. If none suits you, keep your six months' Cash Equivalent Reserve in a regular passbook savings account.

Cash Equivalents

Dealing in cash equivalents can be either complex or simple, however you want to play it. If you have a trustworthy bank manager on your team of experts, probably the simplest technique is to outline your investment objectives to your bank manager and ask for his advice. You tell him: "I have five thousand dollars I want to invest in cash equivalents for ninety days—what will give me the best return on my money?" He'll probably give you several choices and you can decide which you find the most attractive.

If you wish to educate yourself to the nuances and niceties of cash equivalents, you move into a most difficult and sophisticated area. The main reason for this is that cash, like any other commodity, is fluid, not constant. In any one day the value of cash will rise or fall, depending on its supply and the demand for it. The amount of return you receive on a certain kind of cash equivalent today may differ drastically from the return offered 90 days from now.

The government and the general business community both have a constant need for cash, long- and short-term. This creates a marketplace for borrowing and lending money. And in this marketplace every cash equivalent is in competition with every other cash equivalent, as well as with savings accounts and, to a degree, stocks and bonds.

In general, as the Federal Reserve Board's discount rate rises, the interest rates on cash equivalents must rise too, in order to compete. In the same way, as the discount rate drops, money becomes easier to obtain and the returns on cash equivalents become lower. This is by no means a one-to-one relationship since other factors enter in, but it is the trend.

The result is an interesting see-saw effect between cash equivalents and securities—stocks and bonds. High prime rates, which drive down the prices of securities, push up the yields of cash equivalents—and vice versa. So, at a time when stocks and bonds appear to be in jeopardy, cash equivalents will be looking more appealing. For the securities investor who has no desire to risk his capital in a declining market, cash equivalents become a serendipitous place to hide.

The cherished qualities of offerings in the money markets are similar to those in any investment marketplace: safety and yield. Although all cash equivalents are considered to offer a high degree of safety, some are safer than others—and this gives rise to other differences between them. Offerings issued by or guaranteed by the federal government are considered the safest. U.S. Treasury bills, notes and bonds are rated as well-nigh infallible. The government would have to collapse for the investment to be lost. Savings in banks and savings and loans which are insured by the Federal Deposit Insurance Corporation (up to $40,000 per account) are also regarded as virtually risk-free.

Issues by certain federal agencies (the Federal National Mortgage Association's "Fannie Maes," for example) are considered almost as safe.

Some cash equivalents, such as banker's acceptances and time certificates of deposit (TCD's), are guaranteed by the bank that issues them. Since banks, now and then, do collapse, these are only as good as the issuing bank—quite safe, but not as safe as federal offerings.

Certain other cash equivalents, such as "commercial paper," which may be purchased at banks, are not guaranteed by the bank. They are an obligation of the business which is borrowing the money. So the commercial paper of General Motors would be regarded as more secure than that of Fly-by-Night Furniture Company.

The amount of return paid by any cash equivalent is determined roughly by its marketability. A Federal Treasury Note, for example, although eminently secure, will find few takers at a face rate of 3 percent when the rest of the money market is offering rates from 6 to 9 percent. The people who determine money rates are skilled at feeling the pulse of the market and judging the precise rate of interest (down to a few hundredths of a percent) necessary to move an issue. So selecting a cash equivalent is largely a matter of give and take—give up a little safety and take a little more interest, or the reverse.

For persons with modest amounts of cash to invest, especially over short time spans, these small percentage points of difference will play an infinitesimal part in making you richer or poorer. On $1,000, for example, the difference between 5½ and 6 percent interest over three months is only $1.25. On $10,000,000, however, the difference is $12,500.

Other variables among cash equivalents are the time they take to mature and their minimum cash requirements. Here are some rough guidelines:

Treasury bills. Term: 90 days to 1 year. Minimum cash: $1,000.

Treasury notes. Term: 1½ years to 10 years. Minimum cash: $10,000.

Treasury bonds. Term: 5 years to 30 years. Minimum cash: $1,000.

Note: there are two other things you should know about U.S. Treasury issues. First, their interest is subject to federal income tax but not to state income tax—so that may make them worth a few fractions more to you. Second, even though their terms may be far longer than required by your Cash Equivalent Reserve (30 to 90 days), they are readily marketable and can be sold within a few days with only a small loss of interest. Beyond this, you can purchase Treasury issues when they are close to their maturation dates and so cash them out quickly with a few fractions of a percent advantage.

Banker's acceptances. Term: 1 month to 6 months. Minimum cash: $25,000. (This may vary from bank to bank.)

Time Certificates of Deposit. Term: any term you choose. Minimum cash: $500. (Again, different banks have different practices.)

This brings to mind a story the manager of one of my banks recently told to me. One Friday afternoon just before a three-day holiday weekend, a businessman arrived shortly before closing with a certified check for approximately $3,000,000 —payment he had received for a shipment of goods. He asked to take out a TDC for three days, until Tuesday morning. Bank personnel were reluctant to conduct this transaction so late in the day, so the businessman said, "All right, I'll take it in cash." Now, there is not one bank in ten thousand that can come up with $3,000,000 in currency on the spur of the moment. And a man carrying $3,000,000 is not to be treated lightly. They issued him his Time Certificate of Deposit. When the man returned on Tuesday morning, his $3,000,000 had earned a nice little $1,700 in interest. Certainly this was a man who was serious about money.

Commercial paper. Term: 60 days. Minimum cash: $25,000. (These may vary.)

Quasi-government issues. Term: varies. Minimum cash: varies.

Federal intermediate credit in government debentures. Term: 9 months. Minimum cash: $500,000. (These may vary.)

Federal Land Bank Bonds. Term: 18 months to 15 years. Minimum cash: $1,000. (These may vary.)

In dealing with cash equivalents for the short term there comes a time when you have to ask how much your time and effort are worth to you. For example, if you have $5,000 to invest in cash equivalents for a three-month term, and if you are able to better your passbook savings rate by 2 percent—the difference in return over three months is $25. Is this worth a trip to the bank and ten or fifteen minutes of paperwork? It's for you to decide. As your capital investment grows, each trip becomes more worthwhile.

Probably the easiest way to pick up a few fractions of a percent extra interest is through a *30- to 90-day certificate account* at your bank or savings and loan. Once you have it, renewing it is simple. And your Cash Equivalent Reserve is satisfied.

Another relatively new opportunity, which has been recommended to me though I have not yet tried it, is in a special kind of mutual fund called a *liquid asset* or *money market fund*. These funds specialize in short-term money market vehicles—the kinds of cash equivalents I have described. In their short existence, they have earned quite a good reputation for delivering healthy returns (8 to 10 percent) with about as much safety as you could ask.

They are no-load funds—that is, there is no sales fee or commission up front, a serious drawback to many mutual funds. They may call for a small transaction fee for buying or selling shares, or a small monthly service fee. In those I have inspected, administrative costs are minuscule (less than one-half of one percent) compared to their investments.

They seem to be giving the investor what mutual funds are supposed to give—pooled dollars, expertise, and diversification, making for a higher return than the investor can achieve for himself.

The minimum investment in the money market funds I have noted ranges from $1,000 to $5,000. Redemption is invariably simple and quick. The method differs from fund to fund. Some require only a phone call, others a Western Union wire. Still others allow you a check-writing privilege, so that your deposited check automatically debits your investment.

The one main hardship with money market funds is that they are difficult to track down. They do not employ sales forces; their shares are not sold by stockbrokers or banks.

The only way to invest in a money market fund is to locate it; write asking for a prospectus, and then take it from there, dealing directly with the fund. The funds are scattered across the country from Coral Gables, Florida, to Portland, Oregon, and there are few sources of information about them.

One source that I know about is a book: *"The Dow Jones-Irwin Guide to Mutual Funds"* by Donald D. Rugg and Norman B. Hale, published by Dow Jones-Irwin, Homewood, Illinois 60430. Don Rugg gave me a copy. They list 32 money market funds with addresses so that you can contact them. If you are interested in money market funds, I suggest that you make a campaign of it, writing to as many as you can and then comparing them. (The book itself offers an ingenious system of investment in no-load mutual funds. Since I have tended to avoid mutual funds, preferring to do it myself, I have no experience with their system, and thus no recommendations for or against it.)

These, then, are the rough parameters of your opportunities with cash equivalents. As your wealth grows, you will find increasing use for them. For the short run, I suggest you do not become too involved in trying to calculate the intricate and devious ways of the money markets. Rather, depend on your bank manager expert to guide you—or investigate money market funds.

Later you will find your mind fully occupied with the more profitable risks of the stock and bond markets—and with income real estate investment.

You can go through life without fully understanding the mechanisms of the money market—and never miss it at all.

The one-year-and-longer savings accounts offered by savings and loans and commercial banks are not suitable for your Cash Equivalent Reserve. Although they offer attractively higher rates of interest, they do not give you the quick liquidity you desire. If you call on the cash before the expiration date of the certificate, you must pay a stiff penalty.

Stocks and bonds do *not* qualify as cash equivalents. Even though a stock may yield a high dividend relative to its price; even though the corporation may be a securities blue blood; if you need to sell at a time when its price has fluctuated to a low point, your capital will not be returned intact. The same is true for bonds. Corporate and public utilities bonds are interest-sensitive. If interest rates go up, bond prices drop. Some of your capital may be eroded if you are forced to sell during a high-interest period.

Also, it is often the case that the time you wish to call on hard cash is the same time when stocks and bonds are on the ebb.

As your annual expenses grow, your Cash Equivalent Reserve must grow along with them. If you acquire investment real estate, your Cash Equivalent Reserve must be extended to cover six-months' share of such annual and semi-annual bills as taxes and insurance premiums on your property.

You will recall my warning that this step of creating a Cash Equivalent Reserve may be the most difficult of the eight steps I suggest.

It is not so hard in execution. In fact, if you can manage the savings program, the rest is almost automatic. The problem resides with your mental set, your investment temperament.

In the first place, a savings and loan account is far from an ideal investment vehicle for the quick appreciation of your dollars. At 5 to 5½ percent interest, it will scarcely compensate for the inflationary deterioration of your dollars. It is a slow way to get rich.

Through the effects of compounding interest, small differences in interest rates can make huge differences in the amount of return you receive on your capital. Some examples: If you invest $1,000 at a 15 percent rate of return and let it compound, you will double your money in less than five years. (A 15 percent return is hard to come by, but not unheard of.) Your $1,000 at 10 percent will double in less than eight years. At 5¼ percent (current savings and loan passbook rate), it will take nearly 14 years to double your money. That's slow.

Another example. Suppose your gross income is $24,000 a year and your annual expenses are $18,000. You decide to set aside 10 percent of your income toward savings. Assuming the 5¼ percent savings and loan rate, to achieve your Cash Equivalent Reserve goal of six months' expenses will take you nearly forty-one months.

That is a long time in the life of an ambitious wealthbuilder just getting started. Suppose, to make it worse, that during the time you are accumulating your Cash Equivalent Reserve the stock market turns bullish. Your fellow employees in adjacent offices begin talking about the killings they are making in the market.

You are sitting there with your dumb, dreary 5¼ percent interest rate while fabulous investment opportunities seem to be passing you by. You begin to wonder if you will ever get such a good chance again.

How easy is it to maintain your savings and your Reserve discipline then? It's not. It's murder. And yet this is precisely what you should do. I am not deliberately trying to frustrate you. I see it as your only prudent course of action. While some of your friends may have their moments of investment glory, many are bound, sooner or later, to fall from grace—with no reserves to protect them. For them, it will be back to scratching for that capital nut—no longer the ebullient, carefree capitalists of the bull market.

Your Cash Equivalent Reserve is not the end, it is the means. It is the beginning of a train of developments with the greatest probability of getting you where you want to go. Any other course is riddled with chance, no matter how certain or glamorous it might look at the moment.

Console yourself with the knowledge that you are following the basic principles of sound investment. The single most important consideration is the preservation of earned capital (Investment Principle 1). Capital is a precious commodity. If you've sweated for it, you know it. Risk of capital is only for those who can afford to lose it (Investment Principle 2). For you to reach a position where you can manage capital risk (and its potential rewards), you must first create a capital sanctuary. Here no risk is permitted. The fail-safe status of your capital savings is paramount.

In most investment decisions, in this and in subsequent steps, you are faced with a trade-off: perfect safety entails low yields on your investment; high yields require risk.

Yield versus risk is the issue in most of the significant battles among investment professionals. It is no small conflict. How much potential yield is worth how much risk? Should any risk be taken at all? Should you be satisfied with the regular, slow growth of your capital in risk-free situations? Should you go for the big risk and let the bigger profits salve the wounds of loss?

There are no absolute answers to these questions any more than there is one best way to sip soup. However, for the salaried person starting from a small capital base, the only way to become rich is through the assumption of some risk. All other methods are too slow—life too short. The only way to face risk is from a position of financial strength. If a setback would endanger the welfare of you and your family, you are not ready to take on risk. If a loss will delay the growth of your wealth-building program for several years, you are not ready for risk.

So the salaried wealth-builder must construct his financial dream castle with foundations embedded in risk-free granite; however its towers may soar into the clouds of hazard. Then, should a tower tumble—as they well might—the basic structure will remain sound.

Your Cash Equivalent Reserve is your granite base. Once it's established, you can start work on your towers. I wish there were a quicker, surer way to accumulate capital wealth. There are other ways—but they are not so certain.

I will allow the possibility of one alternative. As I see it, the degrees of risk acceptable to the salaried investor are:

1. No-risk (Cash Equivalent Reserve)
2. Low-risk (Liquidity Reserve)
3. Moderate-risk (Optional Investment Fund and Income Real Estate)

(I do not consider high-risk investment since I believe it is outside the realm of the salaried wealth-builder.)

If you have discretionary cash enough to spare after fulfilling your savings requirements, then you might invest in some of the low-risk vehicles of the Liquidity Reserve. If you have spare cash beyond this, you may wish to lower your investment barriers further by taking on moderate-risk (mildly speculative) investments.

While this is more daring than the conservative step-by-step program I recommend, it may have some merit in moving you ahead at a brisker pace. It is only for those with more ready cash than they can conveniently assimilate, and who have all their other fences mended. Do not embark on it to the neglect of your Cash Equivalent Reserve.

You will live (and we hope thrive) with this Reserve for the rest of your life. Develop a healthy respect for it. It will help protect you from financial grief. It will hasten the day of your financial freedom.

7

Step 6—
Build a
Liquidity Reserve

*The rung of the ladder was never meant to rest upon, but only to hold
a man's foot long enough to enable him to put the other somewhat
higher.*

—THOMAS HUXLEY (1825–1895)
"On Medical Education"

*Consider the little mouse, how sagacious an animal it is which never
entrusts its life to one hole only.*

—PLAUTUS (254–186 B.C.) *Truculentus*

Once you have satisfied the requirements of your Cash
Equivalent Reserve, you are ready for the next step up the
wealth-building ladder—the building of your "Liquidity Reserve." Let me pause for a moment to explain what I mean
by "liquidity" and what its use is.

In the simplest terms, "liquidity" describes the ease and
speed with which an asset can be converted into cash. Cash
itself (at least for our purposes) is considered the ultimate
in liquidity—all other assets are less liquid.

Suppose, for example, you travel out of town for a business meeting in Des Moines. On Friday evening, after your

business has been concluded, you go to a small, out-of-the-way steak house that has been recommended to you for a chunk of beef and a touch of spirits. The recommendation proves excellent—the sirloin is succulent, the fried onion rings, crisp, and the spirits, uplifting. But when the check arrives, you discover you have left your money-clip in the hotel dresser.

So you survey your assets. In your wallet you have several bank credit cards, a wad of Swiss francs from a recent European excursion, and a letter from your mother. In your briefcase you find your checkbook on your hometown bank, several stock and bond certificates you had been intending to sell with your broker before this hurried trip, the deed to an apartment house in Encino which you had planned to put in your safe deposit box, and a small ingot of gold you picked up at a Des Moines exchange when you noticed that the price had suddenly dropped.

In any terms, you are loaded with assets.

But then you notice a sign over the bar reading NO CREDIT CARDS ACCEPTED, and another by the cash register, NO CHECKS. The letter from your mother, telling what a good son you have been, although you cherish it, you conclude has limited value in cash negotiations.

The steakhouse owner, although an artist with a sirloin, proves to be a financial primative, calling your Swiss francs (one of the world's most stable, reliable currencies) "funny money." He has a similar opinion of your stocks, bonds and Encino apartment house deed. Your gold ingot "is probably brass."

So for all your potential affluence, you have a serious (although temporary) liquidity problem—no cash.

If you had time enough, you could go to a bank and borrow against your credit cards, clear a check, sell the stocks and bonds at a securities broker, exchange your Swiss francs for U.S. dollars, get your gold ingot assayed and weighed and cash it in, take a second trust deed on your Encino property, or call your mother and have her send some money via Western Union.

To give this liquidity burlesque a happy ending, we'll assume that upon searching further in your briefcase you find an unused American Express Traveler's Check—which is nearly as liquid as hard cash. (Although its worth is not guaranteed by the U.S. government as common currency is, it is guaranteed by American Express, which has a deserved reputation for keeping its financial promises.)

The steakhouse owner accepts the Traveler's Check as payment for the meal, and you are permitted to depart—resolving that ever after you will keep a $50 bill tucked away in your wallet to forestall any such future emergencies.

One consideration in any investment you make, then, is liquidity—the facility with which you can turn your asset into cash. But in investing, liquidity is far from your only concern. The prime purpose of investment is to obtain a return, a profit, on your dollars invested. And as you reach out for higher returns, greater profits, usually some liquidity must be sacrificed.

The Cash Equivalent Reserve (Step 5) aimed at two levels of liquidity. The first, deposits in savings and loans or banks, is highly liquid. It can be immediately converted into cash anytime during weekday business hours. The second level, other kinds of cash equivalents, requires a longer conversion period. At both levels the emphasis is on the safe return of your original cash plus whatever it has earned.

The purpose of your Liquidity Reserve is to supply you with a third level of security. Here the ready conversion of your assets to cash (liquidity) is still a concern, but you are willing to assume a degree of risk in exchange for a hoped-for higher profit on your investment.

The capital for your Liquidity Reserve comes from the excess you have accumulated in your Cash Equivalent Reserve.

Your goals with your Liquidity Reserve will be:

1. To attain a higher yield on your capital than could be gained through cash equivalents
2. To accept a slightly greater degree of risk that goes hand in hand with a potentially higher yield
3. To invest in vehicles with a ready market that can, if needed, be quickly turned into cash.

Two or three times in any investor's financial lifetime there will occur an economic crisis such as happened in 1974–75. This was a particularly harsh fall—the worst since the market breaks of 1929, preamble to the Great Depression. You can count on these periodic economic crises: they *will* happen. You must be prepared to cope with them.

During these crises almost every investor suffers; there are few exceptions. I have known many shrewd, confident investors who have lost a lifetime of effort within a single economic downturn. That is both tragic and unnecessary. The object is to bend but not break.

Your ultimate retreat is your Cash Equivalent Reserve. Your temporary holding action is your Liquidity Reserve. Here you want investment vehicles that will react more slowly to adverse market conditions than will more ambitious investments. And you must be able to cash them out quickly should the ominous turn disastrous.

For capital appreciation on the up side and the ability to retreat quickly on the down side, the best investment vehicles to my mind are conservative securities—stocks and bonds.

Your objective is to create an "investment grade" stock and bond portfolio. This as opposed to "speculative grade" securities, where the wealth-enhancement potential is higher but so is the risk. You are not yet ready to assume a great deal of risk.

Your most recently computed net worth is the basis for the Liquidity Reserve Rule, as follows:

The minimum amount to be allotted to your Liquidity Reserve is equal to 5 percent of your net worth.

Under normal circumstances, the 5 percent should be considered a minimum amount. From time to time, depending on your fortunes and the market's vagaries, you may want to alter it.

If, for example, the market turns chancy, it may be wise to convert some of your later, more aggressive investments into these more conservative vehicles. As you grow older, or if you become fatigued with the extra attention required for speculative investing, you can devote 7 percent, 8 percent, or even 10 percent of your net worth to your Liquidity Reserve.

If the market turns down severely, you may want to abandon even these conservative investments for the sanctuary of your Cash Equivalent Reserve.

It is an iron-clad rule that none of your Liquidity Reserve be margined or pledged as security for loans. Either would defeat the purpose of the Reserve by reducing its safety and flexibility.

The Make-up of Your Liquidity Reserve Portfolio

Your investments here may include stocks (common or preferred) and bonds (corporate, convertible, or tax exempt municipals).

A little basic nomenclature should be introduced here.

Common stocks are the workhorses of the securities markets. They come in greater number and variety than any other form of security. They are the most actively traded. A common stock may or may not pay dividends, depending on the company's objectives and abilities. (A fine growth stock, for example, will often choose not to pay dividends but rather plow back profits to further accelerate growth.) A common stock is secured against no company assets. If a company goes into bankruptcy, its common stock becomes essentially worthless. Common stock does afford voting privileges regarding certain company policies and the election of the Board of Directors. Theoretically, if a company's management is performing badly, you can vote the rascals out. In practice, this is rarely accomplished by the average common stockholder, although it can make for some interesting pyrotechnics at annual stockholders' meetings.

Preferred stocks, technically, represent equity capital of a corporation. If a corporation goes bust, preferred stockholders stand in line for whatever pieces remain, behind the bond holders but ahead of the common stockholders. Preferred stock dividends are usually at a fixed rate, but need not be paid. However, preferred stockholders must be paid their dividends before common stockholders are paid. Changes in tax laws have all but done away with the advantages of preferred stocks.

Bonds are fixed-income securities—that is, they promise to pay a fixed rate of interest through their lifetime or until the company chooses to call them in. Bond holders have first access to company assets in case of bankruptcy since bonds are indeed secured by those assets. Thus they are quite a bit safer than stocks.

Bonds are issued in face value units of $1,000. But their market price may be either greater or lesser than the face amount. Where a bond has a high degree of safety coupled with a high interest rate, it may become so prized that the purchaser may be willing to pay more than the $1,000 for the bond. More normally bonds are sold at discount—for less than their face values. Generally, the lower the quality standing of the issuer and the lower the interest rate paid, the deeper the discount.

Traditionally bonds (along with U.S. government obligations, the safest investments of all) have been considered investment vehicles for old ladies and orphans because of their low yields and lack of risk. In recent years, bonds have become more interesting to the average investor because of higher yields and a greater volume of corporate bond financing.

The majority of corporate bonds issued today pay interest rates higher than you would receive from a savings account in a bank or savings and loan. Rates of 8 and 9 percent are common; 10- and 11-percent rates are not unusual. Because there is an active trading market in bonds, they perform, to a degree, as stocks do—that is, they can appreciate (or depreciate) in value.

Beyond this, because many bonds are sold at a discount, they can take on added value. If you pay less than the face value of the bond, when it matures (or is called), you will get the bonus of the cash difference. Also, by buying a bond at discount you can gain a yield higher than the stated interest rate. For example, if a $1,000 bond with a fixed interest rate of 6 percent can be purchased at a discount price of $600, the return on your cash investment is not 6 percent but 10 percent per year. And at call time you receive an extra $400 profit.

Bond prices fluctuate with economic conditions—they are "interest sensitive." When interest rates rise, bond prices drop. When interest rates go down, bond prices go up. While bonds do not ordinarily have the appreciation potential of common stocks, their combination of possible appreciation, relative safety, and fixed interest rates makes them of more than passing interest to the salaried investor.

Corporate bonds are the cornerstones of the bond business. Not all companies that issue stocks also issue bonds, but many do. The bulk of bonds are issued by public utilities.

They offer a variety of conditions which makes some more attractive than others for any specific investment objectives.

Tax-exempt municipal bonds are issued by communities and are based on the credit and taxing power of the community. As a rule, you are not required to pay federal tax on the interest you receive from these bonds. Most states will not honor the tax-exempt status of another state's bonds, so in this case you might have to pay a state tax. If you buy a municipal bond issued in your own state, the chances are that you will not be liable for either federal or state taxes on the interest earned.

Because of their low rates of interest, municipals are only attractive to persons in very high tax brackets. For example, an investor in a fifty-percent tax bracket will get the same pocket-cash return on a tax-free 5 percent municipal that he would receive on an investment returning 10 percent that is fully taxable.

Convertible bonds offer the extra advantage that you can turn them into the company's common stock at some fixed rate of conversion. Thus the investor has the safety of the bond and the opportunity to gain from the appreciation of the common stock. Because of these attractive features, the bond may be issued at a lower-than-normal interest rate or enjoy a higher-than-normal market price. These, like most kinds of securities, involve trade-offs among the variables.

Securities Ratings

Not all stocks and bonds are created equal—they have different values to the investor even though their face values may appear similar.

The chief variable is the quality of the company issuing the security—its history of earning a good profit and keeping its fiscal promises.

Standard & Poor's is considered one of the authoritative rating services for stocks and bonds.

The highest grade of bond is assigned an AAA rating. A shade under this is AA, and then A. BBB bonds are considered medium grade. Under current federal regulations, banks can only deal in these top four categories of bonds. (This makes for some interesting opportunities, which we will discuss in a later chapter.) Next on the scale comes BB —low-medium grade—and B, which is regarded as speculative. CCC- and CC-rated bonds are considered outright speculations. C is for bonds which are not currently paying the interest promised. DDD, DD and D are ratings for bonds in default, with the single D meaning you have almost no chance of getting any of your money back.

Some newspapers and other publications use Moody's rating service. In this case, the rating scale is: Aaa, Aa, A, Baa, Ba, B, etc. A Moody's Baa is roughly equal to a Standard & Poor's BBB.

Standard & Poor's stock rating system is slightly different from its bond system. A+ is the highest stock rating, followed by A and A−. B+ is considered a median rating; B, speculative; B−, highly speculative. C is reserved for a company with a ton of troubles; D means the company is in reorganization (not necessarily bankrupt but in the hands of its creditors).

The bond ratings reflect the ability of the company to keep the promises of interest payments and redemptions stated on the face of its bonds. The stock ratings reflect a company's asset value—that is, its earnings and dividend performance over an extended period of time.

Quality of Liquidity Reserve Securities

Your goal is to develop a high quality portfolio with minimum risk attached to it. There is safety too in diversifying your investments—between stocks and bonds, different companies and different industries. Somewhere along the way, you are bound to make some judgmental errors. There's almost no way to avoid it. If your mistake is only a piece of your portfolio rather than the whole chunk of it, your investment wound can be treated with a Band-Aid instead of a casket.

Any bond you purchase at this point should be "bank quality"—BBB or better. All stocks for your Liquidity Reserve should be Standard & Poor's A— grade or better.

Ideally, your portfolio should consist of no more than fifteen investment selections. More are hard to keep track of and add little to your safety. It should contain no fewer than five. This is minimum diversification for your protection.

The balance you maintain between your stocks and bonds will alter as economic conditions change. During strong market upswings, as much as 80 percent of your portfolio may be devoted to stocks. During stagnant periods, when the market seems undecided which direction to take, a higher percentage of bonds may be called for.

Then too, as a rule of thumb, you should keep a fairly even balance in dollar amounts among the various securities in your portfolio. Try not to let one or two dominate the rest by weight of dollars invested. That defeats the purpose of diversification. If you have chosen five securities, each should make up approximately 20 percent of the total; if fifteen securities, each about 7 percent of the total.

But here again, let the realities of the situation and common sense prevail. If, for example, you have a net worth of $100,000 and have set aside $5,000 cash for a Liquidity Reserve, you can find yourself immediately boxed in by the rules. Generally, you will want to buy stocks in 100-share ("round") lots. (Less than 100-share purchases are called "odd lots.") The reason for this that you pay a higher price per share when either buying or selling in odd lots. That's money down the drain. So, if you buy one bond for, say,

$800, that leaves you $4,200 to distribute among four 100-share stock purchases, which automatically means you are limited to buying stocks selling for $10 per share or less. This severely limits your options—and that is not the purpose of the rules.

The prudent policy is to know the rules and, even more important, the purposes behind them. Whenever the rules are at odds with things as they are, permit your good judgment to bend them a bit. Just a bit.

BUYING AND SELLING SECURITIES

Your efforts to fulfill the requirements of your Liquidity Reserve may be your first trip into the security markets.

There are some things you should know at the outset. First, you must recognize that as a job-holding wealth-enhancer, in the Wall Street arenas, you are an amateur—and will probably always remain one. Of course you will educate yourself to the basic rules of the game—but one-on-one against the investment professional who spends seven or eight hours a day, five days a week, learning his trade or craft or art or whatever it is, it is no contest. He will beat you hands down every time.

Paradoxically, this can actually be an advantage, as long as you understand it. You can have the advantage of perspective: viewing the battle from the bucolic summit of a green hill may be more enlightening than fighting tooth and claw down on the plain. Moreover, you can have the advantage of time. Where the investment professional may be forced to make thousands of quick decisions as the market turns and churns, you need to make only a few at your leisure. You are not required to squeeze every drop of worth out of your investment; you'll willingly settle for less than the full amount. That puts less pressure on you.

There's more to it, but I won't belabor it. The point is,

if you try to act like the professional when you're only an amateur, I think you are in for some hard knocks. Your strategies must be different. You must play a different game, and that's not so difficult. You can use the tools and materials of Wall Street and build your own apparatus.

The truth is, the last decade has been very hard on the Wall Street professionals. Eliot Janeway says: "In these last ten turbulent years, the individuals making their own money decisions have done immeasurably better than those who have let the 'professionals' do their thinking for them. In the stock market breaks of these years, for example, individual investors have repeatedly anticipated market breaks by 'selling too soon,' as Joe P. Kennedy was fond of doing, while the big institutional investors, though supposedly shrewd, have been left between the devil and the deep blue sea."

Business Week magazine once published a chart entitled: "A Dismal Record for Money Managers." The criterion of performance was the percentage gain (including reinvestment of dividends) of the stocks listed in Standard & Poor's 500 index. This index is one of the broadest and most reliable of stock indexes, more inclusive than the venerable Dow Jones Industrial Average (30 stocks), and therefore a more accurate measure of the stock market as a whole.

Measured against the Standard & Poor's 500 Stocks' performance were the performances of mutual funds (investment companies managed by professionals) and managed employee funds (which include pension and profit-sharing funds managed by banks, insurance companies and investment counselors).

Over the long term, in a ten-year period ending mid-year 1976, the average gain of the "500" stocks was 75 percent, or a mean of 7.5 percent per year, not compounded. For mutual funds the increase was roughly 55 percent, or 5.5 percent per year—just a shade worse than if they had placed their money in the safekeeping of a savings and loan. For managed employee funds, the average gain was about

45 percent or 4.5 percent per year—considerably worse than a savings and loan rate.

Over the last five years, when the stock market was encountering one of its meanest bear markets in forty years, performances were even worse. While Standard & Poor's 500 stocks showed an increase of 5 percent (not too splendid), mutual funds increased about 1.6 percent and managed employee funds increased less than 1 percent.

Now it does not take too much to do better than that. One of the main problems with investment professionals is that they are committed to the market, good times and bad. When the market goes bad, their only satisfaction can be in *losing* less than the Dow Jones.

For you and me, this is not a problem. When the market turns bear, we can get out of it—we have no moral or contractual commitment to it. In the winter of the bear, we can hibernate and live off our fat—our reserves and our paychecks. If we have prepared like the squirrels, we have nuts to spare.

As a salaried person who does not depend on Wall Street for his daily bread, as an investment amateur, you will have investment philosophies quite different from those of the investment professional. You will not try to reach for the maximum gain: you will settle for something less. You will have a tendency to "sell too soon"—locking up your profits or cutting your losses. You will not take on big risks. You don't have to.

You are an enlightened conservative investor—doing your own thing, in your way, in your own time.

Securities Strategies

The two key factors in securities buying and selling are *selection* and *timing*. I would be hard put to say which was the more important, but as an amateur investor going for the longer-range values of the market, I believe I would choose timing.

In any one market day's transactions (whether the market condition is bullish or bearish), you will find some stocks going up, some going down, and some standing still. The gross movements of the market are the sum of thousands of smaller movements.

To attempt to follow the market's minor frenetic movements on a daily basis is enough to send a perfectly sane person to his psychiatrist's couch. It is neither necessary nor desirable. A once-a-week review of the stock market reports is enough. Even then, your interests are limited to the larger movements, the industries you have chosen, and the specific stocks you have bought.

If ever you find your securities investing occupying an inordinant amount of your time and energies or causing you mental anguish, you are doing it wrong.

In Chapter 9 I show you a system of securities record-keeping which will help you make decisions about when to buy or hold or sell. I believe you will find it makes the securities markets a friendlier place for your investment capital.

Timing

The market moves forward by waves—crests and troughs, peaks and valleys. Actually, the profile of market growth is frequently more like the silhouette of a saw blade —a long gentle slope up to the cutting point, followed by a rather sharp drop.

Exhibit 2, page 106, is a chart of roughly twenty-one years of market movement of Standard and Poor's 500 stocks. You will note that while the general movement has been upward (partially the result of inflation), there have been some dramatic rises and falls.

(This chart and the following analyses are presented as a matter of historical interest only and is not intended to

Exhibit 2: Standard & Poor's 500 Stocks — 1955-1977

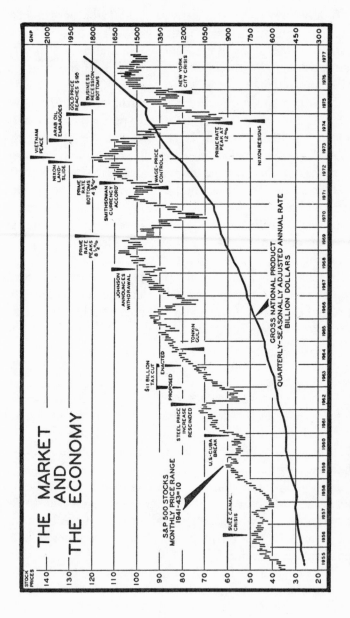

aid in the forecasting of future market events. I am not a chartist—I have been associated with too many of them with less than fortunate results. I have lost patience with slopes, shoulders, penetration levels and other such cabalistic mumbo-jumbo inherent in the rites of the dedicated chartist. I regard charting as having about the same scientific standing as astrology, voodoo and wishes made when blowing out birthday candles.)

The following chart is intended to demonstrate several conditions. Bull markets are invariably followed by bear markets—neither situation prevails indefinitely. The ranges of these market conditions are fairly wide, both in length of time and percentage of gain or loss. Bear markets are generally shorter and more dramatic than bull markets. (It takes less energy to fall down than to stand up.) The ranges of

DATES & (S & P 500 INDEXES)

High Points	Low Points	Market Length	Bear/Bull (Gain/Loss)	% + or −
Jul '56 (49)				
	Oct '57 (39)	1yr/3mo	Bear (−10 pts.)	−20%
Aug '59 (61)		1yr/10mo	Bull (+56 pts.)	+56%
	Nov '60 (53)	1yr/3mo	Bear (−8 pts.)	−13%
Dec '61 (72)		1yr/1mo	Bull (+19 pts.)	+36%
	Jun '62 (53)	7mo	Bear (−19 pts.)	−26%
Feb '66 (95)		3yr/8mo	Bull (+42 pts.)	+79%
	Oct '66 (73)	9mo	Bear (−22 pts.)	−23%
Nov '68 (108)		2yr/1mo	Bull (+35 pts.)	+48%
	May '70 (69)	1yr/7mo	Bear (−39 pts.)	−36%
Apr '71 (106)		9mo	Bull (+37 pts.)	+54%
	Nov '71 (91)	8mo	Bear (−15 pts.)	−14%
Jan '73 (120)		1yr/3mo	Bull (+29 pts.)	+32%
	Oct '74 (63)	1yr/9mo	Bear (−57 pts.)	−47%
Dec '76 (108)°		2yr/2mo	Bull (+45 pts.)	+71%

° This is probably the end of a bull market, but at this writing, there is insufficient evidence to know for certain.

time and of gain or loss frequently differ from the averages by more than 50 percent.

In analyzing this table, we can see that the range of the bull markets is from 9 months to 3 years and 8 months, with a mean of 21.7 months and a median of 22 months. The range of length of bear markets is from 7 months to 1 year and 9 months, with a mean of 13.4 months and a median of 15 months.

There are two important things to be learned by this:

1. It is virtually impossible to prophesy with any degree of accuracy the end of either a bull or bear market. The variables are too great, if not unknowable. Real and unreal factors are intertwined. Real numbers may be attached to such factors as the market's "undersold" or "oversold" condition, the gross national product, the inflation rate, the money supply, short selling, steel production, or a hundred other criteria. The unreal factors are the attitudes of the people who control market movement—and these are hidden from view in dark cranial crannies until evidenced by some overt activity. What is the attitude of the average consumer? Of the government's fiscal and monetary policymakers? Of big corporations? Of big unions? These unreal factors will become every bit as real (and perhaps even more significant) than any collection of number facts.

2. Even though you are doomed to a degree of prophetic failure, you should make a stab at it. The differences in potential rewards are too great.

Here is an example (using the same Standard & Poor's 500 Stocks chart) of what would happen if an investor in the imaginary S&P Index stock bought at the lowest points of the bear markets and sold at the highest points of the bull markets. All profits incurred from a sale are used to buy additional stocks at the next buy time. The numbers ignore all extraneous costs: broker's commissions, transfer fees, odd-

Buy/ Sell	Transaction Date	Shares at Price	Cash Value
Buy	Oct '57	100 @ $39	$ 3,900
Sell	Aug '59	100 @ $61	6,100
Buy	Nov '60	115 @ $53	6,100
Sell	Dec '61	115 @ $72	8,280
Buy	Jan '62	156 @ $53	8,280
Sell	Feb '66	156 @ $95	14,820
Buy	Oct '66	203 @ $73	14,820
Sell	Nov '68	203 @ $108	21,924
Buy	May '70	318 @ $69	21,924
Sell	Apr '71	318 @ $106	32,754
Buy	Nov '71	360 @ $91	32,754
Sell	Jan '73	360 @ $120	43,200
Buy	Oct '74	686 @ $63	43,200
Sell	Dec '76	686 @ $108	74,088

lot penalties, etc. The costs of taxes we shall consider shortly. Since this is my fantasy, I can do whatever I want with it.

If an investor had bought 100 shares of S&P Index stock in October of 1957 and merely held it until December of 1976, he would have received $10,800. This, less his original cost of $3,900, would have netted him $6,900.

Compare this result with our omniscient trader's net gain of $70,188 ($74,088 less $3,900 original cost)—more than ten times better!

But let us bring our balloon a bit closer to terra firma. We'll include consideration of income taxes. Each time our omniscient trader (OT) sold his stocks he would have had to pay an income tax and (where applicable) capital gains tax on his profit, during the current year. So, to maintain the formula he would have had to add fresh cash to make up for that lost by taxes. Assuming a constant 30 percent income tax bracket and no preference tax incurred, OT's total tax over the span would have been $11,031—leaving a net gain after taxes of $59,157

Our stolid investor, on the other hand, would have been taxed only once on his one sale, in the amount of $1,035 (same tax bracket), for a net gain of $5,865—still less than one tenth the gain of OT.

Of course this is a fantasy of the first order. Nobody, but nobody, in true life could achieve OT's phenomenal degree of success.

On the other hand, if OT had been a shrewder *stock selector*, rather than sticking with run-of-the-mill S&P Index —the perfect average stock—he might well have done a great deal better, even with much less power of prognostication.

Let us come even closer to reality. Suppose our investor in S&P Index stock is always late—let's say three months late—in making his decisions to buy and to sell. That probably more closely approximates the abilities of most of us. This is what happens to the late trader (LT) when he always buys three months after a low and sells three months after a high:

Buy/ Sell	Transaction Date	Shares at Price	Cash Value
Buy	Jan '58	100 @ $41	$ 4,100
Sell	Nov '59	100 @ $58	5,800
Buy	Feb '61 (a)	95 @ $61	5,800
Sell	Mar '62	95 @ $69	6,555
Buy	Sep '62	117 @ $56	6,555
Sell	May '66	117 @ $91	10,647
Buy	Jan '67	131 @ $81	10,647
Sell	Feb '68	131 @ $93	12,183
Buy	Aug '70	162 @ $75	12,183
Sell	Jul '71	162 @ $101	16,362
Buy	Feb '72 (b)	162 @ $101	16,362
Sell	Apr '73	162 @ $112	18,144
Buy	Jan '75	267 @ $68	18,144
Sell	Dec '76	267 @ $108	28,944

Note that at (a), Feb '61, LT's tardiness cost him cash by requiring him to buy in at a higher price than he sold. He lost the effect of a short ripple. At (b), Feb '72, LT's buy was a wash with his previous sell. Even fantasy can have its moments of truth.

Still, after tax considerations, LT's net gain for the period was $20,520 as compared to the stolid investor's $5,865 —almost three and a half times better!

The purpose of these exercises is to demonstrate the importance of timing in your use of the stock market as a wealth enhancer. The buyer and holder of the substantial stock can certainly increase his equity in it over a period of years. For the ambitious wealth-builder, however, the process is much too slow. Prudent buying and selling at key moments can multiply the gains many fold.

But how *do* you know when the market is about to reverse its field and run in the other direction? Unfortunately, church bells do not ring to signal the end of a bear market. Neither is there anyone to raise storm warning flags when the bull market is about to run into rough weather.

The market turns by fits and starts, often over weeks or even months. So you must learn how to pay attention— not just to the activity of the stocks you own, but to the market as a whole and the economy as a whole. And, since attitudes play such an important role in market movements, you'll want to know what key people and groups are thinking.

Much of this, you can get by reading. Your Sunday newspaper likely carries a summary of economic indicators showing changes in important commercial activities between this year and last. It charts changes in the Dow Jones averages, or Standard & Poor's 500 Stocks, daily volume of shares traded, daily ratios of advancing to declining stock prices. Usually these are more hints than shouts, but enough hints may help you arrive at a proper answer.

Stockbrokers are not an especially good source of information about timing. As it is with all salesmen, they tend to be optimistic. Better to become an interested reader of some of the business publications I have suggested and learn to be your own bellweather. Ask yourself whether the trend is up or down and move accordingly.

If you are out of the market and want to get into it but do not sense a definite upward trend, stand clear. Mark time with your funds earning modest but secure interest in cash equivalents.

If you have equity in the stock market and fail to sense the upward movement that might carry your stock prices yet higher, perhaps you should begin backing away from it, selling some of your more volatile securities.

(The system I recommend for keeping a current running record of your stock's activities will help a good deal in this.)

Once you've made your plunge into the market and invested in the securities of your choice, undoubtedly you will find some of them trending up and others trending down. What do you do? Follow the Wall Street chestnut—"Let your profits run and cut your losses." The forces that come to bear on any one stock, whether the market as a whole is positively moving up or down, are constantly on the move. If a security loses 15 percent of its market value, you must reassess its industry in general by reviewing the other top securities doing the same kind of business. Are they all losing ground, or is yours the only downer among the group? Either way, you might decide to sell while your loses are minimal. Take the loss, which you can use to offset a gain elsewhere, and buy again, using the same formulas, where the grass appears greener.

Show me an investor who says, "I will not sell such-and-such security until it returns to the price I paid for it," and I will show you someone who does not know where it is at. A security is worth only the price that is quoted for it. It is no more valuable than the price you can obtain from its immediate sale. If the prospects look poor for a security, sell—without a twinge of conscience or regret.

Some stocks by their vigor (or their public relations) defy market trends. If you are lucky enough to select a stock that runs counter to a determined bear market, hang onto it by all means. You may have a gem on your hands. But, by the same token, do not become wedded to a stock merely because it has been a magnificent performer for you in the past. Stocks are things, not people. You have no moral reason to be loyal to them if they fall on hard times. It seems ridiculous to offer this caution, but some investors fall in love with their stocks—"Xerox has been good to me for all these years and I'm not going to desert it now that it's in trouble." Whatever the emotion involved—loyalty, gratitude, dependency, identification—please do not anthropomorphize your stocks. Save your loyalty for your friends. Be cold-blooded and ruthless about your securities.

And the blue chip stocks are not exempt from the rules. The General Motors, the AT&Ts, the U.S. Steels and Du Ponts suffer the indignities of the bear markets just as the plebian stocks do, although perhaps to a lesser degree.

For the ambitious wealth-builder, the conclusion must be that there is no single simple formula for success in the securities market. Capital enhancement comes through the judicious buying and selling of stocks at appropriate times, and there will be a good deal of educated guessing and some luck involved in the whole affair.

Selection

The market is ripe, you have cash in hand, and you are ready to pick a stock for investment. Which one? It's not an easy decision. The New York Stock Exchange does business with over 2,000 stocks, the American Exchange with over

1,100, and the NASD (over-the-counter) with over 1,400—
all together, more than 4,600 stock issues to choose from.

What is the difference between one stock and another?
Considerable. How do the wealth-enhancing (or inhibiting)
potentials vary between one stock and another? It could be
drastically.

For the purposes of the Liquidity Reserve, which has
as its avowed goal the appreciation of capital with a minimum
of investment risk, the task is simpler than for the more
exotic, speculative kinds of programs.

The rules of the Liquidity Reserve in themselves assist
you in your selection of a likely stock. As they limit your
choices to stocks rated by Standard & Poor's at A— or better,
you are assured that the company is of adequate size; that it
has been around for a while; and that it has a history of
reasonable performance. While this may not assure you a
jewel, at least it eliminates a lot of clinkers.

The next step in your selection process may be influenced by the industry in which you are employed. Certainly
you are an insider in your own company and know something
about how it is being run. You may also know your company's main competition—the companies yours is afraid of
or looks up to as models.

I'll give you a personal example of this. All my salaried
life was spent in retail. In my later years, the department
store chain I worked for decided to sell control to Federated
Department Stores, a large retailing conglomerate. I learned
through experience, my own and others', that Federated had
earned a reputation as one of the best-operated, best-con-
trolled operations in retailing. They worked a dollar harder
and better than many of the more familiar names.

On browsing through the *Wall Street Journal* one day
after retirement, I noticed an article telling that Federated
was planning to buy Rich's Department Stores in Atlanta,
Georgia. Since both were members of the same buying

organization, they knew each other's operations thoroughly, so this could be no mere fumbling exploratory courtship. It seemed like the makings of a substantial marriage.

Moreover, at the tentatively agreed exchange ratio between Rich's and Federated stocks, the buyer of Rich's stock stood to receive an automatic 25 percent appreciation the moment the transaction went through. I was surprised that Wall Street did not quickly catch on to this. Further, I felt that retail stocks were generally underpriced, so I had this cushion to fall back on if all else failed.

I put in a bid for 1,000 shares of Rich's at $30—a dollar under the current market—and got it. (Later I added another 150 shares at a higher price to ice the cake.) The deal went through and within a matter of four or five months I had netted a gain of $15,000. So did my broker and another friend I had put on to it.

This is an example of the kind of information that you or I, as Wall Street amateurs, might have that can give us an advantage over the professionals. A certain amount of special knowledge, a certain amount of keeping your eyes open (and your mind open) to opportunities.

From your readings in the *Wall Street Journal, Business Week, Forbes* and other financial media, you may have noted a group of industries mentioned as having a future for investors. With this list of prospects you have gathered, plus others recommended by your broker, you may end up with a handful of industries that look most promising for the appreciation of your investment dollars over the next two to five years. (You may well choose not to hold these stocks that long; however, a bright future could keep them healthier longer.)

Once you have selected your industry prospects, work with your broker in first ranking the industries in order of their apparent appreciation prospects, and then ranking the top two or three companies within each industry. Likely your list of potential stocks for purchase is now down to fifteen or so—a much more manageable number.

Now it is your business to find out as much about these companies as you can. It may take a bit of research. In the end you will have a fair idea of how the experts regard these companies, and will begin to have a feeling as to which ones you would like to have on your side.

Some of the variable statistics you will have to consider are: earnings per share, net asset value per share, price-earnings ratio, and yield.

Earnings per share (total earnings of the company divided by the number of shares outstanding) is one of the most significant measures of the health of the company. Where this figure shows an increase, so, frequently, will the health of the company and the price of its stock.

Net asset value per share—also referred to as the book value per share—is the amount of assets the company has working divided by the total number of shares. This measure is of dubious value, since there are many different reasons why a particular company could have a high ratio. It might be in the nature of the industry, for example, or could reflect simple stagnation.

Price-earnings ratio is one of the most popular criteria, since it directly relates the cost of the stock to the company's earnings per share. For example, where a stock sells for $50 a share and the earnings per share are $5 per year, the P/E ratio would be 10. P/E ratios can be analyzed historically for both the company and its industry, and a judgment can be made as to whether the current price is high or low in relation.

Yield is determined by dividing the price of the stock by its annual cash dividend. A stock selling for $50 with a dividend of $2 would have a yield of 4 percent. Investors seeking high yields are usually income-influenced investors, less interested in taking higher risks for possibly greater appreciation than in getting an assured return on their money. Naturally, there is always the hope of appreciation. Since our primary goal in the securities markets is the quick appreciation of our capital, yield is a nice extra, but not a necessary requirement. Growth companies, for example, often have no yield at all, paying no dividends. When your choice is between two apparently equivalent stocks, one offering greater growth potential and the other offering a higher dividend, you would generally opt for the growth.

When the time comes to purchase a stock, always put in a buy order at a specific price slightly under the market price. This means you will buy the stock when the market sells off a bit. You will save a point or so on each purchase. Only rarely will you miss a purchase.

In selling, if you are in a hurry, sell at market; if not, you can play the same game and perhaps win a few extra dollars.

I imagine many investors and would-be investors will be impatient with the conservative nature of both the Cash Equivalent Reserve and the Liquidity Reserve. Unquestionably, these reserves are geared more to the safety of your capital than to the quick appreciation of it.

When your neighbor, Joe Plunger, tells you that his stock in Gidget International is doubling virtually every other week while your best investment is gaining only 9 or 10 percent a year, you may be strongly tempted to speculate.

I advise you to forbear, have patience. Friend Joe's Gidget Int'l may this week be as sweet as sage honey and next week, when Gigantic Industries announce they are stepuing up their gidget production, as bitter as a lover spurned.

Forbes Magazine has discovered that the most successful investor is characteristically slow on the draw. He buys slower, sells slower, and holds on longer than most other investors.

Before you step into the speculator's shoes, put your business in order. Protect your core capital with a Cash Equivalent Reserve and a Liquidity Reserve. It is the only prudent way to operate.

The rules of the Liquidity Reserve again are:

1. Equal to 5 percent of your net worth
2. Securities made up of bonds rated BBB or better and stocks rated A— or better
3. None may be margined or pledged for a loan.

One final word of advice: When you have accumulated your Liquidity Reserve securities, bundle them in a rubber band, put them in an envelope clearly marked "Liquidity Reserve—not to be margined or pledged," and deposit them in your safe deposit box. This will keep them separate from your other securities, which you will be using for other purposes.

Your leveraged opportunities are waiting in the wings.

8

Step 7– Establish an Optional Investment Fund

The people who get on in this world are the people who get up and look for the circumstances they want; and, if they can't find them, make them.
—GEORGE BERNARD SHAW (1856–1950)
Mrs. Warren's Profession

Life is either daring adventure or nothing.
—HELEN KELLER (1880–1968)
The Story of My Life

When you have fulfilled the obligations of your Cash Equivalent Reserve and your Liquidity Reserve, and your fiscal fences are all in good order, you reach a kind of transition period.

You know that on the horizon is investment in residential income property—a goal we have been pointing to all along. However, it takes time to generate enough cash to provide the nut for your real estate purchase. Neither of your reserves is available for this. And while some properties can be bought for little down, most desirable real estate needs a substantial cash investment at the outset.

Both your Cash Equivalent Reserve and your Liquidity Reserve should be generating cash beyond their minimum requirements. What should you do with it?

Until now, we have been moderately conservative in our wealth-enhancement trip. We have placed the safety of our capital above the possible greater appreciation of it by choosing vehicles that have a respect for capital investment and keep their promises of rewarding it. (A small aside here: Financial labels are as loose and emotion-laden as political labels. What I regard as mild conservatism may seem to some aggressive young bucks downright old-fogeyism, while to the doom-dongers and Chicken Littles of the world, it may seem wild-eyed speculation. I reserve the right to pick my own labels.)

As conservative investors, we have operated by a number of fairly strict rules—six months' worth of this and 5% of that; do do this, don't do that. I hope this hasn't gotten you into the habit of unthinking obedience to instructions. Because now we have arrived at a point where you can shuck some of your chains and find freedom in possibly greener fields. You will need all your wits about you.

The basic goal of Step 7 is to create enough cash to invest in residential income property. (Although later, when you have filled your rucksack with sufficient wealth-building real estate to shelter your income, you may well want to return to some of the practices of this chapter.)

Here all kinds of options are open to you—nearly as many as there are shades of color in a prism. So it seemed only proper to label this investment pool an "Optional Investment Fund." But whatever investment choices appeal to you, you must remind yourself constantly to evaluate the ratio of potential risk to potential reward. The scale ranges from extremely conservative (capital safe) to extremely aggressive (capital hazardous) and from assured modest returns to potential bonanzas.

Obviously, it is not always easy to tell a conservative position from an aggressive position. Take gold, for example. Gold is generally considered a most conservative investment —gold will always be good; it tends to run counter to inflation; it doesn't rot, rust or warp, or break when you drop it. It won't pay interest or dividends, but to gold-lovers that is a minor matter. Yet investors who bought gold in the early 1970s, when the going price was in the $180-an-ounce range, found in the mid-1970s that its value had dropped into the $120-an-ounce range. It was acting just like a despicable aggressive investment: if they had to sell, they would lose money on it.

Then too, it is possible to invest in gold aggressively, just as you can in any other commodity. If you have some inkling that the U.S. Government might want to devalue the dollar by raising the price it is willing to pay for gold, you might buy gold with the idea that you could make a killing quickly.

So gold investment may reflect either an arch-conservative view or a super-aggressive one, depending on the timing and the motives of the investor.

It is that way with most investments. General Motors, IBM, even AT&T were all at one time considered speculative investments. Is U.S. Steel a conservative investment? Its 1960 to 1974 price range was 68 to 16. If you had bought at its high and been forced to sell at its low, you would have lost three-quarters of your capital. That's not a conservative loss.

Van Gogh paintings were once speculative; so were Ming vases and pre-Columbian artifacts. Now they are as good as gold, perhaps better.

The true, legitimate speculator is not the fuzzy-brained fanatic; he is one who sees opportunities that others are unable to see. In other words, before you become too confident about what is conservative and what is aggressive, you had better know your ground.

For your Optional Investment Fund, I suggest that you take a more aggressive stance—but that is not a license to play foolish games.

Later I will discuss briefly a few other wealth-enhancement possibilities, but for the time being, in my view, the greatest opportunities for more aggressive investing still lie in the securities markets.

SECURITIES INVESTMENT STRATEGIES

In your Liquidity Reserve you were limited to a rather narrow band of conservative investments. And, of course, you have the option now of continuing the conservative practices of both the Cash Equivalent Reserve and the Liquidity Reserve. Many financial authorities would advocate just that.

However, as a salaried employee starting from a relatively low capital base, you are probably more eager for success and therefore willing to take on some extra risk.

Following is a micro-discussion of aggressive versus defensive investment stances and something about where I think your best chances lie.

Aggressive vs. Defensive

The *quality of your securities portfolio* is the first consideration. Conservative kinds of stocks might include Blue Chips, Income Stocks and Defensive Stocks. Aggressive kinds of stocks might include Growth Stocks, Depressed Industry Stocks, Cyclical Stocks and Speculative Stocks. The distinctions are not always clear-cut.

Blue Chips are considered the highest grade—a designation assigned only to long-established companies with a continuous history of paying dividends. General Motors would be considered a Blue Chip. But it also acts in a Cyclical manner. When the economy drops, car sales fall off, and so do the prices of GM stocks. Xerox was once a Growth stock. It has done so well for itself and its investors, it is easily Blue Chip.

Income Stocks are bought primarly for the dividend yield they give. Usually they are stable companies with unexciting rates of growth. There may be a few dogs mixed in. Where the market has lost faith in a stock because of its lacklustre future, the stock's price may drop in relation to its dividend, giving the untutored Income investor a false thrill of discovery.

Defensive Stocks tend to remain more stable, especially during recessionary periods. Since eating is a habitual pastime, healthy economy or not, food stocks tend to gather here. So do stocks of banks and utilities.

Growth Stocks belong to companies whose sales and earnings escalate faster than inflation. Usually the companies take an aggressive attitude toward their own growth; plowing back earnings into larger facilities, R&D, and bolder advertising. Since "growth" is such a desirable trait in a stock, the market assigns more brownie points to Growth Stocks, and therefore boosts their prices to high P/E ratios. Thus, at the first sign of a Growth Stock's faltering, its price is apt to tumble precipitously. Certainly "growth" is a desirable attribute in a stock. But by the time the average investor hears of the merits of a particular Growth Stock, the market has already advanced its cause and its price to where its potential appreciation may be marginal. The technique is to locate a Growth Stock while it is still incognito.

Depressed Industry Stocks belong to companies in industries which have taken a beating through one economic quirk or another. Again, the trick is to catch an industry while it still has a bad reputation.

Cyclical Stocks are more sensitive to economic conditions than their ordinary fellows. They are among the first to vault up at the slightest sign of an economic rainbow. Automobile and machine-tool manufacturers fall into this group. Consumers will delay purchase of a new car during hostile economic periods and businesses will be reluctant to invest in added manufacturing capacity.

Speculative Stocks are frequently so only in the eye of the beholder. The title implies that the investor is taking a large gamble with the stock, yet while this is frequently true, if the investor does his homework he may be able to sort out the dangerous speculations from the prudent ones. There is a world of difference. All stocks begin speculative.

For the salaried wealth-builder to chart a course through this maze of labels takes more than a bit of doing. Again, your best bet is to keep yourself informed through reading and frank discussions with your broker, and to keep your eyes open for undiscovered opportunities.

The *diversification* of your portfolio is a clue to your attitude, whether aggressive or conservative. The aggressive investor is inclined to place larger bets on fewer horses. The conservative investor prefers to spread his risks among more contenders. The middle road is to assemble a collection of stocks of more than one industry and more than one label— mixing conservative and aggressive, great and modest expectations, hazard and security.

The various merits of *buying and holding* versus *buying and selling* at critical points have been discussed. The conservative stance is, of course, to buy and hold. I do not advocate this under any circumstances.

This brings us to the concept of the *One-Decision Stock,* a fairy tale that was in vogue during the 1960s. The idea, I suppose, is that once you latch on to a good thing, everything is bound to be peaches and cream from then on. The Price/Earnings ratios of some of these glamour stocks grew to absurdities. They paid dividends based on market value of often 2 percent or less. Investors were persuaded that these stocks, which were continually increasing their earnings quarter after quarter, could go on increasing their earnings forever and were worth the premium prices asked.

But eventually these Prince Charmings turned back into frogs and the honeymoons were over. I'll give you an example. Simplicity Patterns, after a long record of earnings growth, came upon one quarter when its earnings fell slightly. The stock price dropped from a high of 60 in 1973 to a low of 7 in 1974 (a year noted for its increased population of frogs). The one-decision was an illusion—the premium price was not merited.

Blue Chip stocks are not immune from this phenomenon. The idea of making one decision to buy a stock and then putting it away in a closet is at odds with reality. All stocks, like all children, have their nasty moments.

At one time, investors bought and held good, solid common stocks until the day of their death. That way, under then-current tax laws, no capital gains taxes would be paid on the—presumed considerable—gain. The 1976 Tax Reform Act has changed this. Long-term capital gains taxes *may* be applied to estates, along with death taxes. (Check your lawyer or accountant for the exact regulations.) But Tax Reform Act or not, the investor has paid a high price for his inactivity. He has probably been receiving only tiny dividends on the current market values of his securities, which have appreciated greatly. His investments have been stagnating—which should please neither him nor his heirs.

Frequent trading is the sign of the more aggressive investor. But this is a trait largely denied the salaried wealth-builder.

During normal market periods, a "yo-yo" range develops. This has great interest to professional stock traders, who will try to pick up two or three points on a swing. This is their way of making a living—but it is not yours. Following a stock's zigs and zags takes too much attention. It may distract your mind from your job, your primary source of your wealth.

Do not become entranced with the stock ticker display in your brokerage office. That is not a Broadway marquee up there—and you'll not see your name in lights. Concern yourself only with your stocks' broad swings and play for long-term capital gains.

Commodities, options and margin accounts are some of the more exotic forms of investing that fascinate the aggressive investor but are abominated by the conservative investor. Generally these are fast tracks for professionals only and off limits for amateurs. There are some exceptions, which I will elaborate later.

Aggressive versus conservative investing—defining the differences is a job for a team of semanticists and psychologists.

My recommendations (which may be vague to the point of uselessness) are that you *should not* play the traditional role of the conservative investor, settling only for anemic returns from pallid vehicles; and that you *should* venture into areas of risk where the rewards may be more virile, after first checking and evaluating every nuance to know the kinds of odds confronting you. Realize that it is not hazard you are buying, it is opportunity—but to ignore hazard is to challenge the rapids in a cardboard kayak. I also hold that aggressive investments should be accompanied by an equal contingent of somber, serious, even drab investments.

Is this philosophy aggressive or conservative? I do believe it is a tasty blend of both.

DESIGNING AN OPTIONAL INVESTMENT FUND PORTFOLIO

If you are satisfied that the United States is not going out of business, that we are not on the brink of a great depression, that the free world is not going to collapse—if you enjoy these faiths, you may accumulate cash and take the plunge when the time seems right.

You now have more freedom to maneuver your investments. Here are some general recommendations to assist you:

1. You need no longer be restricted to securities of Standard & Poor's A— grade or better. And securities from the American Exchange and the over-the-counter (NASD) market may be included.

2. Review the industries which appear to have the most promise over the next one- to three-year period. The problems of selection here are even more acute than in your choices for your Liquidity Reserve. Discuss the most likely candidates with your broker, research them, take them home and study them thoroughly. Do not buy any securities by whim. Take the time to let the initial excitement wear off and to think up some "why not's." Your considered analysis will prevent many mistakes. You'll avoid emotional buying errors.

3. Predetermine your diversification. Decide on the number of selections and on their personality characteristics. Certainly this will change as new opportunities arise; how-

ever, you should be aware of the balances you are achieving between aggressive and conservative, and match them to your goals.

4. Securities in your Optional Investment Fund may be pledged to a bank for the down payment on investment real estate. However, a word of caution here: Save your solid citizens for pledging and keep your speculations closer at hand. Real estate, for all its attractions, must be considered a speculation until it has proven itself. Piling one speculation on top of another may make for an unsteady stack. Apply the same investment rules you used in your Liquidity Reserve— let your profits run and cut your losses. Be alert to any changes in outlook for securities in which you have accumulated a profit—especially, if you have passed your long-term capital gain requirement. If the future should turn bleak for any given industry or individual security, take your profit and sell. Have your broker keep you posted on any interesting developments that might effect the future of your securities. But remember that he makes his commissions only when you buy or sell. The final decision must rest with you —and you do not want to be an active trader.

You, as a layman, simply cannot become skilled enough to do well consistently as an active trader. Your mind is occupied with other things. Rather, you should train yourself to be skilled at calling general trends. You will do better as a patient investor.

Impatient investors pay lots of brokerage fees. Which brings up another point. Once, brokerage houses had fixed commission schedules which were agreed on industry-wide. Now they do not. Instead, they have individual commission policies. Recently, in idle conversation, I asked my broker whether I was getting the lowest commission rate. "No, you're not," he said, "but I'll get it for you." I had automatically assumed that I was, but I was mistaken. This accidental discovery saved me 20 percent—$200 on every $1,000 in brokerage fees. So ask your broker if you are paying the lowest commission rate. You may not get it unless you ask for it.

5. Buy stocks when the prices are low and the trend looks up. Easier said than done. In the Fall of 1974, stock prices looked extraordinarily low—but could they fall further?

Of course they could. Many did. By any historical yardstick, many fine stocks appeared to be a bargain, selling below book value and at P/E multiples of 4 and 5. They were absolutely at salvage store prices. And yet they fell further. Let history be your guide but not your dictator. Unfortunately, there is no recognizable floor which stops even a good stock from dropping lower. It could end up in the bargain basement. Only the market determines a stock's bottom. Wait until the market tells you where the bottom is. Even then, return to a ravished market slowly, a few investments at a time.

6. Know that the stock market will anticipate the end of a business recession before the business communuity enjoys evidence of it. In most modern recessions, the stock market rises before the economic indicators rise. That is, a healthy stock market and a sick economy may overlap. This is illustrated by the following chart from the *Wall Street Journal.*

DOW JONES INDUSTRIAL AVERAGES
RELATED TO RECESSION PERIODS

Recession Periods	*Start*	*End*	*Change in Points*
1948–49	171	189	+10.5%
1953–54	275	335	+21.8%
1957–58	508	455	−10.4%
1960–61	665	662	+5.9%
1969–70	812	794	−2.2%

Another chart, from *Forbes* Magazine, reinforces the concept of market anticipation. This shows the number of months by which the stock market anticipated business recovery as measured by an upturn in the Dow Jones Industrial Average:

	During Recession of
Four months	1948–49
Eleven months	1953–54
Six months	1957–58
Four months	1960–61
Six months	1969–70

So if you are looking toward economic indicators to tell you when the market is about to turn, save yourself the trouble. By the time the economy has turned around, the market will already have discounted it and be worrying about the next recession. Anticipate at your own risk. The market itself is the ultimate authority on whether it will flip or flop.

7. Choosing the proper time to sell is a more pleasant chore (though no more exact) than choosing the time to buy. It depends to some extent on how great a profit will satisfy you. However, there are several criteria which might assist you in this.

a. You can select a price at which you yourself would lose interest in buying it. Then you install a sell limit order with your broker for this price plus a few points more (there are always investors less sane than you). As the market approaches your price, you can always change your mind and withdraw the order. Or, if you see the stock turning, you can put in a stop loss order to sell for less.

b. You can choose a point on the Dow Jones Industrial Average where you think the selling pressure might become so great as to carry your stock down with the market. Rather than trying to squeeze every drop of value out of the current recovery, you will take your gains and run.

c. Another indication of when to sell is the P/E ratio of your stock compared to its P/E ratio at the time of purchase. Has the price climbed too high without support from increased earnings? What are the P/E ratios for other, similar companies within the industry? If the discrepancies are too great, you may decide that the market's enthusiasm for your stock has gone beyond its merit, and so sell.

d. One of the most useful criteria may be the concept of "energy motivation." If a stock, after a sustained climb, appears to be pooping out, losing its momentum, its energy—it may be due for a stagnant period or even a falling-off of its price. Perhaps at this point you should sell this stock and move to another which is still energy-motivated and has growth left in it.

e. Of course, if the market turns decisively downward, you will want to sell any stock that is not energy-motivated.

One way to hedge your bets in either buying or selling is to "dollar-average" your way in or out of the market.

The salaried investor who senses a cresting period will predetermine that he will sell 10 percent of his holdings each week—or every two weeks, depending on his urgency. No one can know for certain in advance when the market is peaking out. By phasing your selling, you can still gain some up-side action while you are reducing your overall down-side liability.

Conversely, the investor who has stayed out of the market because of recessionary conditions will dollar-average his way back in when he detects the beginnings of an upturn. By investing 10 percent of your stock fund each week, you should be able to catch many stocks near their lows and still retain a hedge against further erosion.

Dollar-averaging in and out of the market is a technique I have practiced for a long time with few regrets.

Dollar cost–averaging (not related to the above) is another technique you should know about for the purchasing of stocks. I don't particularly advocate it, but some investors find it useful. It is a policy more for "buy-and-holders" than "buy-and-sellers."

A securities salesman persuades you it is a good idea to buy a fixed dollar amount of a given security or mutual fund each month. If a particular month's price is up, you buy fewer shares; if the price is down, you buy more shares— either way the dollar amount invested remains the same. In a rising market, you will end up by owning your shares at less than the average price over the period. In a declining market, you succeed only in losing less than average.

However, if we understand the securities market as an appreciation vehicle only, we know there are times when we do not want to be invested in the market at all. From the crest of the bull market through the down-slide of the bear, our dollars should be earning interest with safety elsewhere.

I will reemphasize that the salaried wealth-builder should use the securities markets only as vehicles for growth. This is the main advantage the amateur investor has over the professional. Many investment funds are committed to sticking with the market through thick and thin. You pick up your chips, pay your capital gains taxes, and let the others try to capture the last buck.

When the recession storm has lost its force and you see

signs of blue skies ahead, you will have far more investment dollars to put back into the market to enjoy its burgeoning growth.

LONG- AND SHORT-TERM CAPITAL GAINS AND LOSSES

As I have said elsewhere, the government plays such an important role in wealth-building efforts that its influence must be included in any discussion of moneymaking (or losing).

Capital gains or losses are derived from the sale of any investment. That is, the difference between the buying and selling prices of a stock, bond, business, piece of real estate, is subject to capital gains provisions. Interest and dividends from investments are treated as ordinary income.

A short-term capital gain or loss occurs when the buying and selling were completed within a year or less. A long-term capital gain or loss occurs when the time between buying and selling is more than a year.

A short-term capital gain is taxed as straight income. A short-term capital loss may be deducted from income or used to offset short-term capital gain on a one-to-one basis. In other words, $1 of short-term capital loss washes out $1 of income or $1 of short-term capital gain (maximum $3,000).

Thus, investors who find themselves in an uncomfortable tax bracket near the end of a year may sell a stock for a short-term capital loss to reduce their tax liability. If they wait thirty days to buy it back again (to avoid a "wash" transaction) and its price has not altered significantly, they have gained a tax advantage without sacrificing whatever objectives they had for the stock involved.

I have described the way long-term capital gains are taxed and the advantages in lower taxation to investors. They are a form of tax shelter. After the Tax Reform Act of 1976, there remain only three feasible ways for the average salaried person to get rich: real estate, long-term capital gains, and stealing. Real estate received a few painless wrist slaps. Long-term capital gains took some harsh blows but is still viable. Stealing has always been popular.

Long-term capital losses may also be used to reduce taxes on straight income, but only at a 50 percent rate. That is, $2 of long-term capital loss eliminates $1 of taxable income. You must be fairly desperate for tax reductions to take advantage of it. As long-term capital loss (and short-term too) may be carried forward indefinitely, it might be more judicious to wait until you have a long-term capital gain which it can offset.

Where your long-term capital gains are sufficient to be subject to preference tax, you cannot reduce that tax through "sheltering" as you can with ordinary income. You must either offset it with long-term capital losses or pay it.

These are important conditions to understand. If you are confused by any of them, reread the paragraphs; then if you are still hazy about them, consult either an up-to-date, easy-reading tax book or your accountant.

The point is that whatever investment course you embark on, one of your goals must be to develop long-term capital gains, with their lower-taxed wealth-building advantages. (Unless, of course, you have so much tax shelter available that straight income is no problem to you. For most new investors this is not an impending condition.)

Stock splits come about when the price of a stock rises so high that the issuing company's management decides that the stiff price repels possible buyers. When an IBM sells in the $300-per-share range, for example, it would take $30,000 or more to buy a round lot (100 shares). The number of citizens who have $30,000 to invest in a single stock is considerably fewer than those who have $3,000 to invest.

So the company declares a stock split to reduce the per-share price. The ratio could be anything from three-to-two to ten-to-one.

Resistance to buying appears to begin at about $50 a share. In a recent survey, 95 percent of stocks selling on the New York Exchange were trading below $50. Over 28 percent of the volume of trading is done in the $10 to $20 price range. Over 54 percent of trading is done in stocks priced $30 and under.

Some investors think they have received a bonanza when one of their stocks split. Not so. When a stock splits two shares for one, for example, each of the split shares is worth one-half of the former share. So far, the investor hasn't gained a penny.

One study showed that the *proposal* to split a stock was better than the actuality of it. On the announcement of a stock split, frequently the shares will rise as much as 20 percent. Once the stock splits, it is back to business as usual, the eternal verities of stock worth.

Presumably, if you want to cash in on a stock split, you should buy on the announcement and sell shortly after the event. Whatever the small ripples caused by the announcement of a stock split, they are a minor consideration in your stock selection. There are many more important factors to worry about.

LEVERAGING

Leveraging is the process whereby the investor tries to use fewer cash dollars to accomplish greater purposes. The principle is the same as with a lever—a little weight at one end can move a larger weight at the other end. The problem arises with the fact that levers can move down as well as up. In the same way that upward movement can multiply your capital appreciation, downward movement can magnify your losses. In the majority of cases, leverage is a most aggressive (and therefore hazardous) investment technique. There are a number of ways to apply leveraging to investments. These are some of them:

Margin investing is one of the commonest ways of obtaining leverage. You open a margin account with your brokerage firm and deposit into it either cash or securities. The broker turns your securities over to a "transfer agent" and these are reissued in the name of the brokerage house. These securities are now in what is called a "street name." Technically these securities still belong to you, but they are in the broker's hands. This collection of cash and securities is collateral for borrowing to buy more securities.

The Board of Governors of the Federal Reserve System sets the margin requirements. They might determine, for example, that the margin investor must put up at least 50 percent of the purchase price of any security. This means that if you had opened your account with 100 shares of AT&T, your broker could buy for you another 100 shares of AT&T (or the dollar equivalent in any other security) without your having to put up any cash. Your margin account would then have the power of 200 shares of AT&T although you paid for only 100 shares.

Your brokerage house will charge you interest on the amount borrowed to buy the additional shares. Since brokerage houses are very large borrowers, they usually enjoy the best borrowing rates. The amount of interest charged you depends on the amount you borrow and the amount the brokerage firm itself has to pay during any one period. The amount they pay is termed the "Broker Call Rate." Your interest payments will be from .5 percent to 2 percent above this.

Here is a sample table of the way this works.

Average Debit Balance	Percentage Above Broker Call Rate
Under $10,000	2%
$10,000 to $19,999	1.75%
$20,000 to $29,999	1.5%
$30,000 to $39,999	1.25%
$40,000 to $50,999	1%
$50,000 and over	.5%

You can see that there are real advantages to borrowing $50,000 and over.

Any dividends earned are credited to your account—they are yours.

You can see how this system works. If AT&T should rise a point, your paper profit would be $200 rather than the $100 you would otherwise have earned. The leverage of margin has permitted you to double your profitability. If, on the other hand, AT&T should drop a point, your liability has doubled, and your loss also would be $200 rather than $100.

If the value of your stocks sinks below the 50 percent margin requirement, you will hear from your broker. This is referred to as a "margin call." You must decide whether to give your broker enough cash or additional securities to bring your account up to minimum requirements—or to sell the stocks at loss.

Should you decide to attempt investing on margin, there are some important things to know about it. First, your margin account must be with a reliable brokerage house. Your securities on margin aren't protected by the steel walls of your safe deposit box. They are with your broker in his "street name." If the brokerage house gets into financial trouble you may have long and serious problems in obtaining the return of your securities. Brokerage firms have recently come upon hard times with the introduction of negotiated commission rates. Check with your bank manager if you have any doubt about the financial stability of your brokerage firm.

As I have advised before, use one broker for all your brokerage business. He can keep you abreast of any significant changes which affect your securities.

Next you must ask yourself how much you can afford to lose. How much of your hard cash can you lose without its affecting your standard of living or putting a serious crimp in your wealth-building efforts? If you are not willing or able to lose, steer clear of margin investing. If you regard the possible rewards as worth the risks, you can climb aboard.

Decide on a fixed dollar amount to be so invested. If the worst happens, you will not have sent too much of your precious cash on a suicide mission.

There is an old Wall Street adage—"Never answer a margin call." That means if your stock falls below your margin requirements and your broker calls to tell you to put up or sell out, you tell him to go ahead and sell. It is no fun to take the loss, but the margin game can be played both ways.

Margin buying in stocks is only for bull markets. There is literally no way an investor can win in a bear market. In 1974, margin players were all dealt bad hands. Only when the trend is clearly and convincingly up should you consider margin. Margin is using other people's money to bet that the stocks or bonds you select will rise. You must be thoroughly convinced of the integrity of the current market before you plunge.

Another bit of advice: If you do well on your margin account, your broker may counsel you that you are now playing with the "house's money." The hell you are! That's *your* money. And it does not afford you the luxury of taking bigger chances and greater risks. Every able gambler knows that there is no such thing as "house money." It's either yours or it isn't. When you lose on a security, the brokerage house does not come to your rescue, so don't be persuaded to increase the degree of risk that was your formula for success.

There are only two sensible reasons for getting into margin buying. The investor wants to capitalize on what he sees to be a short-term rise. He wants to get in with the greatest leverage and get out with the greatest profit over a short span of time. In this way, margin interest payments are reduced to a brief period. The other legitimate reason comes about when an investor sees what he believes to be a great opportunity in a stock he wishes to own but does not have sufficient cash at the moment to buy in the quantities he would like. Here he margins for the short term with the intention of accumulating enough cash during the interim to buy the stock outright.

I see no value in long-term margin arrangements for stocks. In buying common stocks on margin, the dividends paid are not enough to cover the costs of financing the margin. If your stock does not appreciate, you must reach down into your pocket for interest payments. The longer you continue on margin, the greater your appreciation must be to come out ahead.

For myself, I prefer to buy common stocks for cash—and sleep well at night.

Buying Bonds on Margin

There are some interesting mechanisms at work in the bond market which make bonds much more likely candidates for margining than stocks.

The objectives, of course, are different. You buy stocks mainly for appreciation; you buy bonds mainly for income. But at the end of the year, when in your bank account shows a large increase, you don't care (except for long-term capital gains provisions) whether the cash came from appreciation or income.

Investment philosophy is more important than a specific method of performance. Methods can change as influenced by interest rates, market prices, business conditions, etc. All business decisions are based on certain assumptions. If your assumptions are that:

1. Business conditions appear fairly stable and are improving
2. Interest rates, short- and long-term, will hold at reasonably low levels
3. Discount bond yields of BBB grade or better are yielding at least 3 points more than your brokerage margin interest rates

—then you can make the decision to place a percentage of your investment funds in a margined bond account for income.

Here are some of the intriguing characteristics of bonds: Traditionally, bonds are cherished for their conservative virtues—safety, reliable income, low volatility. The main market for bonds has been among very conservative safety-minded investors, who tend to shun alphabetical ratings below BBB. Further, banks are restricted from buying bonds rated below BBB or taking them as pledges against loans. Therefore companies that wish to raise capital through bond issues rated BB and below find a slim market for their wares —and are forced to issue bonds with higher-than-normal interest payments and sell them at greater-than-normal discounts. It is not unusual to find these so-called "trash" or "junk" bonds yielding higher than 10 percent with a yield to maturity even higher.

Because of the current state of money markets, most

bond yields have risen, even those of the highest quality, thus pushing up the yields of the lower-grade bonds even higher.

Where bond yields are high and the prime interest rates are low, the spread between the two makes for some fascinating margining opportunities.

Beyond these factors, margin requirements for bonds are lower than for stocks. You may buy a bond for as little as 30 percent of its cost and margin the rest.

Let me pull an example from *Standard & Poor's Stock Guide* to show you the kind of mechanics involved.

Eastern Metal Products (the name has been changed, the numbers rounded off, but otherwise, this is a true case) issues bonds with face values of 10's '95 (10 percent interest per year—redemption date 1995), rated B grade. Their discount price is $750.

If you were to buy this bond for cash, it would yield better than 13 percent per year—not bad. But suppose you buy this bond for 66⅔ percent margin. That is, you put up $250 cash and margin (borrow) $500.

The bond will pay you $100 per year. The rate of interest you pay on the $500 borrowed will vary from month to month, but suppose the prime average is 6 percent and you pay your broker 2 percent above prime for his efforts. Your borrowing cost is $40 per year (8% × $500). The difference between the bond interest paid and the borrowing cost is $60 ($100 − $40 = $60). The rate of return on your $250 cash invested is 24 percent ($60 ÷ $250 = .24).

That is quite an excellent return.

Beyond this, if the price of the bond goes up (appreciates), you can make a nice extra profit here, too.

It sounds too good to be true. What could go wrong with it?

Certainly there are some perils in investing in this manner, as there are perils attached to any investment.

If interest rates go up dramatically, three bad things will happen:

1. Your margin borrowing will cost you more so your yield will be reduced.

2. Since bonds are interest-sensitive, their prices drop when interest rates go up. If your bond price drops too far, you will get a margin call from your broker—come up with more equity or sell out.

3. Rising interest rates foretell greater pressures on weak companies (Eastern Metal Products must have some weakness to have their bonds rated B—the Standard & Poor's people are no dummies), so there is a chance that the company may not pay the bond interest promised (default) or the company could go into bankruptcy.

However, there are some safety factors in your favor. Interest rates normally rise in quarter- or half-point increments. They do not leap up. You will have ample warning. Bonds are less volatile than stocks, so sudden changes in their prices are less frequent. And, if worst comes to worst and the bond goes into default, since it is based on real assets, there should be some recovery value to your investment.

What's more, if you have spread your risks over several of these "deep-discount" low-grade bonds, the odds are that enough will survive to more than make up for your losses.

Yes, it is a gamble; there is risk. But to my mind the greatest risk is attached to a blue-blood triple A bond bought at a premium where the yield is less than the inflation rate and you are automatically assured of the erosion of your equity dollars. It is one of those ironies of investing that the most conservative vehicles can end up being wealth-inhibiting. It is useful to remind yourself of this periodically. As for what you should do with your bond margin account when interest rates rise, you have several alternatives.

You can sell out, pay back your margin borrowings, and move your capital to some safer haven. Close out the margin account until the next business up-cycle.

You can pay back the margin borrowings and keep the bonds (13 percent interest is nothing to sneeze at in hard times), recognizing that you risk default or bankruptcy. As for the price of the bond, you may expect that during the next business recovery the price of your bond will return to your purchase level or higher.

I regard the first choice as more conservative and the second as more speculative.

It seems to me that buying discount bonds on margin during appropriate periods is one of the better ways for a salaried person to enhance his wealth. This is especially true if the investor has ample real estate to shelter his income, since most of the profits of bonds are not protected by the benefits of long-term capital gains.

In the next chapter I show you my methods for securities record-keeping, and include some of my bond pages for 1976. For now, to prove to you that I practice what I preach, I'll summarize the results of my bond investing for that year. Remember that the investment success of 1976 will not automatically ensure the same kind of success in some future year. The year 1976 was a good one for securities investment —not great, but good—one of those all-too-infrequent opportunities to realize better-than-average growth of capital. Also be aware that I had taken care to prepare myself for just such an event and was fully ready when it happened.

The brokerage house I deal with takes a conservative attitude toward bond margins and their maximum allowable margin is 60 percent.

My equity consisted of $42,000 cash and $25,000 in

bonds which I already owned outright and which yielded approximately 10 percent. By using my own bonds as part of the deposit, I accomplished something extra. All the time these bonds are deposited they are still generating dividends for me—they are capital at work. So they can be eliminated from any measure of return on capital. While my apparent leverage was two and a half to one, my true leverage was closer to four to one. This amount of equity enabled me to buy up to $167,500 worth of bonds.

My maximum purchase of any one bond issue was $25,000, and all were B grade, yielding roughly 10 percent. They were all bought at discount. Some were convertible bonds—i.e., they could be converted into the companies' common stocks at a predetermined price. This gave me the opportunity to gain some appreciation should the companies' common stocks be priced higher than the bond option price.

The income from these margined bonds for the year came to $18,455. My margin interest expenses were $6,758. (Margin interest costs during the year ranged from 6 percent to 7.25 percent, which allowed a good spread between cost of borrowed money and my bond yield.) So the net return on my investment of $42,000 cash was $11,696, or 28 percent.

In addition, the market value of my bonds rose so that I enjoyed a paper profit of better than $13,000. If I had sold out my bonds in December of 1976, my profit for the year would have been over $25,000—or almost a 60-percent return on my cash investment. (Lest I give you any wrong impressions, I want you to know that I think paper profits are nice but they are essentially daydreams until you convert them to cash. Actually, I carried my margined bonds over into 1977, when the bond market slumped and some of my paper profits disappeared. I do not regret their loss since my bond portfolio continues to perform far beyond my expectancies of it.)

Since I had no immediate need for cash, I allowed payments from my bonds to accumulate in my margin account. And every dollar added reduced a dollar of debt. At 1976 rates, this amounted to the same thing as getting 6 to 7.25 percent interest on my money (with immediate access to it at any time), which was better than I could have gotten from a regular passbook account in a savings and loan.

A few final thoughts about buying bonds on margin: Essentially, it is a numbers game with the variable factors being the yield of the bond and the interest rate at which you can borrow money for margin. Bond prices are highest when interest rates are lowest; bond prices are lowest when interest rates are highest. Your numbers will tell you when the proper ratios between yield and interest rates are reached.

As for your selection of "junk" bonds, you don't purposely buy trash. Investigate the company issuing the bond just as thoroughly as you would in purchasing any other security. You are bound to come up with some unhappy financial news. Your broker and you may be able to arrive at a reasonable judgment as to whether the condition is temporary or terminal.

Buying options and *commodities futures trading* are hazardous forms of investment with high leverage. I am unconvinced that they have a place in the investment planning of any salaried wealth-builder.

They are fast-moving and require more daily attention than you can probably spare. The techniques for dealing with them are intricate and convolute: matters for professionals, not amateurs. And while there are devices to increase their safety, they also decrease the leverage and therefore the ultimate reward. A lot of hard work and scheming may deliver a handful of dollars.

The world stands ready to separate you from your

money. Many so-called investments and investment techniques are available to you. Stockbrokers will try to tempt you by appealing to your gambling instincts. "Option buying can give you a good swing," they say. Or, if they know you are more conservative, they will suggest you sell options on stock you already own. Through "straddles," "strips," "straps" and other techniques you can play the options game many different ways.

I believe none of these should appeal to you. If you want to find out more about them, get a good book on the subject and then talk to your broker.

Commodities futures are an even more treacherous form of investment. One authority estimates that speculators lose 75 to 80 percent of the time. It takes a lot of leverage to make up for those kinds of losses.

It is a professional's game. Even though your broker tells you he will steer you through the mysterious hazards, if he fails, it is your money which is lost. If he is essentially a nice person, he might tell you that he is sorry it didn't work out. Most brokers don't even show the broken-hearted customer that much courtesy. It is a "tough luck, Charlie," business. For myself, I would rather play the crap tables at Las Vegas, where the action is cleaner and the odds are considerably better.

I have avoided commodities and options for a long time. In 1976, when I was looking around for new adventures in investing, my broker convinced me that the options market was a good place to put my money—and he had a specific option in mind. His firm had an analyst who had made an exhaustive study of the Gillette corporation and thought it was one of the finest growth companies he'd ever seen. On this basis, I bought 1,000 Gillette options at 2⅝ in May of 1976 for a total cost of $2,768.

Now to understand the stakes I was playing for and what I was risking, you must understand at least something of the way options work. An option is an essentially worthless piece of paper, backed by no real assets. It amounts to a contract to buy a certain stock for a certain price by a certain date.

Suppose, for example, Effluvial Gas Corporation stock is currently selling for $17 a share. An option is offered at $2 a share to sell the stock for $20 a share at any time within a six-month period, at the end of which the option expires (is no longer valid, worthless). The seller of the stock has two ways to win. He can sell his stock for $3 more than its current price and also get $2 for the sale of the option— which is very nice. If the option is not exercised (i.e., the option buyer decides not to purchase the option seller's stock), the option seller has his $2 and his stock too—maybe even better.

The option buyer has essentially only one way to win— but it could mean very big winnings. What he is betting is that the price of the optioned stock will rise beyond the optioned sell price and his price of the option combined. In this case, his option can be sold for more than he paid for it. And that is where he expects to make his money. Probably he has no intention of ever laying his hands on the optioned stock or even seeing it. He is playing for leverage.

If Effluvial Gas stock rises to $25 a share during the option period, the option buyer has a valuable piece of paper in his hands. His option now might have a market value of $4 or more. In other words, he could have doubled his investment in just a few months. If, on the other hand, he had bought the stock at $17 and sold at $25 he would have made 47 percent but with a lot more cash tied up in the speculation. That, in crude form, is how options function. In my case, the price of Gillette stock did not even approach my expectations for it. Therefore my option was worth less with each passing day—less to me and less to every other potential Gillette option buyer.

As a novice option buyer, I did not see the message writ large on the wall. What is worse, I did not follow my own sensible advice to cut my losses. Exercising the option and buying the stock, what with brokerage costs and all, would only have deepened the tragedy. In the end, I sold out the last week of the option period for $0.062552 per option—a $17 salvage of a $2,786 mistake, my only big loss of the year. I hope that analyst gets a bad rash in an uncomfortable place.

The only benefit I gained from the transaction is that I can now speak with at least modest authority: despite the growing interest, options are not for the small investor.

Mutual funds are the perfect example of a good idea gone wrong. I frankly don't know what is the matter with them.

The idea is that small investors, who cannot afford to buy round lots or the luxury and protection of diversification, can pool their resources, hire professional money managers, and thereby derive many of the nice benefits of securities investment normally available only to the big guys.

It is a splendid idea, but over the long haul it has worked out poorly. Refer to the statistics of Chapter 7 if you doubt me.

The sad truth probably is that many of the funds are either scams or managed by incompetents. They gathered credibility during the long market rise of the 1960s and did not have what it took to face the hardships of the 1970s.

Of the 400-odd funds offered to the general public, probably no more than a double handful do justice to their customers. These, of course, suffer from the deserved raps the industry as a whole has taken.

One of the drawbacks of the mutual funds is that they have more or less committed themselves to the securities markets no matter what their condition, friendly or hostile. A fund will declare itself "growth," "income," "balanced," "leverage," "hedge," or whatever—and then be stuck with the consequences.

Market conditions change dramatically, but mutual funds only adjust. (Perhaps if they came out with a "We're Doing the Best We Can, Considering the Circumstances" Fund, credibility would return to the industry, and the mutual fund might serve a useful purpose.)

If you are a very small investor, you may want to consider a mutual fund. Compare carefully its long-term record of performance against others in the industry and be suspicious of any premiums charged. If you have the choice, handle it yourself.

There is one kind of recent fund which has possibilities and appears to be a more decent sort. This is the "liquid assets fund." The purpose of this fund is to provide the safest assured appreciation of the customer's capital. The fund's monies are invested in only the highest quality vehicles— U.S. Government Treasury Bills, for example—which are virtually immune to economic diseases. In line with their safety, their returns are modest—but dependable.

This kind of fund could easily fit into your Cash Equivalent Reserve with no problems. Check with your broker or bank manager.

Second trust deeds (or second mortgages) over the years have proven to be conservative investments with a nice return. They are becoming a favorite form of investing among retired families.

There are two possible routes: you can do it yourself, or you can depend on a second trust deed firm to do it for you. I suggest the latter.

In California there are a number of second trust deed

firms with a record of never a penny lost over an impressive number of years. And their steady returns are 10 to 12 percent of your equity. (You should check your local conditions to see if this is also true in your community.)

The main reason a homeowner will apply for a second trust deed loan is that he would like to do improvements on his home but would rather not refinance his first trust deed because he would lose a favorable rate of interest.

When a homeowner applies for a loan, a second-trust-deed-company appraiser is sent out to judge the true market value of the property. The company deducts 25 percent from the true market value, then deducts the balance due on the first trust deed, to arrive at a top amount available for a second trust deed. (The 25 percent is the cushion.)

This is a profession all to itself. The do-it-yourself investor who scans the classified ads in the newspaper seeking second trust deeds is faced by the problems of appraising, the proper legal forms, and, when occasionally necessary, the unpleasant aspects of foreclosure. (Not to mention monthly collections.)

The second trust deed company does it all for you. You are guaranteed (currently) 10-percent return on your investment over a period normally of one to six years. If the homeowner repays the loan sooner, as is often the case, the early payment penalty can raise your rate to as much as 12 percent.

The second trust deed loan done this way is a secure investment. The investor can use it as collateral for a bank loan. As the loan is paid off, it may be converted into a new second trust deed for continued performance.

For my company I once did a study on various methods of investing money for our profit-sharing plan. Over a thirty-year period, second trust deed investment outperformed a stock and bond investment plan by 150 percent. It is an approach to conservative investing you might want to consider.

PROFILE OF A SECURITIES PORTFOLIO

It is always one thing to talk about doing something and entirely another to go about doing it. The world is full of mothers, fathers, teachers and football coaches who tell you, "Don't do as I do, do as I tell you to do." Somehow, they lack credibility. So I will tell you something about my most recent investment, as of the time of this writing, to show you that I do at least some of the things I tell you to do and that they work out all right.

The year is 1976, and that is lucky for me, because among all my many investment years this is the one I would have chosen. I was on my own to do whatever I wanted in my own time. And some of the trepidation about retirement had passed.

There is a fear about retirement, you know. First you look forward to it as the great release from many of your concerns and it shines before you like some cloud-tinged golden city off on the horizon. Then as you approach it you begin to worry that all the good things of your active life will be behind you and that the world will wash around you, going its own busy way, and you will be out of it—a relic, a fossil with an interesting past but no future other than as a decorative and educational exhibit. As you get into it, and push on it a little, retirement can be all the good things you thought it might be and more—especially if you are retired in theory but not in fact, and especially if you have enough money that it is among your least concerns and you can play games you might not have played before because you were in such a hurry to get to where you now are.

It was an active and a hectic year, but that was of my own choosing. The market was behaving itself very nicely.

The Dow Jones Industrial Average in 1976 opened at 852 and closed the year at 1004—a 152-point gain, an increase in the values of these stocks of 18 percent.

My stock portfolio in market value gains plus realized gains increased by $49,640 on an average investment of $102,000 for an average increase of 48 percent.

The 20 Bond Index opened 1976 at approximately 85.71 (an interpolated figure, since the 20 Bond Index was not in use January 1, 1976) and closed the year at 93.20 for a total gain of 7.5 points, which was an average increase of 8.7 percent.

My bond portfolio in market value gain plus realized gain increased by $30,551 on an average investment of $185,492, or a 16.5-percent increase in market value. The net cash earned from my $42,000 cash investment in margined bonds was $12,093, or a return of 28 percent.

I have already told my stories about Federated Department Stores and Rich's Department Stores—and Gillette options.

My broker had information which led him to believe that AVCO Financial Corporation preferred stock might be a candidate for a good run-up. His reasons made sense, so I bought 700 shares in March, 1976, at an average price of 26.5 and sold, when my long-term capital gains period had been satisfied, at 41 for a profit of $9,200. It was simple as that.

I bought 500 shares of Higbee Department Stores, headquartered in Cleveland, Ohio, at 17 in August of 1976. I had three reasons. I still believed retail store stocks were undervalued. Higbee's currently enjoys some rather ordinary management and should be a prime prospect for one of the large, acquisition-minded chains such as Federated or Associated Dry Goods, which would certainly run it up in price. This may take awhile, but in the meantime, the stock pays $1.48 a share for an 8.5 percent return, which is not shabby. I will not be unhappy to wait until the proper suitor arrives.

In April of 1976, I had bought 1,000 shares of TICOR, the Title Insurance and Trust Corporation of Los Angeles.

It is an old and prestigious firm which for years had a lock on most of the title business done in Los Angeles. Its management had become old and soggy and had done a number of foolish things. Also, they suffered during the real estate recession of 1973 through 1975. My broker noted that TICOR had had a change of management and that the new management was aggressive and knowledgeable. Both the industry and the firm were depressed, which drove the stock price down. So I bought it on a speculative basis at 14½ with the idea that new management plus a revitalized industry would give it a lift. At year's end, it was selling for 19 and I would look for it to rise to 22 or more. When it reaches this point, I will be prepared to sell it and move into another opportunity.

While I was involved in some negotiations with a real estate investment trust (REIT), I had the opportunity to look over their inventory of properties they had foreclosed and taken back. When the prime interest rate rose to 12 percent a few years back, many REITs got into terrible trouble. In November 1976 the prime rate was much lower, so I reasoned that the more substantial REITs would make a comeback. They are very interest-sensitive. I bought 10,000 shares of one stock, which then traded on the New York Stock Exchange for 1¼ per share. The management of the firm then represented well-known, respected people in Los Angeles. The book value of the share was about $8.47. If the stock moved up or down by an eighth of a point, it would be worth $1,250 to me. It closed five weeks after my purchase at 2¼. Since REITs were among the most despised stocks on the market at that time, I thought that after some yo-yoing, they might return to confidence and rise higher. I would rather take a flier on a stock like this than stay up all night at a Las Vegas crap table. If the worst happens and the stock doesn't make the grade, I could get a short- or long-term capital loss, which will at least balance some of my gains for tax purposes. Those are better odds than anything the gambling capital of the world has to offer.

Does everything I buy go up? Not by a long shot. Of the seventeen selling transactions I made in 1976, eight of them amounted to losses. In other words, my average was slightly better than 50 percent. Many of these transactions were loss-cutting sales. This is in line with my recommendation for cutting losses fast and letting gains run as long as they are energy-motivated.

Some of the industries I had special knowledge about—retail department stores and real estate. Some stock purchases came about as a result of my broker's advice. I bought stocks in depressed industries, growth, speculation and some blue chips. Standard & Poor's ratings ranged from A+ to C. In other words, I had a diversified portfolio.

Do I do for myself what I tell you to do? I think so.

SOME GENERAL COMMENTS ABOUT SECURITIES INVESTING

Remember that financial adversity is almost always accompanied by opportunity. If the stock market didn't have its recessions, you would not be able to pick up stocks at bargain prices and watch their worth multiply. When you see the clouds of recession gathering, run, don't walk, to convert your sensitive securities into safe cash equivalents.

Once you begin investing, you will find well-meaning friends giving you "inside tips." Any information you receive can be valuable, but you certainly must investigate its quality. Usually your broker is in the best position to give you current, accurate information about potential opportunities and hazards. If he fails you at this, go out and find one who won't.

As to your own financial prowess, you have strengths—play them up. Many market traders, watching the ticker tape every day, tend toward astigmatism. You, operating at arm's length, away from the chatter, may develop the ability to penetrate the mists of the future as well or better than the pros. The average investor really makes most of his profits by being more right than wrong over the long pull—and by being patient in playing for these long-term rewards.

Sophisticated investors don't suffer trauma if the market retreats a bit after they have made a purchase. If you buy a security at what you consider an appropriate price (e.g., below book value or at less than 10 times earnings) and its pays a healthy dividend, don't dump it at the first sign of weakness. Hold it. If it is not margined you can afford to be patient with it. If it continues to try your patience, evacuate.

All market values change, some quickly, some over an extended period of time. Real estate values, too. Your house may be worth more (or less) today than it was yesterday, but since your home is not part of an active documented market, you may not be aware of it. Would you panic if your home suddenly became worth a few hundred dollars less because some city councilman advocated that you be assessed for the fireplugs in your neighborhood? Of course not. Councilmen come and go. Stock values fluctuate. It is the long run that matters. In investing, patience is wealth-enhancing; impatience is wealth-inhibiting.

You must understand that what I give you here is only the briefest of capsules concerning the many and varied opportunities and pitfalls of the securities markets. Thousands of volumes have been written on the subject—and in their entirety still do not encompass it. Experts who have been students of securities investment for dozens of years still don't know everything there is to know about it. It's impossible.

Still, this complexity should not cause you to shun this

most valuable area of capital appreciation. If you are not too greedy, too emotional, too phelgmatic, you can do well with securities investing and never be distressed by the incompleteness of your knowledge.

Do as well as you can within your limits and you will, with reasonable certainty, be rewarded for your efforts.

OTHER INVESTMENT OPPORTUNITIES

This must of necessity be an abbreviated section. It is a hanging of flags over various other areas of wealth-enhancement merely to show where they are. I have dabbled in or investigated these areas only to return to the securities markets and real estate as my choice of wealth-enhancement vehicles.

Collecting for Fun and Profit

Inflation has been particularly evident in the art, artifact and antique markets. It stands to reason that as more people desire and can afford the accouterments of wealth, the limited supply of precious objects must enhance their worth.

There is no longer a Renoir to render his unique interpretation of beauty in oil on canvas. There are only so many pieces of Etruscan ware yet to be discovered. Chippendale is long dead, although his memory lingers on in countless thousands of inferior imitations.

The supply is finite.

Items that are one-of-a-kind or genuinely good pieces sold in limited editions are in brisk demand. But beware of the salesman's "limited edition" pitch. Many charlatans are selling shoddy works of art under the "limited edition" banner. One can only say, "Thank God, they're limited!"

Some companies are in the business of manufacturing instant collectibles: classic books bound in fine leathers and stamped in genuine 14K gold; commemorative coins and medallions stamped into "precious" metals, antique furniture with the drilled wormholes fresh upon them. These, for the most part, make bogus claim to worth. One day they may have some nostalgia value, much like a pillow with "Welcome to Niagara Falls" embroidered on it. But in the short run you would do as well collecting beer cans or campaign buttons.

There is a serious problem in any kind of collecting. Personally, I enjoy collecting eighteenth-century English furniture, porcelains, Oriental artifacts and what I believe to be good contemporary art. They have added to my net worth but have not contributed a penny to my cash flow.

If you buy something you love and admire, you are naturally going to be reluctant to part with it—unless you are more enamored with trading than with collecting.

On the positive side, if you select well, you can personalize your home or office and at the same time watch your selections appreciate in value, whether you ever intend to reap their appreciation or not.

As in other forms of investment, it pays to become well-acquainted with the area you are interested in—and to locate an expert you can trust for backup support. This is especially true when you are buying a high-ticket item. When you discover that the expensive "antique" you bought on a whim is actually worth far less than you paid for it, somehow it loses a portion of its charm.

For practical reasons, whatever collection you maintain, your appraiser should review these items from time to time. They do influence your net worth. Most important, your insurance policies should include coverage at current values. Your bank manager should be able to direct you to a competent appraiser.

Collections of coins, stamps, guns, first editions, all have their place as investments. And I recommend collecting, even if only as a recreation. Once you become a collector, you gain an understanding of, and enjoy a common bond with, all collectors.

Gold and silver jewelry have become excellent collector's pieces. They have increased in value both for their artistry (or antiquity) and for the inflated prices of their precious metals. Authentic Oriental rugs have demonstrated great appreciation.

Furs do not qualify as legitimate investments. They become outmoded and wear out. Contrary to popular conception, they do not have a built-in wealth-enhancement value. They are but a fleeting show of affluence.

For all collecting's delights, unless you decide to become professional at it, it is not a major area of wealth-enhancement. *Do* collect. *Don't* depend on it to make you rich.

Investing in a Business

For some people securities investments hold no appeal. They would rather venture into areas where the assets are more tangible and amenable to personal manipulation.

Perhaps you would rather invest in a small business. Do you have a special area of expertise or a talent which you believe could make you successful at it?

Franchises have become a popular means of getting a start in business in a small way. Many have been disasters; some have been gold mines.

Certainly your business will require many more hours of work than you currently spend as a salaried employee. The countless regulations and forms, personnel, buying, promotion and the thousand-and-one other things that a business entrepreneur must attend to will keep you busy. You may enjoy this enough that it compensates for your effort. One day your business may grow to a point where you can turn it into a corporation with the accompanying tax advantages.

Every business was started by someone who wanted to do for himself—and that is just another variation of what this book is about.

It is a matter of personal abilities and tastes. A business of your own could be precisely the vehicle you need to increase your wealth. Perhaps you can do both—conduct your own personal wealth-enhancement program and run a profitable business too.

Investing in Oil

Some years ago I talked with a very successful independent oil operator. At that time he had an income of about $300,000 a year and a stable of racehorses and was completely successful and secure. This was before I had discovered real estate and was investigating all possible ways of becoming rich.

I asked him if he thought I might profit by investing in oil speculations. He told me that, owing to his large income, he could drill nine dry holes and hit on the tenth and come home a winner. (In recent years, I believe the odds have grown to more like one-in-fifteen for success.) But the average salaried person does not have the resources necessary to enter this game. The odds favor the well-heeled operator or promoter. I have friends who have done well in oil speculations, but many more fail than succeed. I did not like the percentages.

Since the 1976 Tax Reform Act, oil has become an even less attractive speculation. Many of its side benefits have been taken away or severely reduced. For the near future, unless you find oil seeping up in your back yard, I would avoid the oil business.

The 1976 Tax Act has eliminated many of the popular tax shelters that were previously employed (and abused)by the high-incomed and rich. A good lot of them proved chimercial anyway—especially those where the emphasis was on tax shelter to the neglect of the principle of capital equity protection.

There's not much left but real estate and long-term capital gains—the rest have been straitjacketed. Perhaps some new ones will sprout up.

Investing in Gold

During one period recently when it appeared that the economic world was falling apart, gold was of extraordinary interest. That interest has tapered off but will never disappear entirely. There's something about gold.

Traditionally, gold soars in price when the public has low confidence in government. Political upheavals, uncontrolled inflation, energy crises, high interest rates, unsettled international conditions—all are reasons to buy gold. When these factors came into conjunction they sent gold prices shooting through the roof.

When these conditions ease, gold prices drop—as they have done. When uneasiness returns, gold prices will rise.

American citizens can now legally own gold for the first time since 1933, when President Roosevelt took it out of circulation. Yet there has been no great rush for it. This, I believe, shows a great deal of common sense.

Buying and selling gold and silver for speculation is a fast track—too tricky for most salaried persons. The commodities market as a whole (which includes gold and silver) is a one-way ticket to capital oblivion for all but the professionals.

Gold is a messy thing to buy and sell. If you buy ingots,

their gold content must be assayed at each transaction. Gold does not produce an income for you. It is in some ways similar to the one-decision stocks I spoke of earlier. All is lovely when the price is going up—but all hell breaks loose when the price begins to fall.

Gold coins are easier to buy and sell. However, their prices are invariably higher than their gold content merits.

As far as I'm concerned, gold is for speculators, recluses, and for admiring around a lady's neck.

I said at the start of this chapter that the main purpose of Step 7 was to give you more investment freedom while you are accumulating capital to invest in real estate. I have shown you, briefly, a number of the more common investment opportunities. Certainly there are many, many more.

For me, the most direct line to my goals was through the securities markets and then on to real estate. Although my real estate investments have grown to considerable size, I still invest in securities and cash equivalents. I still maintain my Cash Equivalent Reserve and my Liquidity Reserve. And I am satisfied with my decisions.

For you, the band may play a different tune. The excitement of the Big Board may stir your blood. An ingot of the yellow stuff may send chills down your spine. A store, a factory, a franchise of your own may tickle your fancy.

The options are yours, but before you limit yourself to these alone, let me tell you about real estate. That is coming up in the chapter after next.

The next chapter is devoted to my system for securities record-keeping and controls. It interrupts the wealth-building steps, but it is so important, I don't want you to ignore it.

If you have any intention of investing in the securities market, read the next chapter—now or later.

9

The Investment Mentality— Securities Record-Keeping

Economic distress will teach men, if anything can, that realities are less dangerous than fancies, that fact-finding is more effective than fault-finding.
—CARL LOTUS BECKER (1873–1945)
Progress and Power

It takes less time to do a thing right than to explain why you did it wrong.
HENRY WADSWORTH LONGFELLOW (1807–1882)

In my experience, most amateur investors, when the whim and the spare cash coincide, buy a security, drop it into their safe deposit box—and then go on about their business as if nothing happened, or need happen further.

Occasionally they will check their stock's quotation in the financial pages of their newspaper. They will feel good if the price has gone up. They will feel bad if the price has gone down. And that is the extent of it.

Where the amateur investor owns more than two or three securities, the confusion begins. I have known few who could offer an accurate account of their securities' movements over the past several weeks or months, or of how they have performed in relation to the overall market indicators.

This is an exceedingly haphazard way to do business. It is asking for trouble.

I suspect that much of the fear of the securities markets comes from this feeling of uncertainty—not knowing precisely what is happening and therefore not knowing what to do. Having no system.

I have already told you that my career was in retailing. As you may know, retail is an intense and fast-moving numbers business. It has gotten that way of necessity—for survival. So much of retail is based on best guesses—Which will be the selling fashion trends? How many gross of sheets will be wanted in blue and how many in pink? Will men this year be buying shirts in plains, plaids, or polka dots? There is no sure way to know.

So a retail business survives and prospers by keeping accurate records of exactly what is happening at the moment—how the customer is reacting to the buyers' best guesses, what is selling and what is not. These are not merely passive numbers, history. These are action numbers. They tell you what must be done and, often, how quickly.

The numbers tell you that this item is a dog—to be marked down immediately, to be sold at a smaller profit or even a loss. Dead inventory is worthless—get the dollars back into circulation. Other numbers tell you that the item is a success, it's selling. So run with it, order more quickly, get it out on the floor so the customer can buy.

I believe there are direct and illuminating parallels between the processes of retailing and the processes of securities investment. Securities are purchased as best bets with no guarantees of performance. Some selections will be good and some will be rotten. Some need to be dumped at a loss and some need to be let ride or expanded.

How can you know just what is to be done and when unless you have the record of numbers to support your decisions? You can't.

For the wage-earning wealth-builder, for the amateur investor (such as you and I are, and always will be), there is only one solution—accurate, up-to-date records of your securities' performances. I believe firmly in productive score-keeping. It sets in motion the decision-making process.

Ownership of any item of value presumes certain responsibilities toward it. This is in your own interest. If you deny this responsibility, you might as well pack up your valuables in a sack, toss it over your shoulder, and walk off into the sunset. End of scenario. Drop the curtain.

A wealth-builder with the investment mentality wants to know what is happening. And what to do about it.

He wants to know what happened this week to his securities in particular and to the market in general.

More important, he wants to know how what happened this week relates to what happened in prior weeks.

Most important, he wants to know how this information affects what action, if any, he will take in the following week.

I have no greater fondness for paperwork than the next person, so I always try to limit it to the least amount necessary to do the job. I was unable to find printed forms to suit my purposes (with one exception) so I developed my own. I offer them to you for your use:

1. *A detailed securities record* is commercially available. The one I like is called "Securities & Income Records at a Glance," published by the Shaeffer-Eaton Division of Textron, Inc. It sells for about $5 in most stationery stores. I show samples of a page front and back from my book in Exhibit 3.

2. *Weekly Stock Summary*—consisting of a Master Page and Weekly Summary Pages. (Exhibits 4 and 5.)

Exhibit 3: Securities & Income Records at a Glance

Income Record

QUARTERLY INCOME RECORD

YEAR	DATE	RATE	1st QUARTER AMOUNT	DATE	RATE	2nd QUARTER AMOUNT	DATE	RATE	3rd QUARTER AMOUNT	DATE	RATE	4th QUARTER AMOUNT		TOTAL	
1976				9/7	.25	250	-	9/7	.25	250	-	12/6	.25	250	-	750	-
1977	3/6	.275	275	-													

Securities Bought and Sold

COMPANY **TICOR**   PAR VALUE

ADDRESS

SHARES OF ☒ COMMON   ☐ PREFERRED   ☐ DEBENTURES   ☐ BONDS

DIVIDEND OR INTEREST   RATE **1.10**   YIELD **1100 52**

REMARKS

PURCHASES

DATE	NUMBER OF SHARES OR BONDS	CERTIFICATE NUMBER	UNIT PRICE	TAX	BROKER'S COMMISSION	COST	TOTAL INVESTMENT	
4/5/76	700	LC 1968/4/5/6/7/8/9	14½		192.99		10343	54
4/9/76	300	NC 39364/5/6	14	.60	85.58		4286	18
						TOTAL	14629	72

SALES

DATE SOLD	NUMBER OF SHARES OR BONDS	CERTIFICATE NUMBER	UNIT PRICE	TAX	BROKER'S COMMISSION	AMOUNT RECEIVED	PROFIT OR LOSS

FORM BF-1

Courtesy Shaeffer-Eaton Division of Textron, Inc.

3. *Weekly Bond Summary*—consisting of a Master Page and Weekly Summary Pages. (Exhibits 6 and 7.)

4. *Weekly Securities Recap—Gain or (Loss)*—adds stocks and bonds gains or losses to achieve a total. (Exhibit 8.)

5. *Monthly Margin Account Recapitulation,* a running record derived from the broker's monthly report of various margin activities. (Exhibit 9.)

The "Securities & Income Records at a Glance" comes in its own book. The rest are kept in a three-ring binder with spacers to separate the sections. The form paper is 8½″ by 11″ with blue lines horizontally and red lines vertically. There are wide columns left and right and twelve smaller columns through the middle. (One brand is "Efficiency Data Pad" #1636-3.)

WEEKLY STOCK SUMMARY

Master Page (Exhibit 4)

Beginning on the second blue line down, on the far left and far right sides of the page, number the lines 1, 2, 3, 4, etc., for as many stocks as you own.

Across the top of the page, starting from the left, these are your column headings:

1. (The wide column) "Security Description."

2. (The first narrow column) "Standard & Poor's Earnings & Dividend Rating." You'll get this from your broker's Standard & Poors Stock Guide.

3. "Nine-Year HI-LOW." From Standard & Poors Stock Guide.

4. "Last Year HI-LOW." From Standard & Poors Stock Guide.

5. "Probably Sell At." (It is not necessary to put in this year's high and low, since you can get that from your daily newspaper or the *Wall Street Journal.*) This column is left blank when you purchase the stock unless you have a clear idea in your mind as to the price you wish to sell at. It is a good idea every six months to make an appointment with your broker to meet before or after market closing hours and review your list of securities with him. (I've found securities brokers remarkably cooperative in this. They welcome the opportunity of educating and assisting their clients—at least partly because successful clients are likely to increase their future business.) From the accumulated information in your Weekly Stock Summary and his input, you may be able mutually to decide at what price it would be best to sell each security. You may decide to sell none until they have qualified for long-term capital gains. Or, if a stock appears energy-motivated with no top in sight, you may postpone any decision. You may decide that at a given price a security will be fully valued. Select one or two securities that you feel are your least desirable. If a better opportunity comes up, these will be the first ones to sell to raise cash for your new purchase.

If you feel a stock is approaching its peak, a good method in selling is to set a price "above the market"—especially if it qualifies for a long-term capital gain—even if you have no other new purchase in mind. Give you broker a "limited order" on a "Good 'Til Canceled" (GTC) basis. This means that if your stock reaches your chosen price, your broker is authorized to sell at that price or higher—but at no lower price.

6. "Shares of Stock." Pencil this number, as you may want to buy more or sell part over the course of a year. Keep the number current.

7. "Average Purchase Price Per Share." When more than one transaction is involved, average them: 100 shares of XYZ

Exhibit 4: Master Page – 1976 Stocks

(LEFT HAND PAGE)

Security Description	Standard & Poors Earnings & Dividend Ranking	9-Year Hi-Low	Last Year Hi-Low	Probably Sell @	Shares of Stock	Average Purchase Price per Share	Total Dollars of Investment	Last Date Purchased	Sold - Number of Shares	Sold @ Quoted Price	Sold For Total Dollars	Dollars (Gain or Loss)	
1. ~~Arcata Nat.~~	B	53-5	11-6		300	12⅛	~~3718~~	1/23/76	300	13	3817	99	1.
2. ~~Ariz. Pub. Serv.~~	B+	43-11	16-11		300	16¾	~~5131~~	1/23/76	300	17	4993	(138)	2.
3. Aetna Life & C.	–	41-15	29-17		200	24½	4986	2/9/76					3.
4. ~~Avco Pfd. 3.20~~	C	130-9	26-9	40	700	26½	~~16493~~	3/9/76	700	39½	27764	9271	4.
5. ~~Exeter Oil~~	–	–	–		2000	2	~~4174~~	1/28/76	2000	2¼	4321	147	5.
6. Fed. Dept. Stores	A	59-15	56-25		50	18¾	937	7/10/50					6.
7. ~~Firestone T&R.~~	A–	33-12	23-12	25	100	18⅛	~~1855~~	3/26/75	100	22⅛	2167	312	7.
8. ~~1st S&L (Denver)~~	–	29-5	9-5	15	1000	8.3	~~8321~~	5/5/76	1000	7⅛	6927	(1394)	8.
9. ~~General Motors~~	A–	113-28	59-31	70	100	42⅜	~~4308~~	3/26/75	100	69½	6869	2561	9.
10. ITT	A–	67-12	25-19		200	23½	4796	2/6/76					10.
11. ~~Johns Manville~~	A–	46-14	26-19	30	100	22¼	~~2273~~	3/27/75	100	31¾	3116	843	11.
12. Mt. Fuel & Sup.	A–	53-11	44-25		100	30¼	3083	2/27/75					12.
13. ~~RCA~~	B+	65-9	21-10	30	100	19⅞	~~2032~~	7/2/75	100	25	2497	415	13.
14. ~~G.D. Searle~~	A+	40-5	25-13	25	200	16⅛	~~3301~~	2/6/76	200	14¾	2878	(423)	14.
15. Sec. Pac. Nat. Bk.	–	42-13	20-14		100	17⅞	1787	7/27/75					15.
16. Std. Oil-Cal.	A+	45-15	33-22		200	28⅛	5619	2/23/76					16.
17. Tyler Corp.	B+	17-1	12-6		split 200	11	2197	7/2/75					17.
18. ~~United Tel.~~	A–	33-9	16-12	20	100	13⅝	~~1397~~	6/20/75	100	15⅞	1551	154	18.
19. ~~Va. Elec. Pwr.~~	A–	39-6	13-8		200	14	~~2870~~	2/11/76	200	14¼	2779	(91)	19.
20. Puget So. P&L	A–	44-18	27-18		100	30⅛	3012	3/11/76					20.
21. Ticor	–	61-9	19-9		1000	14.63	14630	4/19/76					21.
22. ~~Merrill Lynch~~	A–	46-6	20-10	35	100	28¾	~~2937~~	1/6/76	100	29½	2397	(531)	22.
23. ~~E.F. Hutton~~	–	21-3	15-5	25	200	18⅞	~~3850~~	5/13/76	200	16½	3224	(626)	23.
24. ~~Anixter (Options)~~	–	–	–	4	1000	2⅝	~~2768~~	3/4/76	1000	.062552	17	(2751)	24.
25. Bicks (EPS.) Options	A	59-15	56-25		977	36½	35816	9/10/76					25.
26. ~~Pressley~~	–	35-1	6-1		1000	12⅜	~~12665~~	8/6/76	1000	12	11740	(875)	26.
27. Hibbee	B+	38-10	14-10		500	17	8660	8/26/76					27.
28. Umet	–	33-1	3-⅞		10,000	1¼	13159	11/8/76					28.
29. Kewanee	A–	24-5	19-11		200	31⅞	6489	11/17/76					29.
30. ~~Fed. Dept. Stores~~	A–	59-15	56-25		156	51¼	~~7995~~	2/29/76	156	55¾	8563	668	30.
31.													31.
					TOTAL $ INVESTMENT = $ 105171			TOTAL REALIZED GAIN = $ 7541					

Exhibit 5: Weekly Stock Summary
Closing Stock Prices by Week + Market Summary

(RIGHT HAND PAGE)

	12/3/76		12/10/76		12/17/76		12/22/76		12/30/76				
1.													
2.													
3.	34 5/8	6925	35 1/2	7100	34 1/4	6850	34 1/2	6900	35 5/8	7125			
4.													
5.													
6.	48 3/8	2419	49 1/8	2456	48 1/2	2425	48 5/8	2431	49	2450			
7.													
8.													
9.													
10.	32 1/4	6450	33 5/8	6725	33 3/8	6675	33	6600	33 7/8	6775			
11.													
12.	41 5/8	4162	42 1/2	4250	44 3/8	4436	43 1/2	4350	44 1/2	4450			
13.													
14.													
15.	26 3/8	2634	27 7/8	2788	26 3/4	2675	27 1/8	2712	27	2700			
16.	37 3/8	7475	38 1/2	7700	38 7/8	7775	39 1/2	7900	41	8200			
17.	22 1/2	4500	22 3/8	4475	21 3/8	4350	22 1/4	4450	22 3/4	4550			
18.													
19.													
20.	29 5/8	2962	30	3000	30 5/8	3062	31	3100	33 5/8	3362			
21.	18 1/8	18120	18 1/2	18500	19 1/8	19120	18 3/4	18750	19 1/4	19250			
22.													
23.													
24.													
25.	48 3/8	47262	49 1/8	47995	48 1/2	47384	48 5/8	47506	49	47873			
26.													
27.	22 1/4	11125	21	10500	20 1/2	10250	21 1/4	10625	22 1/4	11125			
28.	1 3/8	13750	1 5/8	16250	1 5/8	16250	1 7/8	18750	2 1/4	22500			
29.	33	6600	33 5/8	6725	32	6400	32 3/8	6475	34 1/8	6825			
30.													
31.													
MKT. VALUE TOTAL		134386		138464		137652		140549		147185			
DOW JONES	950		973		979		985		1004				
MKT. VALUE GAIN		29215		33293		32481		35378		42014			
REALIZED GAIN		7541		7541		7541		7541		7541			
TOTAL GAIN		36756		40834		40022		42919		49555			

Corporation at $90 and 100 shares at $80 averages to $85 per share.

8. "Total Dollars of Investment." This includes the price you paid for the shares of stock listed in column 7, brokerage commissions, taxes, etc.—all costs.

9. "Last Date Purchased." This is to prevent you from selling a stock before it qualifies for long-term capital gains— where you have a choice. The specific information about purchase dates is contained in your "Securities & Income Records at a Glance" book. Here it is important that you keep a record of the specific certificate numbers next to the dates purchased. If you sell the wrong certificate, you could lose your long-term capital gains benefits.

10. "Sold—Number of Shares." No explanations necessary.

11. "Sold @ Quoted Price." This gives you a quick evaluation of the points made or lost when you compare it with your "Average Purchase Price Per Share" column.

12. "Sold for Total Dollars." This is a net price—after deductions of brokerage commission, taxes, etc.

13. "Dollars Gain or (Loss)." No need to differentiate here between long- or short-term capital gain or loss. You'll put together your tax information from your "Securities & Income Records at a Glance."

At the very bottom of this sheet, add up the column "Total Dollars of Investment" and write the grand total in very light pencil. (This may change many times.) Also add up the column "Dollars Gain or (Loss)," to achieve a Total Realized Gain. These are locked up—not paper—profits or losses. These two are concrete figures—hard cash totals. They will change frequently over the course of the year.

At the beginning of each year, you will set up a new Master Page. The old page gets too messy through cross-outs and erasures. I suggest you write your stocks down in alphabetical order, simply because it makes it easier for you to run through the stock columns of your newspaper to tabulate results. Otherwise you must skip all over the place.

As you purchase new stocks, just post them in the first blank space. As you sell them, run a line through the name of the security and the total dollar investment figure. This investment figure should be subtracted from the grand total at the bottom of the page. The "Dollars Gain or (Loss)" figure should be added or subtracted from this bottom page total, too.

This is your completed Master Page. It is a lefthand page.

Weekly Stock Summary Sheets (Exhibit 5)

This is a righthand page. The heading is "Closing Stock Prices by Week Plus Total Market Value—Weekly Stock Summary."

Number the far-left side of the page to match the numbers on your Master Page. Leave the wide column blank.

Two narrow columns are used for each week's record. Above the top blue line, post the Friday date for the week concerned (12-3-76).

In the left of the two narrow columns, list the price at Friday closing for each of the stocks you still own. You'll get the Friday closing quotes from your daily newspaper. Wherever you have sold a stock and lined it through, skip the space.

Take out your pocket calculator (or a sharp pencil and piece of scrap paper) and multiply each closing quote for a stock by the number of shares owned in that stock. If this is not too elementary for you, here is some help in converting fractions to calculator-usable decimals.

$$\frac{1}{8} = .125$$
$$\frac{1}{4} = .250$$
$$\frac{3}{8} = .375$$
$$\frac{1}{2} = .500$$
$$\frac{5}{8} = .625$$
$$\frac{3}{4} = .750$$
$$\frac{7}{8} = .875$$

Thus, 300 shares at $37\frac{7}{8}$ would be 300×37.875, and if your calculator batteries still have juice in them, the LED readout should display 11362.500.

The product of your multiplication is posted next to the closing quote in the column to the right of it.

The bottom five lines of this page are reserved for totaling and one other thing. Count five lines up from the bottom and start titling the lines down in order like this:

Market Value Total
Dow Jones
Market Value Gain
Realized Gain
Total Gain

The "Market Value Total" is reached by adding up all the products of your multiplication and then posting the number in the same column. This is what all your stocks are currently worth (or what they were worth if you had sold them at Friday close—a lot of investors change their minds over the weekend).

"Dow Jones" means the Dow Jones Industrial Average at closing. This is posted in its proper line in the same column as the closing quotes. It does nothing for your numbers but gives you a running account of how your stocks are reacting compared with the Dow.

The "Market Value Gain" is the difference between your "Market Value Total" on this page and the "Total Dollar Investment" at the bottom of your Master Page. This is your "paper" gain—you haven't locked it up yet.

The "Realized Gain" is merely the "Total Realized Gain" from the bottom of your Master Page.

"Total Gain" is the result of adding "Market Value Gain" and "Realized Gain." This is the number that can make or break your week.

When you have completed this, you will scan the whole page for significant information. What has been happening? Is there a stock going sour? Is the Dow Jones moving into dangerous territory? Is one stock pooping along doing nothing? Is there a hard-charging stock you would like to own more of? Is it a time to sell or a time to buy? Are there some pregnant questions you would like to ask your broker?

Frequently you will find yourself making some notes about points you will want to discuss with your broker on Monday morning, a discussion that may lead to decisive and profitable action.

I find that this entire exercise, including the record-keeping that follows, takes no more than fifteen to twenty minutes of a Sunday morning—about the time it takes to sip a cup of coffee. What it accomplishes is of enormous benefit, and I know of nothing else that will do so much for you. It is the difference between making it and not making it; between wealth-enhancing and wealth-inhibiting.

WEEKLY BOND SUMMARY

This record is a kissin' cousin of your Weekly Stock Summary with only minor differences.

Master Page (Exhibit 6)

Same blank forms, same arrangement. Number the extreme right and left sides of the page down, beginning on the second line as before.

These are the headings across the top of the page:

1. "Bond Description." This includes the name of the issuing company, the declared interest rate, and the year of redemption. "Am. Fin. Corp. 9½ 88" means the bond was issued by the American Financial Corporation, promises to pay 9½ percent annual interest, and will come due for redemption in 1988. This information takes up the first wide column and the first narrow column.

2. "Standard & Poor's Quality Rating." What it says.

3. "1960–74 HI-LOW." From Standard & Poor's Bond Guide.

4. "1975 HI-LOW." From Standard & Poor's Bond Guide.

5. "Probably Sell @." Same as for stocks.

6. "No. of Bonds Purchased." Since bonds normally are issued in increments of $1,000, a "40" in this column indicates $40,000 worth of bonds purchased.

7. "Average Purchase Quote (Less Interest)." This needs some explanation for anyone who has never bought a bond. In the first place, you must add a decimal place to every number in this column to arrive at a dollar amount. Therefore, a purchase quote of 62¾ means a buying price in dollars of $627.50. About the "Less Interest": when you buy a bond at any time between interest payment periods (which is most of the time), you pay the seller of the bond the amount of interest he has earned from the last payment date until the date of sale to you. This does not mean that the bond costs you more, even though you have to come up with more cash than the purchase quote indicates. Come the next interest payment date, you receive interest for the full period,

which includes the amount you advanced the seller. It seems the only just and fair way to do it. Since this interest advanced is only a temporary condition and not part of the cost of the bond, it is excluded from this column.

8. "Dollars of Investment." Again, exclude interest paid. *Do* include broker's commissions, taxes, etc.

9. "Last Date Purchased." Although less important here than with stocks, bond appreciation (or depreciation) may be treated as long-term capital gain (or loss), so the one-year holding period is still important.

10. "Sold No. of Bonds." You can sell all or part of your holdings—indicate how much in this column.

11. "Sold @ Quoted Price." This is the price quoted on your brokerage slip and does not include earned interest paid to you by the new buyer.

12. "Sold for Total $ (Less Interest)." You know what that means by now. It also means minus brokerage commissions, taxes, etc.

13. "Dollars of Gain or (Loss)."

At the very bottom of the page in the "Dollars of Investment" column, insert the total of the column. This is your "Total $ Investment." Also add up the "Dollars of Gain or (Loss)" and post the figure at the bottom of the column. This is your "Total Realized Gain."

As before, post your numbers in pencil to permit changes when they occur. Again, run a line through any bonds sold.

This completes your Master Page for bonds, a lefthand page.

Weekly Bond Summary Sheets (Exhibit 7)

This is a righthand page. The heading is "Closing Bond Prices by Week Plus Total Market Value—Weekly Bond Summary."

Exhibit 6: Master Page—1976 Bonds

(LEFT HAND PAGE)

BOND	DESCRIPTION	STANDARD & POORS QUALITY RATING	1960-1974 HI-LOW	1975 HI-LOW	PROBABLY SELL @	NO. OF BONDS PURCHASED	AVERAGE PURCHASE QUOTE (LESS INTEREST)	DOLLARS OF INVESTMENT	LAST DATE PURCHASED	SOLD NO. OF BONDS	SOLD @ QUOTED PRICE	SOLD FOR TOTAL DOLLARS (LESS INTEREST)	DOLLARS OF GAIN OR (LOSS)	
1. AM. FIN. CORP.	9½-88	—	83-53	70-55		40	62¾	25250	1/16/76					1.
2. ~~AVCO FIN.~~	~~7½-93~~	B	94-30	60-33	72	39	61	~~23982~~	1/15/76	39	72¼	27983	4195	2.
3. ~~AVCO FIN.~~	~~7½-93~~	B	94-30	60-33	72	25	66½	~~16250~~	2/17/76	25	72¼	18062	1312	3.
4. FUQUA.	9½-98	B	96-55	72-55		35	80	27828	2/11/76					4.
5. GEN TEL (OHIO)	10¼-04	A	99-96	103-94		5	99½	4988	11/26/74					5.
6. MGM	10-94	B	67-59	80-60		30	84½	25507	1/15/76					6.
7. MT. DAK. UTIL.	10¾-99	A	102-95	105-98		5	100	5031	10/29/74					7.
8. NIAG. MO. PWR	10.2-05	BBB	–	100-88		5	90½	4586	4/7/75					8.
9. SO. CAL. GAS	10¼-81	A	109-100	108-101		5	100	5032	10/16/74					9.
10. TWA CV.	5-94	B	–	–		25	45⅜	11969	2/18/76					10.
11. GENESCO	10⅜-84	BB	–	–		5	99½	4975	3/12/76					11.
12. ITEL CV.	8-96	B	–	–		10	96	9675	4/12/76					12.
13. TWA CV.	5-94	B	–	–		25	49	12375	7/12/76					13.
14. CAVENHAM	11½-00	—	–	–		15	99	15012	8/27/76					14.
15. AVCO CV.	9⅞-01	—	–	–		25	99	24750	9/7/76					15.
16. COMP. SCI. CV.	6-94	CCC	–	–		15	60½	9187	9/16/76					16.
17.														17.
18.														18.
19.														19.
20.														20.
21.														21.
22.														22.
23.														23.
24.														24.
25.														25.
			TOTAL $ INVESTMENT = $ 185,665							TOTAL REALIZED GAIN = $5507				

Exhibit 7: Weekly Bond Summary
Closing Bond Prices by Week + Total Market Value
(RIGHT HAND PAGE)

	12/3/76		12/10/76		12/17/76		12/23/76		12/31/76	
1.	72	28800	73½	29400	78¾	29800	75⅛	30050	79½	31800
2.										
3.										
4.	93½	32725	95½	33425	95	33250	95½	33425	97	33950
5.	108	5400	108	5400	108	5400	108	5400	108	5400
6.	95¼	28675	95½	28650	96⅞	29063	97⅛	29177	99⅜	29812
7.	111	5550	111	5550	111	5550	111	5550	111	5550
8.	108⅝	5431	108⅝	5431	108⅝	5431	108⅝	5431	108⅝	5431
9.	108¼	5412	108¼	5412	108¼	5412	108¼	5412	108¼	5412
10.	49⅜	12344	50½	12625	50½	12625	47⅛	11781	49	12250
11.	104¼	5212	104¼	5212	104¼	5212	104¼	5212	104¼	5212
12.	100½	10050	102⅜	10234	102	10200	101⅛	10112	103	10300
13.	49⅜	12344	50½	12625	50½	12625	47⅛	11781	49	12250
14.	103⅛	15469	104	15600	104½	15675	104½	15675	106	15900
15.	105½	26375	104⅞	26219	105	26250	106¼	26562	108⅜	27187
16.	63	9450	64	9600	65	9750	65	9760	67¼	10125
17.										
18.										
19.										
20.										
21.										
22.										
23.										
24.										
25.										
MKT. VALUE		203157		205383		206943		206278		210579
20 BONDS	91.32		91.76		91.96		92.27		93.20	
MKT.VAL.GAIN		17972		19718		20278		19613		24914
REALIZED GAIN		5507		5507		5507		5507		5507
TOTAL GAIN		22979		25225		25785		25120		30421

Number the extreme left side of the page to match your Master Page. The setup of the columns is the same as for stocks—two narrow columns for each week. The top of the two-column heading is the Friday date for the week concerned.

The left column of the two is for Friday bond market closing quotes. Remember, these numbers are less one decimal place (93½ = $935).

After you have posted the quotes, multiply the quote (plus a decimal place) times the number of bonds held, to get the total current value of the bonds. This goes in the righthand column of the two.

As before, count five lines up from the bottom and insert these line titles in order going down:

> Market Value
> 20 Bonds
> Market Value Gain
> Realized Gain
> Total Gain

"Market Value" is the grand total of all the bond market values.

The weekly bond price index, "20 Bonds," serves the same function as the Dow Jones Industrial Average for stocks.

"Market Value Gain" is the difference between the "Market Value" figure and the "Total $ Investment" figure from the bottom of the Master Bond Page.

"Realized Gain" is a pickup from the "Total Realized Gain" at the bottom of the Master Bond Page.

"Total Gain" is the sum of "Market Value Gain" and "Realized Gain."

The purpose of these pages is to show the movements of your bond prices—the appreciation or (depreciation) they are enjoying. It has nothing to do with the interest income derived from them.

While the movements of bond prices take second place to their interest income yield, they are still most important. When a bond price drops below what you paid for it, it is equity lost, even though it may continue to deliver a charming yield.

Any sudden movement of a bond price should be a cause for alarm, or joy, depending in which direction it is suddenly moving. Whenever there is abrupt change, it is worth calling your broker on Monday morning to find out why.

Both stock and bond Weekly Summary sheets have enough columns to handle five weeks of activity. I suggest you start fresh sheets the first Friday of each month to keep things neat.

WEEKLY SECURITIES GAIN OR (LOSS) RECAP (EXHIBIT 8)

For this I use a separate page (actually two pages per year) inserted at the back of the three-ring binder. In starting each new year, I drop the previous year's Realized Gains (they are now old business) but keep the Market Value Gains and carry them forward. Their relationship to Total Dollars Invested is still valid.

The wide left column carries the Friday date of each week. The first three narrow columns are devoted to stocks. Leave an empty column, then the next three narrow columns are given over to bonds.

The column headings are all old friends.

Left to right under "Stocks": "Market Value Gain," "Realized Gain" and "Total Gain." The same headings go for the three bond columns.

The numbers are straight pickups from the bottom lines

Exhibit 8: Weekly Securities Gain or (Loss) Recap—1976

1976 DATE	STOCKS			BONDS			TOTAL GAIN STOCKS & BONDS
	MARKET VALUE GAIN	REALIZED GAIN	TOTAL GAIN	MARKET VALUE GAIN	REALIZED GAIN	TOTAL GAIN	
6/4	10265	1700	11965	7054	5507	12561	24526
6/11	12825	1700	14525	7261	5507	12768	27293
6/18	17937	1700	19637	8758	5507	14265	33902
6/25	17783	1700	19483	9758	5507	15265	34748
7/9	20497	1700	22197	10828	5507	16335	38532
7/16	20329	1700	22029	10192	5507	15699	37728
7/23	20328	1700	22028	10769	5507	16276	38304
7/30	20309	1700	22009	10644	5507	16151	38160
8/6	23924	543	24467	10834	5507	16341	40808
8/13	19506	4992	24498	11099	5507	16606	41099
8/20	17160	7828	24988	9724	5507	15231	40219
8/27	16959	7828	24787	7447	5507	12954	37741
9/3	17066	7828	24894	11639	5507	17146	42040
9/10	17908	7828	25736	7941	5507	13448	39184
9/17	18860	7828	26688	9787	5507	15294	41982
9/24	17440	9536	26976	12057	5507	17564	44540
10/1	14527	9536	24063	12252	5507	17759	41822
10/8	10270	6785	17055	12167	5507	17674	34729
10/15	9618	6785	16403	11395	5507	16902	33305
10/23	13746	6785	20531	11700	5507	17207	37738
10/29	17429	6785	24214	12745	5507	18252	42466
11/5	19800	6785	26585	12199	5507	17706	44291
11/12	18295	6603	24898	11540	5507	17047	41945
11/19	24988	6972	31960	13004	5507	18511	50471
11/26	27067	6972	34039	16088	5507	21595	55634
12/3	29215	7541	36756	17472	5507	22979	59735
12/10	33293	7541	40834	19718	5507	25225	66059
12/17	32481	7541	40022	20278	5507	25785	65807
12/23	35378	7541	42919	19613	5507	25120	68039
12/31	42014	7541	49555	24914	5507	30421	79976

of the weekly stock and bond summary sheets—no additional mathematics asked for.

As the three totals columns grow through the weeks, you begin to see the profile of your success or disappointment. I think it is more entertaining and illuminating than either the Dow or the 20 Bond Index.

MONTHLY MARGIN ACCOUNT RECAPITULATION (EXHIBIT 9)

If you are buying bonds on margin, this is a form which takes some of the mystery out of maintaining a margin account. It is all there before you.

Each month your broker sends you a statement of your margin account. It shows the total dollar amount you have borrowed on margin, broken down by the amount devoted to straight bonds and that for convertible bonds. (My brokerage house assigns the number 7 to indicate straight bond accounts and 8 to indicate convertible bond accounts.) The statement also shows the amount of interest charged to each account number, the total dollars of interest credited (paid to my account by my bonds), any cash deposits or withdrawals from my account, and the cash that is left on deposit in my account. (This last is designated account 2.)

This is the way you set up the page:

The main top heading is "Monthly Margin Account Recapitulation," and then the year.

The wide left column carries the dates as expressed on your broker's statement.

The secondary headings, which bridge one or more columns, are:

"$ Amount Total Margin" (3 columns)
"$ Amount Interest Charged" (3 columns)

Exhibit 9: Monthly Margin Account Recap

1976 DATE	$ AMOUNT TOTAL MARGIN			$ AMOUNT INTEREST CHGD.			MARGIN INTEREST % FOR PAST MONTH	$ AMOUNT INT. CREDITED			PERSONAL		DEPOSIT BALANCE
	#7 BONDS	#8 CONV. BONDS	TOTAL	#7 BONDS	#8 CONV. BONDS	TOTAL	%	#7 BONDS	#8 CONV. BONDS	TOTAL	DEPOSIT	WITHDRAWN	#2 ACCOUNT
6/25	95868	12791	108369	506	72	578	6.75	2781	400	3181			8444.05
7/30	96063	21240	117303	494	73	567	7.00	1500	625	2125			6474.57
8/27	96063	21339	117402	504	99	603	6.75	1662	—	1662			8137.07
9/24	75865	38305	114170	535	112	647	6.75	255	—	255			1645.62
10/29	76258	38501	114759	392	196	588	6.50	525	—	525			2170.62
11/26	76666	38714	115380	408	212	620	6.50	—	—	—			2170.62
12/31	76758	39306	116064	351	191	542	6.00	5178	1202	6380			8692.50
'76 TOTAL				3190	955	4145		11901	2227	14128			

"Margin Interest % for Past Month" (1 column)
"$ Amount of Interest Credited" (3 columns)
"Personal" (2 columns)
"Deposit Balance" (final wide column)

Under "$ Amount Total Margin," the three columns are subheaded: "#7 Bonds," "#8 Convertible Bonds" and "Total." The same three headings hold true for columns under "$ Amount Interest Charged" and "$ Amount Interest Credited."

The subheadings under the two "Personal" columns are "Deposited" and "Withdrawal."

The subheading under "Deposit Balance" is "#2 Account."

I think all these headings and their purposes become clear when you relate them to Exhibit 9.

You'll notice that the margin interest rate charged to me each month ranged from 6.00 percent to 7.00 percent.

I made no cash deposits or withdrawals during the period of this report.

I allowed my dollars of interest credit to accumlate in my deposit balance and only withdrew to buy additional bonds. Under my broker's margin requirements, $4,000 in cash would buy $10,000 worth of bonds. I made several purchases during the year. After the new year, I withdrew some of the surplus cash to pay tax bills.

This money left on deposit is not mere carelessness. Each dollar in the deposit account reduces a dollar of margin debt. That is the same thing as getting 6 to 7 percent on my money. And the money is instantly available to me. A telephone call to my broker, and a check for the amount I want will be in the next mail.

These five record-keeping forms are all you will ever need throughout your securities investing career. The con-

trol over the destiny of your investments is absolutely in-
dispensable.

Once the forms are set up, the time required to keep
them up-to-date is minimal. The difference between tight,
action-inducing record-keeping and other, slap-dash methods
could amount to thousands of dollars to you over the years.

If I had to do my securities investing without these five
forms, I would feel as if someone had severed my right arm.
I strongly suggest that you not try to do *your* securities
investing one-handed. Once you gain experience with this
dynamic decision-making technique of securities record-
keeping, you will not be satisfied to be the passive, unin-
formed investor ever again.

10

Step 8– Invest in Residential Income Real Estate

No man feels more of a man in the world if he have a bit of ground that he can call his own. However small it is on the surface, it is four thousand miles deep; and that is a very handsome property.
—CHARLES DUDLEY WARNER (1829–1900)
My Summer in a Garden

It is a comfortable feeling to know that you stand on your own ground. Land is about the only thing that can't fly away.
—ANTHONY TROLLOPE (1815–1882)
The Last Chronicle of Barset

I did not fully comprehend the wealth-enhancing power of residential income real estate until I owned my first apartment house. It is one thing to know about it in the abstract; it is another to see the wealth-building numbers actually working for you.

Investment in residential income property brings a number of strong wealth-enhancing factors into confluence—more than I know of in any other single investment opportunity. This concentration of energy is so great, so beneficial to the appreciation of capital and net worth—I do not see how any ambitious salaried wealth-builder can accomplish his goals without it.

Of course, there are hazards to real estate investment as there are to any aggressive wealth-building program. You cannot go into it with your eyes half-open and your brain in low gear. On the other hand, there are safety factors at work that help protect you.

I'll show you both sides—the risks and the potential rewards. Measure them by your own yardstick and decide for yourself whether I am right or wrong in my judgment.

The government is kind to the owners of investment real estate, and for good reasons.

In a growing economy there is a constant need for new living space. The natural deterioration (and ultimate demolition) of older buildings, population movement, birth rates that grow and death rates that diminish—all these contribute to an ever-expanding need for residential buildings.

In a major sense, governmental tax laws which provide benefits for the real estate investor are, in actuality, subsidies for the individual renter. To my view, this is a good arrangement. Everyone benefits. For the owners of investment real estate, the blessings are multiple. Let us begin enumerating them.

Tax Benefits—A Shelter for Your Income

We have noted before the disastrous effects of taxation on wealth-enhancing ambitions. It removes capital from your pocket; it breaks the pyramid of compounding, essential to wealth-building.

In recent years many otherwise shrewd investors and high achievers sought tax relief through one or another dubious tax-sheltering device. Many of these devices ignored the primary principle of the preservation of capital; they lost huge sums of equity in the scramble to salvage fewer tax dollars.

Further, a good portion of these "shelters" offered only temporary relief—a delayed tax payment. When the piper arrived at the front door to be paid, the "sheltered" investor suffered either the repayment of postponed taxes or diminished (or totally lost) equity in his investment. It was a bitter and costly truth.

No tax shelter is of any worth unless it is a wise investment of itself.

The 1976 Tax Reform Act put the ax to most of these shady shelters and sent them to a deserved demise. But the act has left residential income real estate relatively untouched—at least to the extent required for the particular strategies that I propose, which I believe are the wisest and most beneficial in the long run.

Ownership of residential income property can help you reduce your burden of federal and state income taxes. This is perfectly honorable and legal. It is the government's deliberate and concerned effort to provide new housing and buildings for our population. It is not a tax loophole.

For you as an owner, it can mean that a considerable portion of your normal federal and state taxes can be offset. Two tax concessions provide for it.

One: you can deduct the interests on your real estate loan payments directly from your gross income. Two: you can take depreciation credits on the total value of your building (but not the land under it) directly from your gross income.

It is the second of these, depreciation, that supplies the greatest immediate financial benefits. Depreciation is truly a tax deferral. It allows you to retain and make use of your investment capital for now and pay the tax at some future date (or never).

Depreciation is explained in detail in Chapter XI, but here is a simple example of it: You own a property on which the improvements (building, etc.) are worth $250,000. You decide to take straight-line depreciation over the life of the mortgage, twenty-five years. This means you can "shelter" (remove from taxation) each year $10,000 of income. The income may come from the property itself, from your salary, from short-term capital gains, or from one-half of your long-term capital gains. (The "preference tax" portion of your long-term capital gains can not be sheltered—the tax must be paid.)

At its worst, depreciation allows you to keep today's hard dollars and then pay back in softer dollars that have been eroded by inflation. At its best, depreciation will never be paid back at all. If you do not sell your building during your lifetime, or if you trade up (or even) to another piece of property, the taxes on depreciation will not come due.

Your real estate investment helps you beat the treacherous game of inflation. Inflation runs counter to depreciation, for as dollars get cheaper, prices rise. Your rents rise and the value of your building goes up. You have the ability to manipulate your dollars now, make your score, and pay back (if at all) out of winnings.

In real estate investment you can have your cake and eat it, too: retain (or enhance) your financial equity and also depreciate it.

There is a penalty you must pay for all this. The cash flow (income) from your real estate investment will be normally somewhat less than you could achieve in other investment areas. In today's market, with financing costs so high, you may do well to get a 6 to 10 percent income from the equity in your investment property.

Yet, when you begin adding up the benefits, perhaps the penalty is not so severe as it might seem.

Prepayment Benefits

If you have a very profitable year and a large amount of your income is subject to tax, you can prepay the second property tax installment (due in the next calendar year) in the current year. You can paint your building, spend money to improve your property, and thereby obtain a better future income from it. All these payments will reduce your tax burden for the year in which they are incurred.

In other words, you are offered far more flexible control of your tax obligations than you could achieve with most other investments you could find.

Equity Build-up

Each month that goes by increases the value of your real estate to you. You will pay down on your loan with the cash generated by the building itself. This is a continuing contribution to your net worth.

Because of this, real estate is a fabulous estate-builder. Most loans are amortized to zero in twenty-five to thirty years. Your principal payments grow as your interest payments diminish, until in the end the building is yours, free and clear. Then, instead of sending three or four thousand dollars a month to the lending institution, you keep it or use it to help finance another building.

An acquaintance of mine in Chicago, a third-generation descendant of a real estate–oriented family, now owns some 20,000 units of apartments. Many of the buildings, he owns free and clear. Rather than take mortgages or trust deeds on the buildings he owns, when he wishes to build or buy a new building, he negotiates a bank loan using one or several of his buildings as collateral. He does not pay points for his loan.

This is the ultimate concept in estate-building, one that any salaried person can adopt and make work for him.

Leveraging

Investment in residential income real estate offers you one of the highest ratios of leverage available in legitimate investing—without the immense risk that usually accompanies high-leverage situations.

This is what I mean by high leverage: A good piece of real estate can generally be bought for 10 to 29 percent of its purchase price as a down payment. If you were able to buy an income property for 10 percent down, this would mean that each dollar of your invested capital would be producing a return roughly equal to $10. If the site has been wisely selected and the numbers (rents, expenses, vacancy rates, taxes, maintenance, etc.) are as they should be, this should be the first and only cash you will ever put into your property. Loan payments, property taxes, maintenance—all costs of operation plus the equity build-up—should be paid for by the income generated by the building.

That is a lot of "go"—a lot of leverage—for your capital investment.

Summary of Benefits

These, then, are some of the wealth-enhancing benefits you should expect to achieve from investment in residential income property:

1. *Tax relief.* Apartment houses offer the best depreciation advantages as an offset to salary. By adjusting real estate tax prepayments and maintenance spending, you gain flexibility in your tax obligations.

2. *Inflation protection.* A residential income property is a hedge against inflation. Rents increase during inflationary periods, and so the market value of your building automatically increases.

3. *Capital leverage.* Since your building is highly leveraged, any increase in its value is accelerated as a percentage of your investment. What's more, you receive 100 percent of the increase in value while your trust deed or mortgage holder is paid back in fixed-rate, inflation-cheapened dollars.

4. *Equity build-up.* The building pays for itself out of its own income. Each month your equity in the building is increased, and where the value of the building rises, your equity is increased even further. This is a real wealth-builder —a major contributor to the growth of your net worth.

Beyond these, there are other advantages for the salaried person:

1. *Management of the investment.* With most businesses you might buy, it would be folly to turn the management over to others. Yet for you, with a full-time job on your hands, any other alternative would be out of the question. The business of residential income property is highly structured and relatively slow-paced. It can safely be run by others while you keep a firm hand on the controls during your off hours. A resident manager can take care of day-to-day affairs. You can employ a professional property management company for about 4 percent of the gross rentals to oversee the major management decisions. Thus you are relieved of the daily burdens of bookkeeping and decision-making and still are confident that your investment is being properly cared for. When you choose to retire from your primary job, you can take over management of your properties and add the 4 percent to your retirement income. Few business investments offer this much flexibility.

2. *Apartment houses versus business properties.* Residential property usually reflects the highest ratio of building to land value. Since depreciation may be taken only on the building portion of the investment, the invester gains the greatest depreciation for his dollars of investment. Further, apartment houses are not subject to becoming 100 percent vacant all at once as are single-tenant industrial and office buildings. If you own such a commercial building and do not have sufficient diversification to withstand the loss of income, it could be disastrous to your investment.

3. *Pyramiding.* After you have owned your building for six to ten years, and if you still approve of its location, you can refinance your loan. Your rents will have increased over this time and so will the market value of your property. Since your present loan has been amortized down, your equity has been increased. With these conditions, refinancing can return to you a large chunk of capital which can be put down on another building. There is, of course, a price tag for this. You will pay the lender one or two points (percentage points of the total loan which are an advance payment). These points, under the new Tax Act, may no longer be deducted from income incurred in the year but must be deducted in equal increments over the length of the loan.

With the new buildings you have bought with your cash from refinancing, you will enjoy immediately the advantages of an added depreciation schedule to help offset more of your income. This depreciation may also be used to offset that portion of your long-term capital gains which would ordinarily be taxed as straight income.

4. *Increased depreciation option.* A furnished apartment house or complex will spin off more immediate depreciation benefits than if it were unfurnished. This is an advantage for a highly paid executive who wants to shelter more of his income during his last high-earning years prior to retirement. Furnishings can be depreciated over a four- to five-

year period. (I do not advocate taking accelerated depreciation on the building itself, and I will explain why later.)

The investor who seeks the most depreciation will try, when he is purchasing the property, to ascribe the maximum amount of the purchase price to the improvements (i.e., the building) and the least to the land it sits on, since the land is not depreciable. A good system for handling this is to investigate the property's last tax bill. Whatever value the current owner assigns to the land, the generally acceptable authority is the tax assessor, who will usually undervalue the land. The price of the total property remains the same, but that portion which is depreciable is increased. Then too, your accountant can further your depreciation rate by setting up component depreciation. This means he figures your air conditioning, elevators, roof, etc. with different life expectancies than the structure itself, so you can enjoy a quicker write-off on them.

As a salaried person, you can see that owning residential income property offers many varied and substantial benefits.

Now that I've highlighted the benefits, let us take a step back and review some of the prerequisites to owning residential income property.

Preparing a Secure Base for Property Ownership

I want to return to Steps 5 and 6 in your wealth-building program—your Cash Equivalent Reserve and your Liquidity Reserve. However much I applaud the virtues of real estate investment, I implore you not to neglect these two financial necessities in your enthusiasm for real estate.

You may be tempted by friends or circumstances to break from your wealth-building criteria and to abscond with your reserves in pursuit of some other goal. Don't do it.

By imprinting your reserve guidelines on your investment mentality, you will avoid the many bear traps that any investor risks.

A credit crunch, such as the ones we had in 1970 and in 1974, when large corporations teetered on the brink of bankruptcy for lack of cash or inability to pay 16 percent borrowing rates—this is reason enough for "fail-safe" reserves. It can happen, it *will* happen, again.

If you maintain your secure reserves, you will be better able to fend off adverse conditions so as to take advantage of the great buying opportunities in some future bargain market.

The conservative investor might even consider increasing his Liquidity Reserve to as much as the balance of his mortgages or trust deeds, although the total would exceed his standard 5 percent of net worth. This would offer an extra degree of safety.

Real Estate Syndication

I know there is a great temptation for investors with small amounts of capital to be attracted by real estate syndications. You can get into the game for a smaller stake and someone else is doing most of the work for you, while you may possibly enjoy many of the benefits.

My advice to you is to steer clear of syndications or multiple ownership syndicates—for several reasons.

In recent years, Real Estate Investment Trusts (REITs) have been disasters and the major scandal of the investment and banking businesses. These REITs, and the banks that lent money to them, are still today trying to get out from under the landslide of bad judgment, incompetent management and insane risk.

Many of the REITs, especially those that concentrated on the potentially more lucrative construction mortgage business, were pyramids standing on their tips—doomed to topple at the first ill breeze. Hundreds of millions of dollars either have been written off as losses or continue to undergo attempts at salvage.

For the small investor it has been capital hazard to the extreme.

From the resulting shake-out, we can hope that REITs will come under reasonable restraints so that they can offer a degree of safety. For the time being, they are no place to have your money.

REITs that concentrated on equity and management in large, established properties where the honest values prevailed have done a respectable job and should not be condemned for it. They appear to be in the minority.

But even where a real estate syndicate is honestly and capably managed and its properties are sound investments, I would still advise you against it. Your investments are not in your own hands and you lose some of the benefits you would otherwise have as a private investor. For example:

1. You cannot pick the year in which to sell. The syndicate picks the year. The resultant income may come in a high tax year for you and complicate your taxes.

2. You sacrifice the opportunity of trading up a property and further delaying the payment of capital gains taxes. This is the single greatest advantage that real estate has over investment in stocks and bonds. Many real estate investors never pay a capital gains tax in their lifetimes. The heirs to the estate will pay neither capital gains nor depreciation on the real estate as long as they do not have to sell the property to settle the estate. If the property is held or traded up, the estate will be liable only for death taxes. This is not true of stocks and bonds. (This may be the subject of some further interpretation, so check with your accountant for the current taxation policy.)

3. The syndicate, in most cases, will take the fastest depreciation available, which will force a sale in six or seven years, when the depreciation runs out. This brings into play a number of undesirable factors.

4. In this kind of shared ownership you are not building the kind of annuity for yourself that is the option of individual ownership.

5. You lose the flexibility of prepayments of taxes and anticipatory maintenance, so useful in adjusting your taxes. You are at the mercy of group decision.

All things considered, you might do better to keep your funds working in your Optional Investment Fund until the day when you can afford to buy property for yourself.

I will make one exception to this. In some areas, the costs of viable residential income property have risen to such heights, it is difficult for the individual to collect enough capital for a suitable down payment. Here, I would suggest you form your own syndicate with one, two, three or four friends of about the same income level, age and ambitions as you (so that you will all be talking on the same wavelength) and pool your resources as partners in an investment.

You will need all the help of your individual lawyers to assure that this will come off as you expect it to. But the effort could be worth the trouble. The benefit of a partnership is that of pooled resources: together you may be able to buy a desirable property that one alone could not bring off. Then too, the liabilities of the investment are shared— you don't carry the full burden of risk alone.

The most common vehicle of the unincorporated business arrangement is the general partnership. Typically, each partner has a voice in its management and any one can bind the business by his actions.

The general partnership in itself is not a taxable entity (unlike the corporation). Each partner shares the profit or loss as part of his personal tax liability or asset. If the partnership enjoys long-term capital gains, these are shared. If depreciation is incurred, the benefits are shared.

The general partnership arrangement is becoming more and more common in real estate investment as the costs of attractive properties rise. For some, it is the only way to get into substantial real estate investment.

I offer these suggestions:

1. Any partnership agreement should have a definite termination date—anywhere from five to ten years from its inception. There are several reasons for this. At best, the real estate partnership is a short-term solution. By far the most advantageous wealth-building occurs when you own your property alone. As time goes by, the financial requirements of the partners could differ radically. One might need immediate cash flow while another needs tax shelter. Thus, management decisions would be poles apart. A definite termination date assures that all partners leave the enterprise with equal gain or loss. Otherwise, if one partner wishes to sell and the other does not, the selling partner usually suffers some loss of equity build-up.

Where the partners are close to retirement age, the termination date might well be set beyond the retirement dates. This allows the partners to reduce their tax liabilities because of reduced income.

2. Partnerships should take straight-line depreciation only. Since the intent is not to hold the property for an indefinite period but to sell it at the termination of the partnership, any depreciation taken that is greater than straight-line will be penalized by being taxed as straight income.

Partnership arrangements in purchasing real estate have some shortcomings. The most serious of these is that it is difficult, if not impossible, to trade even or up to another piece of property and thus avoid the taxes incurred on depreciation taken. Disagreements occur between the best of friends and there is bound to be some friction. If there is a serious falling-out, it may end up in a law court, a wealth-inhibiting place if there ever was one. Then too, a settlement may force the sale of the property at a time when it cannot achieve its greatest worth.

For you, a partnership may be the only way to launch yourself into real estate. But before you take the step, understand clearly what you are gaining and what you are giving up.

Real Estate Investment Goals

Your first goal is to own enough improved real estate to offset your taxable adjusted gross income through depreciation. Apartment houses and duplexes offer this opportunity for maximum depreciation since the building-to-land ratio is generally the most favorable.

Geographical diversification is most desirable. All your peaches are not on one bough. Should the bough break—should the hazards of nature, fire or social change damage your investment—you have other investments in other locations to console you for your losses.

Where possible, you should choose an apartment house of sufficient size that it will justify the costs of an on-premises manager to attend to immediate problems. Residential income property should no more be a distraction from your job than you would allow the securities market to be. I have chosen apartment houses with thirty-three units and it has worked out well for me. You probably can get by with fewer units.

For young people of limited means who, after satisfying their two reserve requirements, wish to own real estate, a duplex apartment may be the answer. The owner can live in one apartment and lease the other. He can gain experience with a rental unit and begin to enjoy some of the pleasures of depreciation (but only on the half he is renting out, not on the half in which he resides).

One of your main objectives in selecting a real estate property to own is to buy one you will want to keep for a long time.

This is the exact opposite of the advice I gave to you for the securities markets. With securities, you buy and sell in appropriate seasons. With real estate, you buy and hold.

This naturally places an extra strain on your selection process. Choosing a location that will weather the storms of change and the caprices of society is not the easiest job you will ever undertake, but it's preferable to the alternatives.

Trading real estate is time-consuming. You can't afford it. Not frequently, at any rate.

By selling outright, you invite all sorts of wraths down on your head. I'll give you a personal example. On one of my buildings I am taking straight-line depreciation even though, since I built the building, I could take much more. Had I taken 200 percent depreciation, I would now, with the depreciation used up, be forced to trade up or sell outright. Either way I would have to pay a real estate commission of $48,000. Then too, I would have to sacrifice my 7¾ percent loan for a much higher rate on the trade-up—and pay a new set of points. I would also have to pay a new escrow fee plus a lawyer's fee for checking the contract. And a penalty for loan prepayment.

What's more, I would have to go out and find another building. If I could not find one to put into escrow with the one I was selling and I had to sell outright, I would be subject to a huge capital gains tax plus ordinary income tax on the excess depreciation taken.

If you had paid $100 for this book and accepted only

this single bit of advice, you could save one hundred times the price of one transaction.

Select your real estate investments for the long pull.

Real Estate Investment Strategies

For this I will call upon the assistance of a recognized real estate authority in this area—George Elkins. Elkins was a pioneer in Southern California real estate, having moved there fresh out of college in 1921. He is the founder of the George Elkins Company, realtors and mortgage bankers, with nine offices in California, headquartered in Beverly Hills. The company conducts real estate transactions around the country.

Elkins is one of the most knowledgeable and honorable men I have met in the real estate business. I came to know him through working out of his Beverly Hills office as an independent, unsalaried real estate salesman in his investment division—a "retirement" occupation I enjoy immensely.

When George Elkins came to Beverly Hills in 1922, the community comprised no more than 700 people. The "city" was made up chiefly of vacant lots.

Beverly Hills is blessed uniquely in a number of ways. Historically, it has elected city councils with a predilection for strict building and zoning codes. It came to be viewed as a green oasis in the midst of Los Angeles' clutter and sprawl.

By location, it is about midway between downtown Los Angeles and the Pacific surf—a midpoint between commerce and recreation.

Most significant, it was centrally located among the growing wealth of the burgeoning young motion picture industry—a short drive from Paramount, Columbia and RKO studios in Hollywood, Warner Brothers in Burbank, Metro-Goldwyn-Mayer in Culver City, and right next door to Twentieth Century Fox. It became the home of the Hollywood rich.

When George Elkins arrived, it seemed to him that selling lots in Beverly Hills had a future in it. So he toured the studios, talking to movie people, great and small, of the benefits of undeveloped real estate.

George Elkins recalls: "During the year 1925, I had occasion to sell a successful real estate subdivider a lot in the 800 block on Alpine Drive in Beverly Hills. The price of the lot was about $6,500."

Today there are no vacant parcels in this area. But if this lot, or one similar to it, were selling unimproved, it would command $250,000 in this year's currency. (Of course, Beverly Hills is a community that compares with few. Small in size, limited in growth, intensely in demand—it has almost no peers in land appreciation.)

George Elkins told me about his early selling technique. "I sometimes assured the buyers," he said, "without reasonable justification for doing so, that they would be able to double their money and not have to make another payment—which at that time would be six months away.

"Because of the general conditions in the United States at that time, it was quite possible to do so—and it happened. I'd sell them a lot, come to them before the six months, double their money for them, and they'd get out. As time went on, I became interested in buying real estate for myself. I went very strongly into unimproved properties—both some acreage and lots.

"Unfortunately, when the depression hit, I found that such money as I had been able to accumulate, I had in equities and unimproved real estate, which very quickly ate me out of the remaining capital I had, trying to keep it.

"I felt I had paid a very sizable price for a lesson—that if I was smart enough, I could get some benefit out of the lesson instead of feeling bitter about having lost a lot of money. It would do me no good to dwell on that—it was gone. So I did try to figure out why I had made this kind of mistake.

"I came to this conclusion," said George Elkins, "which I think is a sound one—I still employ it. If you buy good, well-located *improved* real estate that shows a healthy income, borrow as much as you can borrow at the time you acquire it, and have your loan spread out over as long a period of time as you can have it, and then look after the property and have patience—oftentimes that property will do unbelievable things for you . . . if you have selected wisely in the first place."

Here in a few sentences are encapsulated some of the basic principles of real estate investment, as valid for the part-time investor as they are for the professional:

1. Well-located, improved real estate, bought and held, can make a phenomenal contribution to your wealth.

2. One obvious difference between an apartment house and vacant land is that one produces an income and the other, an expense. When hard times hit, this difference can have monumental consequences.

3. In real estate, the name of the game is location selection—everything else is secondary.

4. When you borrow to invest in real estate, borrow as much as you can on the property for as long a time as the lender will allow.

Several important factors come into play in location selection.

Where a neighborhood appears to be deteriorating, approaching the point where it might be hard to get and keep good, sound tenants, your real estate investment decision must be carefully weighed. When environmental, economic and political conditions are right, the neighborhood may rebound, vastly increasing the worth of your investment. On the other hand, if conditions are not benevolent, the erosion of your property value, the decline of rents, the increase of crime and vandalism, all will contribute to making your investment a burden, not an asset.

As you might expect, rent control is a specter that frightens every prospective investor in real estate. In New York City, for example, rent control has been probably one of the greatest disasters to hit the town. Because of rent control, owners have been literally forced to abandon their properties. As costs of remodeling, of keeping properties in respectable condition, kept accelerating, while rents were kept level, property owners found it ever more difficult to finance the costs of maintenance. They finally arrived at the point where they tired of reaching into their pockets, trying to hang on to their properties, so they abandoned them to the lender or the city. Tens of thousands of these units belong to the City of New York right now. No one is paying taxes on them. Many thousands of them have been demolished.

Millions of tax revenue dollars lost, tens of thousands of dwelling units that might have served the residents of a great city destroyed—these are the lessons of rent control. Dr. Stuart Butler, a British economist, commenting on his country's experience with rent control, said, "Rent control is probably the most effective way to destroy a city, short of bombing—but at least in bombing, you reduce the demand as well as the supply."

A third vital factor in property selection is diversification. If you plan to own more than one piece of investment real estate, it is wisest to select your holdings in different neighborhoods. Should one location turn sour, the percentages are with you that your others will more than make up the loss.

So add these three to your scrapbook of basic real estate principles:

5. Practice extreme caution when considering a purchase in a deteriorating neighborhood. Your golden opportunity may turn into a lead weight.

6. Avoid communities with rent control, either in force or threatened. Rent control is good for no one—property owner or tenant—except for politicians near election time.

7. Diversify your real estate investments into varied areas so that a single neighborhood's decline will not jeopardize your entire estate.

No matter how much more you learn about real estate in your lifetime, if you remember these seven principles, you cannot go too far wrong.

A Few Other Real Estate Strategies

Often it is possible to buy a building from an older owner who no longer wants the responsibility of ownership. In many cases, this former owner will be willing to carry the first trust deed at an interest rate lower than is available on the market and will not charge the additional points. If he approves of you and your credit standing, he and you can do each other a favor by amortizing the loan over a longer period of time. You recognize a greater immediate income flow and he enjoys an eased capital gains tax burden by spreading it out.

I urge you to find a reputable property management firm to handle your property. They charge roughly 4 to 5 percent of the gross rental income for this service and will send you a monthly statement and check. They eliminate most of the routine obligations of the property owner, which are necessary but irksome, and too much for you as a salaried person with plenty of regular job preoccupations.

Upon retirement you can decide whether or not you wish

to take over management of the property to gain extra income.

If your spouse has a flair, and a desire, to manage property, certainly this is a possibility. I recommend you join a local apartment house owners' association to obtain information about proper forms, tax rulings and legal situations. Where you employ a property management firm, you will get part of this education through discussions with your account manager—which can serve you well at a later date.

And a Few Observations

You may have read some of the recent headlines about the increase of foreign investment in this country. One of the favorite forms of investment for cash-rich Japanese, West Europeans and Arabs is improved real estate.

In some especially choice areas, this competition for land and buildings has driven prices up to unprecedented levels relative to the amount of cash generated.

At this time, some investors are buying apartment houses in Beverly Hills that are priced so high they have a negative cash flow. That is, the rents generated by the properties are not sufficient to cover the expenses. The owner must burrow in his pocket to keep his buildings operating. He *pays* for the privilege of owning his building.

This is not so lunatic as it might seem from a distance. The strategies involved point to the power of residential income real estate in a strong location.

Because of the stringent Beverly Hills building and zoning codes, the investor is assured that the property values will not be allowed to decline through reckless development. He is reasonably convinced that as the pressure of Los Angeles City squeezes around, Beverly Hills property becomes more and more wanted. Every time a property changes hands, it is sold at a higher price. In recent history in this area, property has increased in value at better than 1 percent per month.

The purchaser of a negative-cash-flow apartment house is convinced that this trend will continue—that his investment may appreciate (depending upon whether he pays down 29 percent or 10 percent) by as much as 41 to 120 percent in a year. His investment is secure.

Hollywood has earned a reputation as a kind of never-never fantasy land. When it comes to real estate, Beverly Hills wins the title. It is not your ordinary, everyday American community. As the evaluation rises on Beverly Hills apartment houses, so must the rents. Within two or three years, through rental increases, the owner may expect the cash flow to turn from negative to positive. The money flows back into his pocket.

In the meantime, the buyer has taken full advantage of deductions from his federal and state income taxes for:

1. Business losses—the cash paid out in excess of cash received from his property
2. Interest paid on property mortgages
3. Depreciation allowances.

All the while these negative-cash-flow properties appear to be *money-losers* on their books, actually they are *money-enhancers* for their owners. Besides doing wonderful things for the owners' net worths.

No fools, these buyers. Their sanity is not in question.

But before you get excited about the possibilities of negative cash flow, I'll warn you that it is not generally a condition you search out. The location of the property must be considered so prime that its continued growth is assured not just for years but for decades. It must have nigh perfect safety as an investment. The buyer must be generating plenty of income on his own so he can afford what may be heavy out-of-pocket costs . . . and give confidence to the lending institutions, who are not thrilled about lending money on negative-cash-flow investments. Most important, he must be able to take advantage of depreciation to protect his taxable income.

I must give you a word of extreme warning here. Some areas of the country have been so struck by real estate speculation that property prices have soared beyond hopes of a reasonable return on the investment. This is true in many areas along the West Coast, around Washington, D.C., and in a number of other locations. Los Angeles investors, for example, have become disenchanted with high property prices and are beginning to buy into areas in Arizona, Texas and Florida. As a result, properties around Dallas and Houston (among others), which once yielded a 10 percent cash flow, are now priced by the market competition to yield 7 to 8 percent on the investment.

Property investment in the United States is no longer insulated from distant interests. Your objective should be never to buy into an inflated market—but to find locations uncontaminated by speculation. Then when the speculators come, it's all to your benefit.

OTHER REAL ESTATE INVESTMENTS

Your Home

Your home is a wealth-enhancer—no matter what sort of damage it seems to be doing to your checkbook. If you have selected your home with foresight, it is increasing your net worth even though it produces no income for you. The other real estate virtues take care of it.

In the study I mentioned, about the typical wage earner

from Detroit, the worker who owned his own home had a net worth of about $38,000, while the worker who lived in an apartment had a net worth closer to $13,000. Same income, same life-style—different result.

The time-honored rule that your house should represent an investment of no more than two-and-one-half years of income has been invalidated by inflation. Today it takes a good deal more than that to own a fair home. Of course, the size of your income affects this ratio, too. There is no one rule of thumb that covers all people in all circumstances in all parts of the country. You can buy a fine home in the backwoods of Michigan or on the remote lakes of Maine for a small price. But for the average urban citizen today, the typical price of a home is in the $40,000 to $45,000 range. If the average income is $13,000, this becomes a most burdensome purchase.

A home of your own means capital taken out of the investment action. Dormant dollars. Yes, there are tax advantages and appreciation and increased equity. But these are invisible until you cash them in.

Some people have built up their real estate equity by home-hopping—by taking undervalued or under-maintained properties, fixing them up in their off hours, and reselling them at a profit. This is certainly an avenue of possible real estate growth—if you can stand the constant upheaval.

On the one hand, owning a home of your own means that you can enjoy the intangible assets—the pleasure, the sense of family security and well-being—which cannot be measured by a formula. On the other, a home purchased at a price beyond your means can be a financial albatross, limiting your opportunities. Clearly the goal is to find the right property that permits pleasures of home ownership with real financial enhancement.

Estée Lauder, the cosmetics tycoon—a lovely lady— once told me that her father advised her always to own her own home free and clear. This is noble advice, but frequently not possible for many.

All my life I have lived in homes with large mortgages. But finally I took Estée Lauder's father's advice and paid off the trust deed on my new home. I made it a condition of the first trust deed (mortgage) that I could pay it off in the first year without penalty. When interest rates retreated to about the same rate I was paying on my trust deed, I paid it off.

I must say that it is a great feeling to know that you own your home outright with no obligations but to the county property tax collector. I am fortunate that I can afford this luxury. In today's world, it *is* a luxury.

Unimproved Property

If you have a collection of residential income properties, raw land could make a nice addition to your real estate family. Rarely should it be your first real estate acquisition— only an extra added attraction.

As a rule, any time you have to hold a piece of property (vacant property) for as much as ten years to double your money, it has not been a good investment. You should double your money every seven years—at worst—to get 10 percent net on your cash invested.

Raw land seems to hold the same hypnotic appeal for the novice real estate investor as a shapeless lump of clay does for a sculptor. It seems to have *so many* possibilities! But I have found from my own bitter experience that land which does not produce an income can be a terrible drag and very expensive to cling to.

Vacant land, while you hold it, adds a cost, not an income. It is attractive because it requires no management; it is latent wealth like an undiscovered gold nugget; it is pristine in its lack of man-made structures. But until it reaches its moment of marketability it is Prometheus chained —potentially great wealth-building power with no place to go.

Raw land is for those who can afford to sit and wait on their assets. The only viable land is that which is directly in the path of urban growth—and the growth had better come with reasonable haste. Farmland has its points—it may produce an income while you wait. But if the farm's management is in Neanderthal hands (and how's a city slicker to know?) the losses could be greater than if the land just rested there doing nothing.

The idea of buying a large piece of raw land and then subdividing it is largely a daydream for the novice investor. Today more than ever before, subdivision is a business for professionals, not for amateurs. It is very tricky.

If you are considering buying a vacation site, building on it, using it yourself part of the year and renting it out the rest, you should know the rules. A vacation home is considered personal property and not residential income property if the owner uses it for more than fourteen days a year or 10 percent of the number of days during the year for which the residence is rented, whichever is greater. This rule makes it somewhat awkward to achieve both a personal vacation home and an investment property in the same package. At the same time, the low ratio of improvement to land offers minimum depreciation relative to investment. A multi-use vacation home is not one of your better ways to make money in real estate. (As with every other real estate dogma, exceptions do occur.)

Recent legislation concerning ecological factors adds another dimension of uncertainty to raw land acquisition. You can't be sure what you will be allowed to use your land for. However, if you live in a non-ecologically-sensitive area, it should affect your purchase not in the least.

My recommendation is that undeveloped property should be valued at no more than 5 percent of your net worth. It should be selected for its potential for development in the not-too-distant future.

Mineral Rights

Check your properties' title rights reports to see if there are mineral rights contained in them. You could be sitting on a mother lode.

Where the rights are intact, I suggest you see your lawyer about setting up a trust to skim the mineral rights out from under any property you own or purchase. There is no tax on these rights. They can be separated from your property with ease. The legal fees are minimal. And who is to say how valuable they might be in the future?

Potential buyers of your property will be disappointed to find mineral rights gone, but their absence will not diminish the price you obtain.

The trust can be for children or grandchildren, or can be combined with any trust currently in force. Since you are adding nothing of current value, it will not disturb the viability of the trust.

The recent urgency to obtain new sources of energy and basic minerals could someday make the dirt under your property worth a great deal. Since it costs next to nothing, preserve these rights for your family's future.

A General Evaluation of Income Property as an Investment?

A fair report card of income property as an investment might look something like this:

Current income on equity $= C+$
Tax benefits $= A$
Capital growth $= A+$

The nonprofessional investor can easily learn and implement the requirements of real estate investment. It does not take a superior brain to see whether the numbers are working or not working.

Real estate is a commodity with a limited supply and an ever-increasing demand. Currently in this country there are about 150,000,000 people living in urban areas. By the year 2000, the number is expected to grow to over 220,000,000. The estimated number of new U.S. housing units required between now and 2000 A.D. is over 50,000,000, with an additional 14,000,000 units needed to replace obsolete units. Some 26,000,000 of these will be apartment house units located in suburbs near or within the limits of large cities.

Will the housing industry be able to meet these challenges? Doubtful. It is therefore probable that there will continue to be an increasing demand for rental units and higher prices for land.

The mathematics of population are on the real estate investor's side. And the mathematics of real estate are on the wealth-builder's side.

If I have convinced you that income property deserves a dominant place in your wealth-building strategies, you'll find in the next two chapters some important guides to buying and managing residential income real estate.

11

How to Buy an Apartment House

Three things are to be looked for in a building: that it stand in the right spot; that it be securely founded; that it be successfully executed.
—JOHANN WOLFGANG VON GOETHE (1749–1832)
Elective Affinities

No man acquires property without acquiring with it a little arithmetic, also.
—RALPH WALDO EMERSON (1803–1882)
Society and Solitude

If buying an apartment house were totally simple, then all the world would be landlords and there would be no tenants. On the other hand, people who think that one must be highly sophisticated to buy residential income property are wrong. Anyone capable of buying his own home should be able to grasp the few fundamentals of buying a piece of residential income property successfully.

There is a small group of rules and formulas to guide you; you'll call on your team of experts to help carry you through the more complex processes; the rest is a matter of judgment.

If you have a natural feel for land and buildings, if you can put yourself in the place of your potential tenant and

see the kind of dwelling place that might excite him—all
to the good. If real estate leaves you cold, if you can't see
the romance of a structure or the relative merits of one piece
of land over another—you could need the help of someone
you trust who does have an appetite for property.

Buying real estate is not an art form, it is a business.
But an appreciation for some of the intangible values helps.

How Much to Invest

Your first real estate investment is made from your Optional Investment Fund. It must not diminish your Cash
Equivalent Reserve or your Liquidity Reserve. As an owner
of income property, you will in fact have greater need for
these reserves than before.

The range of your cash investment as a percentage of
the total selling price of a property will be from a low of 10
percent to a high of 29 percent.

If you seek immediate income, you'll want to pay the
larger amount down. If your salary takes care of your current financial needs, you will choose to buy more property
for less cash.

The wealth-building rule in real estate is to obtain the
largest loan possible to be amortized over the longest period
of time.

The lending institution will have something to say about
this. They are even more dedicated than you to the security
of capital. They don't want your building back on their
hands. If you have an impressive financial statement with
prudent reserves, they should be more inclined to lend you
what you want. If you are buying on a shoestring, you will
probably have to settle for less than the ideal amount, or an
increased interest rate, or both.

But the goal is worth pursuing; shop for money as you would shop for any other large purchase—or put a mortgage broker to work for you.

When I want to seek a loan for a building I intend to buy and keep, I will trot around from bank to bank—beginning with the ones I normally do business with—talking to loan managers.

These are my criteria in order of priority:

1. Largest loan
2. Longest period of amortization (30 years, hopefully)
3. Lowest interest rates
4. Fewest points
5. Least prepayment penalties

The relative charm of the loan managers has no place in the judgments.

Where I am dissatisfied with the loan terms offered (or just want to check that I am doing the best I can), I will seek the services of a mortgage broker. A mortgage broker is, in essence, the middle man between the borrower and the lender. You employ him to do your loan shopping for you. He has resources and contacts that you might not be able to discover on your own. He knows who is eager to lend money and who is satiated with loans. He is paid by the lender and his fee is only a fraction of a point so it makes small difference in your final terms. Do both—shop for your own money *and* consult a mortgage broker. That way you will get a broader view of the money market, and have more arrangements from which to choose.

The large-property, small-cash-down formula provides you with the greatest leverage, the highest depreciation, and the best equity build-up.

Selecting a Geographical Location

The three most important factors in selecting a piece of real estate are:

1. Location
2. Location
3. Location.

It is just *that* important.

Among the main location considerations are the potential deterioration of the neighborhood and the presence (or threat) of rent controls. Either can diminish the value of your asset.

The problems facing today's huge, sprawling megalopolises are colossal and difficult. The lack of solutions has forced movement from the central cities to the suburbs. The natural trend of neighborhoods is cyclical: they are born, grow old, are revitalized as land costs rise, and so on. These changes take place over decades. But where economic incentives for revitalization are destroyed, as with rent controls, the cycle is cut—the neighborhood's downward path to decay and abandonment continues unchecked.

Rent controls aren't evil in themselves. When properly applied with well-conceived, enforced building codes, they can drive the slumlords and rent gougers out of business. But too often they are misconceived and misapplied—ignoring the city's paired obligations: supplying its citizens with respectable housing, and private enterprise with a fair and just return on its capital investment.

The city is an investment marketplace just as much as is the New York Stock Exchange. And in exactly the way I advised you to take your cash out of a faltering securities market, I'll tell you that if you have a city in decline, it is a wealth-inhibiting investment market. Take your dollars to a healthier investment climate in the suburbs.

If you are considering investing in your city, look around. If you see rent controls that are not working, if you see neglect and decay and people living beneath their dignity—know that the city is a sick marketplace. No place for you and your precious cash.

Now for my general strategies for selection of real estate location. Every area has its own real estate personality— its own opportunities and hazards—so there can be no one fixed formula, but only general guidelines.

I prefer locations in growth areas with lids on them, in or around centers of commerce—that is, within a city or in a nearby suburb. By a lid, I mean some limit to further growth—a mountain range, an ocean, a river, travel time, an industrial area, anything that would discourage further development in that direction.

In many areas of Florida, Texas and Arizona, for example, where vigorous cities are surrounded by areas of apparently unlimited land, apartment structures have been overbuilt, far in excess of the demands of the population. The result is vacancy rates (and rental rates, because of the competition) at unacceptable levels.

Where urban properties are found in areas of limited geographic growth, they generally will increase in value as raw land in the vicinity is used up.

My two apartment houses are both west of downtown Los Angeles—one in the city proper in the so-called "Wilshire District" and the other in Culver City (a pocket city, surrounded by Los Angeles, the same as Beverly Hills is a pocket city). The barrier to the west is the Pacific Ocean, and to the north the Santa Monica Mountains.

Property on the West Side of Los Angeles has increased dramatically in value over the past decade or so. One reason is that the prevailing westerly breezes from the ocean usually sweep this area clean of smog. Proximity to an ocean is considered an asset. Zoning laws have kept this area relatively uncluttered and have sustained property values. There is also a fairly low level of crime.

Every large population center is subject to human pollutants. Several years ago we saw the beginnings of a crime problem in the area of my Culver City apartment house. It was going downhill fast. We, the owners of apartment houses in this section, formed an association in self-defense. We had some muscle, since our members contributed one-quarter of the property tax bill in Culver City. We obtained the cooperation of the police chief to have a black-and-white patrol car in the apartment house area twenty-four hours a day. This reduced the crime rate by better than 50 percent and really saved the area from deterioration. It is now on its way back up and property prices have escalated.

My Wilshire District apartment house enjoyed steady growth until a year or so ago, when the neighborhood appeared to be starting the process of decay. But as apartment rental prices soared along the coast and the mountain foothills, there was a rebound effect. The neighborhood is again upgrading itself and prices are increasing.

I have always taken special care to plow back rental dollars into the maintenance of my buildings so they stay in first-class condition. This serves the practical purposes of making these buildings more desirable to tenants and contributing to the quality of the neighborhood.

I have chosen to build quality apartments that will attract a more stable, reliable tenant. Part of my motive, of course, is that I wish to hold onto these buildings a long time and quality contruction shows its age with more grace.

Every city has its main direction of movement for high-income growth. It's north in Chicago, west in Philadelphia, south in Kansas City, and north in Dallas and Miami Beach (where they have just about run out of north). New York in its dynamic prime pressed north to Westchester and

Connecticut, east to the far reaches of Long Island, and hopped the Hudson River west to New Jersey.

Undoubtedly you can see these movements at work in or near your community. The trick is to anticipate them. To be a little ahead, rather than behind, the center of progress.

If you choose a first-class location you will likely pay a premium for it; but for the long hold, it could well be worth it. Where you select a second-choice location, you may be able to get a higher cash flow as the outset. However, if this lower-quality location does not fulfill its promise of appreciation, you could be trading up to another building sooner than you wish.

. In picking the proper community and neighborhood you are the best judge. I think it is safest to choose an area where you would be happy to live yourself. You know the kinds of living values you want—look around and see if they are there. If you try to guess other people's idiosyncrasies, you'll be operating at a disadvantage.

There is a consensus among tenant wants: the quality of the community, closeness of shopping facilities, proximity to schools, convenient transportation, and social class of neighbors. These are the kinds of benefits they will be looking for, so your job is to anticipate them.

Once you have settled on a community (which may or may not be your own) and a particular area within it, now you begin the detective work. Ride the streets of the area, locating the schools, shopping centers, transportation lines—evaluating the personalities of the different sections.

Circle the area for several miles around and explore its perimeter. Are there signs of growth or obsolescence? Is there vitality or just tired, old construction? Are there young newly-marrieds on the streets or old folks? What kinds of people are in the shopping centers? How are they dressed? What kinds of cars do you see on the streets?

Before long, if you keep your senses tuned, you will begin to get the smell and the feel of the place and will know how you would rate the different sub-areas for potential investment.

Now it's time to call in an expert. Locate a broker in the area who specializes in apartment houses. He'll have more exclusive listings than an ordinary broker and this works to your advantage. When you make an offer to the listing broker, he has more influence with the seller. If you make an offer to a broker with an open listing on the property, you run the risk of having the seller use your offer to increase the price another interested prospect may have submitted. The listing broker has more control.

From the collection of listings your broker lays out before you, you may be able to eliminate some at the outset. You've done your homework in advance. Where you have the choice, you should look for a building that is relatively new. Three to eight years is a good bet. It has been a common practice on new buildings for the owner to take some form of accelerated depreciation to obtain greater tax shelter. As the amount of depreciation diminishes (after eight to ten years), the owner, who still wants high shelter, may be forced to sell. This usually puts a large group of eight-to-ten-year-old buildings on the market with the seller so eager to move to other properties that you might be able to negotiate a better-than-average selling price.

Older buildings are not excluded from among your choices, but with these you must be more careful in evaluating their present condition and the amount of revitalization required to bring them up to standard.

Personally, I prefer unfurnished buildings. Tenants do not move so often if they must pay a moving company to transport their furniture. If you have a desperate need for depreciation, you can always change your mind and furnish a number of apartments, the furnishings of which you can depreciate over a period of five years or so.

You, as a buyer, should be alert to the possibility of finding an owner who is willing, or eager, to carry the financing, without the usual points charged and at a reasonable rate of interest. This can be a good deal for both the seller and the buyer. Some owners prefer to sell direct, thus avoiding a broker's commission. The classified ads of the newspaper covering your area of interest should be scanned for such opportunities.

Finally you are down to a handful of residential income properties you might be interested in owning.

What do you do from here? I'll show you.

FACTORS OF REAL ESTATE ANALYSIS

You've found one or more buildings that interest you in an area that meets your requirements. It appears you have enough cash to put a down payment on any of them. But which of these buildings (if any of them) is the best investment for you?

Beyond the intangibles and unmeasurables, which must be left to your judgment, there are some specific considerations in determining just exactly what the building is worth to you.

Fixed Expense Items

Real estate men are fond of quoting the value of a property as determined by the gross multiplier. They will tell you that a certain property can be bought for "six-times gross" or "eight-times gross," etc. This number is obtained by dividing the price of the property by the gross annual rentals. For example: if a property was selling for $105,000 and was producing $15,000 in rents, it would be selling for seven-times gross.

This is a simplistic and inaccurate approach to value. Most vitally, it ignores the fixed expense items, which will drastically affect the productivity of the building.

For example: energy costs have risen so high in my area I would not consider any building that does not have individually metered electricity to each unit—and the tenant pays the cost. Central air conditioning can be a monstrous electrical expense to the landlord. Without the responsibility of paying for it, tenants will be careless with it—often leaving it on year round, even with the windows open. With air-conditioning units of the so-called "window-box" type, the tenant pays for the amount he wants and uses. (In some areas of the country, it is not the practice to meter apartments individually. This, I'm afraid, the owner will have to live with. Not only is the cost of converting to individual metering prohibitive, but the community's practice sets the standard; you would be less competitive if you tried it. Therefore, you should be sure to calculate this expense in your overall costs.)

All expenses which are presented to you should be verified by actual bills. For you to estimate the fixed expense of a property under consideration, you should know, by month and year, the following:

1. Utilities
2. Gardener (if any)
3. Resident manager's salary plus fair market value of his apartment and utilities
4. Rubbish hauling
5. Pool maintenance (if any)
6. Elevator service
7. Licenses and permits
8. Property taxes
9. Fire and liability insurance
10. Petty cash

11. Pest control
12. Property manager's fee
13. Janitorial service

In the purchase agreement, the seller must warrant the accuracy of these figures. The scheduled gross income, if 100 percent full, must be warranted as well. If the seller tries to duck these warranties, be on your guard.

Vacancy and Maintenance Allowances

The vacancy factor must always be considered. This will vary by building. Allow a minimum of 5 percent of the gross scheduled income for a good building in a good location. Allow a greater percentage for a less desirable building in a poorer location. Recently, because of curtailed building in most areas, the vacancy factor in most quality buildings has been reduced.

Allow no less than 6 percent of gross scheduled income for annual maintenance on unfurnished buildings with carpets and drapes. This is a minimum. It should be increased, as your judgment dictates, to reasonably offset the higher maintenance costs of older buildings. Add another 3.5 percent for a furnished apartment house.

Rent Schedules

Ask the seller or your broker for a warranted rent schedule of the building. This must be listed by apartment and should specify: furnished or unfurnished; number of baths, bedrooms, etc. You'll insist that the seller supply a written warranty that no rent concessions have been made to any tenants.

Also be certain to get the rentable square footage for each apartment. This should not include balconies or any external hallways. The rentable square footage for any apartment is measured from wall to wall and includes living areas, kitchen, bedrooms, bathrooms and halls within the apartment, closets, etc.

The total rentable area is added up and divided into the monthly rental to achieve a monthly rental cost per square foot. This is a handy gauge to determine whether this building's rentals are high, low or competitive in the neighborhood.

Once you've done these exercises, check several competitive apartment houses in the area to see how your rental rates compare. If you rents appear to be low in relation to the competition, you're in luck. Rents may be raised to the going standard and your building will be worth more. You have an instant profit.

Building Inspection

Obtain the name of a professional and reliable contractor who will inspect the building for any defects. This must be done if you don't want any expensive surprises such as a new furnace, air-conditioning unit, or roof—or the discovery that your building is a cafeteria for termites.

But you'll want to do your own inspection too. As the potential owner of a substantial piece of property, as a merchant of dwelling space, you can see some of the things you would like to have done to make it more attractive, more desirable to tenants. And you can put your finger on any sore spots that might cost you in the long run—or might become a talking point on getting the asking price down a few thousand.

All posted selling prices are negotiable, unless the owner

is unrealistic. If you can point out his building's frailties, you may negotiate from a stronger position.

Here's a checklist of some of the things to look for, starting with the exterior:

1. *Building surface.* If natural (brick, stone, unpainted wood), does it need sandblasting to return its luster? If painted, is the color bilious, the paint faded, peeling, chipped or cracked? Check surfaces and trim. This is both a potential cost and an opportunity. Your investment in refinishing the building's exterior in a tasteful way is a justification for increased rents. The return can be immediate and profitable.

2. *Windows.* Clean or dirty? Cracked, broken? Costly to replace? If applicable—same questions for storm windows. (Ask your consultant contractor.)

3. *Screens.* Rusted, torn? What kinds of replacement costs would you face?

4. *Weather damage.* Look for cracks, chips, sagging, rust spots, water stains. Check around windows and doors, up under the roof and down near the foundation.

5. *Garage area.* Inspect the type and condition of the structure.

6. *Trash area.* Check condition, size and adequacy of bins or cans and the general maintenance of the area.

7. *Grounds.* Well-maintained or gone to seed? A few purchases from the local nursery might improve things immeasurably. How about walks and decking?

8. *Roof.* Notice the type, age, condition and drainage pattern. If there's an attic, get up into it. It is a rain-shedder or a sieve? New roofs can be costly. Get a repair estimate.

9. *Utilities.* Locate furnaces, air conditioners, gas, water and electric meters. What shape are they in?

10. *Miscellaneous.* If a communal entrance, is it a welcome or a turn-off? Does it need remodeling? What about location and condition of mailboxes? Do the entrance doors

work properly? Are all steps and handrails safe? What is the condition and appearance of all community areas? If safety is a problem in this neighborhood, does your building provide for it? Are the ground-floor apartments too accessible to burglars? How do tenants escape if there's a fire? Are there any fire code violations that you can see? Is it properly insulated to save energy—to keep out summer's heat and winter's cold? Are the walls between apartments insulated for tenant peace and serenity?

These suggestions do not necessarily cover all the features and conditions you might want to inspect, but they're a start. They can tell you a lot about the current owner, the tenants and what it takes to maintain a marketable dwelling in this area.

Where the owner has achieved good cash flow figures by deferring needed maintenance, you certainly will not pay top dollar for the building. And you will want to develop your own set of figures about what is needed to keep your building viable, wanted property.

Checking the inside of the building will confirm many of your impressions of its exterior. Remember that you inspect tenants' apartments only at their courtesy. Where they have a lease, they have the right to tell you to go away. Use your charm, imply an interest in improving their living conditions but commit yourself to no specifics—and certainly don't admit to thoughts of raised rents. Here you will want to consider:

1. *Paint.* Check the color and condition of walls and ceilings. Look for stains, watermarks, chips or cracks. Is it due for a repaint? Or replaster?

2. *Room size and amenities.* Do the rooms appear cramped or spacious? Do the ceilings crowd in? Enough closets of sufficient size? Are the living rooms and bedrooms

so designed that it is impossible to arrange furniture? Is the kitchen large enough to move around in? Does it have feminine appeal? Stove, dishwasher, garbage disposal—in working order? Enough cabinet space? Enough counter space? What kind of surface? Floor surface? Quality, convenience and size of bathrooms? Enough mirrors? Are there sufficient electrical outlets or do you see "octopus plugs"? What is the taste level of the tenants?

3. *Carpets and draperies* (if supplied). Check quality and condition—rips, stains, holes, watermarks.

4. *Plumbing.* Inspect type of pipe, color of water flow, pressure from sinks, showers, toilets; condition of sinks, showers, tubs and toilets. Check age of water heaters; ask tenants about quantity of hot water available to them.

5. *General.* Note squeaks in subflooring, signs of decay in halls and stairwells, condition of doors, locks and knobs. Is there a pride of tenancy? Or don't the tenants care?

Be nosy. Some insignificant bit of information may give you a clue to a potential problem—and its possible solution.

Between you and your professional, you can find out a lot about your possible purchase—and whether or not it is likely to be a good investment for you.

How Much Do You Pay?

Although there may be emotional considerations in buying any piece of property, pride of ownership is not a main concern with an investment building. If you wish to entertain your friends, rather than running them past your buildings, take them on a Sunday afternoon drive through the country or to a local museum or park.

Your building is for go, not for show. It's a business. Your pride is in the bottom line. (I don't mean this to be as harsh as it sounds; of course there are human values involved.) You have the right to expect a cash return of 6 percent to 10 percent on your investment. Your loan should be amortized to increase your equity by about 4 percent a year. The depreciation should be enough to shelter your building income and a portion of your salary, to boot. You'll recall my admonitions about straight-line depreciation.

Here are the methods of arriving at the price you should pay for your apartment house.

ALL-CASH METHOD OF PURCHASE

1. *Total gross scheduled income.* (Include the market value rental of the manager's apartment—it is included as an expense item with the manager's salary.)

2. *LESS vacancy factor.* (This is your predetermined judgment—5 percent or more.)

3. *EQUALS effective rental income.* (True gross.)

4. *DEDUCT total expense.* (Include a factor based on past year's records as a percent for maintenance, but do not include loan costs.)

5. *EQUALS net income.* (Spendable cash.)

6. Using a capitalization rate of 9 percent—*DIVIDE net income by .09.*

This is the proper amount to pay for the property.

Note: This is the amount you could afford to pay for the property if you were to pay all cash and were satisfied to have a 9 percent cash flow on your investment.

FINANCING METHOD OF PURCHASE

1. *Total gross scheduled income.* (Include manager's apartment, as above.)

2. *LESS vacancy factor.*

3. *EQUALS effective rental income.*

4. *DEDUCT total expense.* (Including maintenance estimate.)

5. *DEDUCT proposed loan payments.*

6. *EQUALS net income.* (Spendable cash.)

7. Using a capitalization rate of 9 percent—*DIVIDE net income by .09.*

This is the amount you can afford to invest in cash to achieve a 9 percent return on your investment.

If this amount falls below the lending institution's minimum requirements, you have problems. If it exceeds the requirements, you have two choices. You can put down this full amount and be satisfied with a 9-percent return on your investment plus all the other good stuff. Or you can put down less (as little as the lending institution will allow) and enjoy the confidence that the greater leverage will increase your net worth faster. It is an option and it is yours to take.

These two formulas—the "All-Cash Method" and the "Financing Method" of purchase—are both subject to adjustment but offer reasonably sound parameters for guiding your purchase.

Every day millions of dollars are invested unwisely by investors ignorant of these two simple, logical formulas.

Depreciation

Since the depreciation is such an important reason for buying residential income property, let me explain in a little more detail what it is and how it works, and what kinds of options you have in using it.

The concept of depreciation is that every man-made object of business use declines in value through wear, obsolescence or the forces of nature over time. So the government allows you to account for this loss of value through a tax deduction for depreciation. Theoretically, this man-made object is of no value at the end of its depreciation period. In reality, this object still usually has some value to it. In the case of a building, the value has actually been enhanced in most instances.

The day of reckoning for depreciation occurs only when the object or building is sold. Wherever the depreciated value is less than the selling price, the difference becomes taxable. So depreciation is truly a deferred tax—and remains an obligation on the piece of property until it is sold.

If you bought a piece of machinery, for example, took depreciation (a tax write-off) against its full purchase price, and then threw the machine away when it was no longer of use to you—you would never have any further tax obligations against that machine. If, however, you sold that old, fully depreciated machine for scap for $200, that $200 would be taxable.

It's the same way with real estate. If you buy a piece of property for $100,000, take, over the years, $30,000 depreciation on it, and sell it for the same price you paid for it ($100,000), you are liable for a capital gains tax (or straight income tax) on the $30,000 of depreciation even though you did not make any gain between the purchase and the sale.

Do you understand that? The tax has been delayed, but you will pay it in the end if you sell the property and it still has some cash value.

If you never sell the property, or if you (or your estate) trade it up into a property that is worth the same or more, you will never pay the capital gains tax on the depreciation that has been deferred.

I know it can be confusing, but it makes sense if you think it through.

In short, depreciation is marvelous to have even at its very worst. It will let you keep today's dollars and pay them back sometime later in cheaper, inflation-nibbled dollars—

and, if you've held your property long enough, at a long-term capital gain rate. That's not too bad in itself. When you can keep stalling depreciation's day of reckoning, it's even better.

There are about three different ways you can take depreciation, depending on the conditions. These are: *straight-line* and *accelerated* (which includes *sum-of-years-digits*). A third way is *component*.

Straight-line. For real estate purposes, you assume the life of your property is the length of the loan period. As you know, depreciation cannot be taken on land, only the improvements to the land. You will depreciate 100 percent of the cost of the improvements over their normal life—generally twenty-five to thirty years. Assuming a twenty-five-year life, you may deduct 100 percent divided by 25 to discover what your depreciation might be in any one year.

This is an example:

Value of property	$200,000
Less land	−40,000
Net improvements	$160,000

Life of property 25 years.

$$\frac{100\%}{25} = 4\% \text{ per year.}$$

Annual depreciation: $160,000 \times .04 = $6,400 per year.

Accelerated depreciation. This works just about the same way as straight-line, except that you are speeding up the depreciation—getting more at the beginning and using it up faster. There are two conditions here—old apartment buildings in which the maximum depreciation rate is 125 percent; and new apartment buildings in which you can take as much as 200 percent depreciation.

OLD APARTMENT BUILDING

Same conditions as before. Depreciation 125 percent.

$$4\% \times 125\% = 5\%$$

1st year depreciation
$160,000 × .05 = $8,000

2nd year depreciation
$160,000 − $8,000 = $152,000
$152,000 × .05 = $7,600

3rd year depreciation
$152,000 − $7,600 = $144,400
$144,400 × .05 = $7,220

The progression continues, growing smaller with each passing year. Total depreciation ends up being the same as straight-line, but it is taken quicker and is used up faster.

NEW APARTMENT BUILDING

Same conditions as before, but this time you have built your own building. Maximum depreciation rate is 200 percent.

$$4\% \times 200\% = 8\%$$

1st year depreciation
$160,000 × .08 = $12,800

2nd year depreciation
$160,000 − $12,800 = $147,200
$147,200 × .08 = $11,776

3rd year depreciation
$147,200 − $11,776 = $135,424
$135,424 × .08 = $10,833.92

And so forth. In this case, more than half the depreciation has been used up by the ninth year—and thereafter, the annual depreciation allowance is less than if the owner had applied straight-line depreciation.

Sum-of-years-digits. This depreciation system is allowable on new residential property only—and uses up depreciation at an even faster clip than the accelerated 200 percent rate.

The formula for this system is derived as a fraction. To get the bottom number—the denominator—of the fraction, add up the digits of your building's years of remaining life. Assuming a life of 25 years, this would amount to $25 + 24 + 23 + 22 + 21 +$ etc. $= 325$. The denominator for any particular year is the number of years of remaining life.

Here's how it works out for a depreciation life of twenty-five years:

1st year depreciation

$$\frac{25}{325} = 7.69\%$$

$160,000 \times .0769 = $12,304$

2nd year depreciation

$$\frac{24}{325} = 7.38\%$$

$160,000 \times .0738 = $11,808$

25th year depreciation

$$\frac{1}{325} = .31\%$$

$160,000 \times .0031 = 492.16

As you can see, there's not a whole lot of depreciation left in the building's later years.

Component depreciation. Each of the parts of your apartment building has a different life expectancy. Elevators, carpets and draperies, roof, wiring, etc.—each one deteriorates at its own particular rate. Your accountant can separate these building components and depreciate them at the current allowable rate. This permits you to increase your depreciation in the building's earlier years. When an item, say, carpet wears out, a new depreciation schedule can begin when you replace it. Although this involves more bookkeeping, it is a reasonable system for taking depreciation.

Recapture. Since depreciation is a tax deferral and not an outright gift, all depreciation taken is subject to recapture in one form or another unless the depreciated item becomes completely worthless.

Where a building is sold after twelve months, all depreciation taken as straight-line is subject to a long-term capital gains tax.

Under various legislation since 1964, the amount of excess depreciation over straight-line has been increasingly subject to recapture as *ordinary income.* (You lose the benefits of long-term capital gain.) Currently, for example, all excess depreciation taken after December 31, 1975, is fully recapturable as ordinary income.

However, there still is the substantial benefit of postponement—so that the owner retains possession of the dollars saved in taxes. When, and if, he sells the building, assuming continuing inflation, any tax paid would be in cheaper dollars. Of course, if the building is traded even or up, the tax is deferred indefinitely.

I will reemphasize that I believe in buying residential income property to hold; so I advocate the use of straight-line depreciation only.

Sample Return on Apartment House Investment

Here is an example of the sources of capital growth in a typical apartment house investment.

These are the kinds of figures you might expect to see in the *first year*.

Let us assume the price of the property to be $200,000, of which $40,000 is attributed to land and $160,000 to improvements (building, etc.). The down payment is $30,000; the loan is $170,000 for thirty years at an annual interest rate of 9 percent. We will take straight-line depreciation, assuming a thirty-year life.

First year depreciation: $160,000 × 3.33% =	$ 5,328
Annual loan payment:	16,422
Less first year interest: $170,000 × .09 =	15,300
First year principal payoff:	$ 1,122

I. CASH FLOW

Annual gross rental income		$29,700
Less expenses:		
Fixed	$8,316	
Variable	3,564	11,880
Net operating profit		17,820
Annual loan payments		16,422
Net cash flow (spendable)		$ 1,398
(Equals 4.7% return on cash down)		

II. TAX CALCULATON

Net operating profit (forward)		$17,820
Less loan *interest* (only)	$15,300	
Depreciation	5,328	
		20,628
Taxable, or (tax loss)		($ 2,808)

Although the net cash flow is paltry (4.7 percent return on capital invested), the depreciation taken has supplied a tax loss which may be applied to outside income for a further cash benefit through tax savings.

III. AFTER-TAX CASH RECAPITULATION

Assuming a 32% tax bracket:

First year tax loss: $2,808 × .32 =	$ 899
Plus net cash flow (spendable)	1,398
Total first year cash flow	$2,297

$$\frac{\$\ 2,297\ \text{(cash flow)}}{\$30,000\ \text{(cash down)}} = \text{return on cash} \qquad 7.6\%$$

Thus:

First year equity growth (principal payoff)	$ 1,122
First year cash flow (from above)	2,297
Total first year yield	$ 3,419

$$\frac{\$\ 3,419\ \text{(total yield)}}{\$30,000\ \text{(cash down)}} = \text{total return on cash} \qquad 11.4\%$$

So in this example the total return on the investment is adequate, though not sensational.

But let us investigate what happens to your investment as your building matures.

These are the kinds of figures you might expect to see in the *fifth year*. It is the same property example, but in these intervening years inflation has played its expected role. Rents have been increased each year by 6 percent, and both fixed and variable costs have increased by 3 percent.

Depreciation (same as first year)	$5,328
Annual loan payment (the same):	16,422
Less fifth year interest	14,841
Fifth year principal payoff	$ 1,581

I. CASH FLOW (FIFTH YEAR)

Annual gross rental income		$37,495
Less expenses:		
Fixed	$9,360	
Variable	4,111	
		13,471

Net operating profit		$24,024
Annual loan payments		$16,422
Net cash flow (spendable)		$ 7,602
(Equals 25.3% return on cash down)		

II. TAX CALCULATION (FIFTH YEAR)

Net operating profit (forward)		$24,024
Less loan *interest* (only)	$14,841	
Depreciation	5,328	
		20,169
Taxable or (tax loss)		$ 3,855

In this case, the net cash flow has exceeded the limits of the tax shelter. $3,765 of the net cash flow is tax free and $3,855 is subject to tax.

III. AFTER-TAX CASH RECAPITULATION

Again assuming a 32% tax bracket:

Taxable income	$3,855	
Less 32% tax	1,234	
Income after taxes		$ 2,621
Untaxed income		3,765
Net cash flow (spendable) after taxes		$ 6,386
(Return on cash down = 21.3%)		
Add fifth year equity growth		1,581
Total fifth year yield		$7,967
(Yield on cash down = 26.6%)		

This is a very handsome after-tax yield on your capital investment, although the property no longer serves as a shelter for your salary.

But this is not the end of the story. As a result of your increased rentals, the value of your building has appreciated. This has contributed mightily to the resale price of the building and also to your net worth.

You bought your building at a price 6.7 times its gross rental income—an apparent bargain, since a more normal gross multiple today in many parts of the country would be 7.5 times gross rental income.

See what happens as the result of the increase of the resale price of your building together with your equity build-up.

Year	Annual Rental	Building Value	Value Increase	Mortgage Equity Increase
1st	$29,700	$200,000	—	$1,114
2nd	31,482	236,115	$36,115	1,214
3rd	33,371	250,282	14,167	1,324
4th	35,373	265,297	15,015	1,443
5th	37,495	281,212	15,915	1,573
			$ 81,212	$6,668

Five year total net worth build-up = $87,880
(Equals 293% appreciation on $30,000 capital investment)

The foregoing examples do not imply that these are the kind of results you may expect from every investment in income property. The possible variables are too numerous.

In the examples above, when the property produced more cash flow than was sheltered, the owner had the option to pay for extensive maintenance, which would make the building more desirable to tenants, justifying further rent increases.

Because of the increased resale price of the building due to higher rents, the owner might choose to refinance for a larger amount and put the extra capital down on a second building, which could then generate additional depreciation.

Your apartment property is in competition with every other apartment property in your area. It can generate no more rental income than the market will allow. Where an area becomes overbuilt, where a neighborhood deteriorates, increased rents may be out of the question. In fact, rent reductions may be called for. Vacancies are accounted as costs. If ever your vacancy rate becomes too high, you must look for solutions—which may include reducing rents.

My Two Apartments

To prove to you that the examples I have provided are not made up out of whole cloth, I'll give you some figures taken right out of my record books concerning the performance of my two buildings from 1972 to 1977. (See next page.)

You'll note that in 1973, due to some overbuilding and neighborhood problems in both building areas, values either fell off or stood still. Then the problems were solved and the values again moved ahead.

By today's standards, these building values are quite conservatively stated.

You can see why residential income real estate in the proper location is considered such a tremendous wealth-builder.

Many sophisticated investors who have previously bet the stock market on the "come" (rapid appreciation) are discovering that residential income property frequently has more "come" to it.

They would, for example, invest heavily in an IBM, where the dividends produced a very low cash flow (2 percent or so), in the faith that the stock would appreciate to the point where they would get a far greater price when they sold it. They were betting on IBM's "come"—and "come" it did.

But actually, they might have done considerably better, and received tax sheltering too, if they had placed their bets

BUILDING "A"

Year	Building Value	Loan Balance Due	My Equity in Building
1972	$686,000	$479,480	$206,520
1973	684,000	470,136	213,864
1974	725,580	460,935	264,645
1975	777,345	450,152	327,193
1976	820,845	438,531	382,314
1977	869,400	426,008	443,392

Increase in net worth 1972–1977 (Bldg. A) = $236,872   (+114.7%)

BUILDING "B"

Year	Building Value	Loan Balance Due	My Equity in Building
1972	$616,000	$455,899	$160,101
1973	616,000	449,209	166,791
1974	644,235	442,036	202,199
1975	679,035	434,287	244,748
1976	705,135	425,914	279,221
1977	766,350	416,869	349,481

Increase in net worth 1972–1977 (Bldg. B) = $189,380   (+118.3%)

Total increase Bldgs. A & B 1972–1977 = $426,252   (+116.3%)

as wisely with apartment houses. The awareness of residential income property as a wealth-enhancement vehicle is growing; and I would expect in future years more competition for choice properties from former stock market investors.

As the discretionary income from your real estate investments grows, you may want to return to the securities markets, as I have done. There obviously is a place for both kinds of investments when you have accomplished your eight wealth-building steps and are reaching out for more.

But any investor who does not include income-producing property in his investment portfolio is short-changing himself.

The young investor may wish to start with a duplex or triplex and live in one unit while renting the rest. This gives experience in owner-tenant relationships and the whole mechanics of income property investment.

I suggest you limit yourself to one investment in a small property. Every other apartment house you buy should be large enough to sustain a manager living on-premises. Twenty units is a good next step up. This will not only enable you to have a live-in manager but will allow for a professional management concern to insulate you from the stress of daily decisions, complaints and concerns.

Geographical Diversification

We have discussed before the advantages of geographical diversification of your properties. Keep this in mind as a precept before you buy your first piece of property.

I know that many professionals will tell you it is best to own all your properties within one carefully selected locality. Their rationale is that it is easier for you to get around to visit your buildings. But areas can change quickly. Riot, fire, flood, earthquake, or any number of other uncertainties striking in one area can diminish your assets in a hurry. The wise investor hedges his bet. Wouldn't you consider the extra safety of diversification worth the extra effort?

A dozen or so years ago, here in the Los Angeles area, apartment builders looked some 70 miles south of the Civic Center to Newport Beach as a Mecca. More and more Angelenos, looking for breathing space, were willing to travel the long miles daily to achieve it. As soon as an apartment house was completed, it was fully rented. It looked as if the appetite for living space was insatiable. Yet in a few short years the traffic congestion in the Newport Beach area became worse than in the areas the expatriates had left. While the condition is still far from intolerable, the building boom in Newport Beach has peaked. Any investor with too many eggs in this basket would be smart to search out some diversified nests.

FINANCING YOUR PROPERTY

Your best bet is a first trust deed or mortgage that will amortize itself over the longest period of years. A payoff period of twenty-five to thirty years is most desirable. If you require a second trust deed (or second mortgage) to accomplish your purpose, you will find a five- to ten-year payoff period more than standard. You should be advised that it is customary in many parts of the country for second trust deeds (second mortgages) to be repayable in shorter periods of time than needed to fully amortize them—so a final balloon payment (see Glossary) of the balance is called for at the end of the payment period. With either type of second, this additional debt service will reduce your income during the life of the loan. It is a good idea to insist on a fairly substantial positive income as a safety factor on a cash investment, even though it might not be currently needed. (I have noted possible exceptions to this elsewhere.)

If you finance without a second, you can predetermine easily the yield you hope to receive on your cash investment. You'll expect a cash flow of between 6 and 10 percent. But don't allow this low rate to discourage you. In addition to cash flow, you enjoy the advantages of depreciation and interest deductions, total payment of all property taxes and expenses connected with the property, and most important, equity build-up as your loan is paid down.

Taking all factors into consideration, your true benefits could be enabling you to achieve a real 17-to-20-percent return on your investment. Be aware, too, that good residential real estate has an historical tendency to appreciate in value over a period of time—it should have a higher resale value when you sell it (if you ever do) than when you bought it. Rent increases to keep pace with inflation practically insure increasing property values.

Check all your mathematics with your accountant when the time comes to make an offer. He must be a partner in your deliberations.

During the earlier part of this decade, interest rates rose to inordinate heights—as high as 12 percent in some states without usury laws. During 1974–75, apartment building construction was stifled by these high interest rates and growing building costs. In many areas of the country this has created a shortage of apartment units, forcing an increase in rents.

The real estate "boom" of 1977 has done little to alleviate this shortage. Excessive costs of construction have made new buildings uncompetitive with older buildings unless rents are pegged to return less-than-ideal cash flows. All this has tended to dampen the enthusiasm for new building. The shortage still exists and vacancy rates remain low—below 5 percent in many areas.

Certainly you should try to make your long-term loan commitments at a time when interest rates are close to bottom. But how low is low? And how long can you wait? With today's patterns of interest gyrations, there are no easy answers. The current useful range seems to be between 8 and 9.5 percent. Double-digit rates are close to unbearable, sucking up too much cash flow. One alternative is to borrow at the prevailing rates and then refinance when the rates decline. The penalties of prepayment plus points for the new loan must be weighed against the other alternative.

There are a number of ways to finance an apartment house. Here are some of the more common:

1. *Savings and loan associations and commercial banks.* These are the most common places for an investor to find his financing. If you buy your property through a broker, have him check the loan market and obtain a commitment for you. Most lending institutions will ask for points—that is, in addition to the agreed amount of interest, you must pay 1 to 3 percent of the amount of the loan up front as a fee merely to get the loan. This is regrettable but normal.

2. *Life insurance companies.* These institutions are relatively active lenders on apartment buildings. While their loan amounts, terms and interest rates are comparable to those of banks and savings and loans, their policies generally lock up a loan for five to ten years, thereby preventing any payoff during that period. This is compensated for, as a rule, by having lower prepayment penalties after the "lock-up" period. If you anticipate a period of lower interest rates in five to ten years (if anyone can anticipate that far ahead in today's economic climate), this kind of loan could offer you benefits. You might then refinance at a lower rate and improve your yield. You could expect that, with rents increased and your old loan paid down, you will be able to obtain a larger loan, returning some of your principal, which you can then use to finance another building.

3. *Former owner carries back trust deed (or mortgage).* This can be the best of both worlds. As I have said before, this type of transaction can be beneficial to both the seller and the buyer. The seller can stretch out his capital gains liabilities over a period of years under an installment sale, while he receives a substantial annual income from the interest and principal payments by the buyer. The buyer, perhaps, can get a more favorable loan agreement and avoid the penalty of paying points. In this kind of installment sale

the owner accepts no more than 29 percent of the purchase price of his property (more would invalidate it as an installment sale), and the balance of the principal is amortized with interest over a period of years. When the numbers and conditions are right, this is one of the better ways of buying an apartment house. Your attorney and tax accountant should approve the conditions of any loan agreement. Never, never, try to save the professional fees and negotiate in ignorance. Your team must always be consulted.

4. *An assumable loan.* Few savings and loans or banks will write loan agreements that permit a new buyer to assume the existing property loan. However, many insurance company loans are assumable at the original interest rate. These loans are usually—though not always—paid down to a rather low figure. The low loan is generally reflected in the price of the property, and the owner will take back a generous second trust deed (mortgage) at a rate of interest and period of years to be negotiated. This method of financing is a bit more complicated than the preceding three, but definitely worth investigating.

5. *Wraparound financing.* It is possible, if the owner's present loan agreement is sufficiently attractive, to negotiate a special agreement called "wraparound" financing, which will enable you to keep this favorable loan. The borrower actually assumes two loans—the old favorable loan, and a new, high-interest loan. Assume a property is priced at $125,000 and you will pay $25,000 down, financing the $100,000. The current interest rate is 10 percent, which will give you too low a yield on your cash flow. The old mortgage is $75,000 at 6.5 percent. You go to a new lender (or to the owner himself) and offer to "wrap around" the old loan with a new $25,000 loan at 11 percent (higher than the current rate). Your net rate is thus lower than the prevailing rate. Many lending institutions will not permit this kind of creative financing. Some first-loan agreements contain an *aliena-*

tion clause which dictates that the balance of the loan comes due upon the sale of the property. If you can not talk the lender into waiving the alienation clause, the deal can not be made.

6. *Contract of sale.* When an investor wants to buy a property and financing money is scarce or too costly, one solution that is becoming increasingly common is a "contract of sale." In this you can close the sale while the owner continues to pay down on the existing mortgage—and the land title remains with him. The purchaser puts down a certain amount on the contract and agrees to monthly payments of both interest and amortization. When the time comes that the purchaser chooses to apply for refinancing, the rest of the transaction proceeds as it would normally. This is the chanciest way of purchasing a property, since the title does not change hands. Also, some lending institutions specifically prohibit it. Best have your lawyer check it out thoroughly before you get too far along with it.

These are a few of the recognized methods of financing. There are many more which are both artistic and financially successful. You may come up with a unique variation tailor-made for your particular circumstances.

In General

I'll repeat that you should only own enough income real estate to obtain sufficient straight-line depreciation to shelter your income. While its wealth-building aspects are unexcelled, its cash flow is simply not as good as that from some other kinds of investments. It is possible to become property poor, with all your wealth tied up in the future and none of it at your disposal today.

I know of a man who lived across the mountains from me in the San Fernando Valley whose home was a tumble-down shack in the middle of what appeared to be a garbage dump. Doorless refrigerators, rusted water heaters, torn screens, bent piping—these were the cast-offs of hundreds of houses and apartments.

Across the sunshades of the man's decrepit Cadillac were two parallel strips of wood, behind which were tagged keys —keys, keys and more keys—several hundred of them. Each one represented a house or an apartment dwelling that he owned and rented.

He explained that he was a sucker for a good property buy—and a terrible property salesman. Every time he got a few dollars ahead, another irresistible property cropped up and he was off to the savings and loan for another mortgage.

Certainly, his net worth was in the millions of dollars, but until he sold something, or paid off some of his mortgages, he was strapped—a property-coholic, living in apparent poverty.

Now that's a real estate enthusiast!

When you are careful in your selection of location and building, your risks with apartment house investment are minimal.

My apartments are almost always fully leased. On the other hand, I had a one-tenant office building in the Irvine, California, area which was a great income-producer for five years. It was a handsome building of 10,000 square feet. When my tenant moved out during the 1973–74 recession, I could find no other tenants for it.

The only interested firms demanded such extensive leasehold improvements and low rent that there was no way I could make out. The costs of owning a vacant office building investment mounted alarmingly. I cut the price and then cut it again. After the building had stood vacant for a year, I sold it on an installment sale to a law school. Although it is worth $100,000 more today than when I sold it, I was happy to get it off my back.

Remember that your apartment house is a fine inflation hedge. If inflation races, rents must go up. As this cancer erodes the dollar, you will pay back the lender in ever-cheaper dollars. And the value of your building will increase.

Should you become involved in an exchange of properties, be sure to pay no premium for the property acquired. Always adhere to the market price.

If you plan to buy residential income property, these are the factors that should be imprinted on your investment mentality:

1. Buy only residential income-producing property (at least until you are in a position to speculate in a small way on vacant land).

2. Select your property on the basis of location, location, location.

3. Maximize financing. Use O.P.M. (Other People's Money)—the most you can get over the longest period.

4. Make sure that the building is sound. Pay to have the building inspected by a professional. Find a reputable contractor who will check the plumbing, wiring, roof; inspect for water damage, termites, dry rot, etc. The fee is worth every penny. You should make such an inspection a condition of your escrow.

5. Determine how you can improve the building cosmetically to upgrade its appearance and make it more attractive to tenants.

6. Obtain a good real estate management company and they will get a good resident manager.

7. Raise rents on December 1 of each year (if merited). Send notices out at the end of October. Your residents will

be reluctant to move during the holidays; by the new year, they become accustomed to the new rent schedule.

8. Take straight-line depreciation.

9. Refinance and buy another building in six to ten years.

10. Repeat the process. Live a long, healthy life. Teach your children to hold on to these buildings or to trade up after you have gone to that great residential real estate in the sky.

12

Managing Your Own Property

The great thing in the world is to know how to be sufficient unto oneself.
—MICHEL DE MONTAIGNE (1533–1592) *Works*

I never did anything worth doing by accident, nor did any of my inventions come by accident; they came by work.
—THOMAS ALVA EDISON (1847–1931)

This chapter is concerned with the many small details, systems and strategies of property management. They are important details: necessary to know. However, much of the discussion may seem premature to the investor whose first real estate purchase is still beyond the horizon. For any owner who contemplates managing his own property, I believe it will ultimately prove an invaluable reference.

For the last five or six years prior to my retirement, I used a highly qualified property management company to manage my apartment houses. They did a good job.

Each of my buildings contains thirty-three apartment units; each I had built for me. I remember thinking at the time of building that the costs seemed astronomically high and the interest on the loans, devastatingly severe.

250

Today in retrospect, nearly a decade later, neither condition looks so bad. The buildings have made extraordinary
contributions to my net worth. I never could have cracked
the million dollar barrier, I never could have had an early,
financially secure retirement, without them.

Inflation has played its role over these years—and every
investor must condition himself to the realities of it. Undoubtedly, building costs will continue to escalate, as will
the costs of land. Interest rates have eased somewhat, but
lenders have become cagey about dropping them too quickly
lest they get caught up in long-range fixed-rate commitments
where their interest income lags behind inflation rates.

So the fantastic prices of yesterday are often the bar-
gains of today, as the fantastic prices of today may well be
the parsimonies of tomorrow.

My first adventure into residential income real estate
was a third interest in an older twenty-seven-unit apartment
house in South Pasadena.

I decided to act as property manager myself, although
I had no real credentials for the job. The resident manager
was an old English gentleman who lived there with his wife.
They were lovely, reliable people—but he was tough.

Periodically, after a hard day's work, I would visit them
to check up on the building's business. The Englishman
would courteously ask me to be seated. Those were the last
agreeable words I would hear. In cultured Oxford tones, he
would recite in intricate and exhaustive detail the innumer-
able frailties of our tenants and how they had misbehaved,
and the heroic efforts he had put forth to handle the situations; and the extensive and Herculean chores he had performed around the building; and the poverty of his calling;
and the lack of quid pro quo on my part; and that he was
overworked, underpaid and that he should have a raise in
salary as of this moment, effective retroactively.

Invariably, I left a beaten man (although, if I gave in at all, it was only in inches), thoroughly drubbed by a Machiavelli of the King's English. I always drove home with a throbbing, pulsating headache. So I took to popping two Excedrin tablets before knocking on their door. Most often these were not enough.

Because I didn't have the time or the know-how to search for a new manager, he sensed he had me over a barrel —and took full advantage of it. He was the toughest negotiator I ever faced, and in one way or another, sooner or later, he won every round.

When I traded the apartment house, he and I parted, never to see each other again. But I had learned my lessons in apartment house management in spades. I got my Ph.D. from a tough old Englishman in South Pasadena.

Over my years of property ownership, I have developed a philosophy and a variety of techniques for effective property management. I had learned a great deal from the ways professional property managers go about their business. But I think I have improved on their methods—for ease, simplicity and greater control.

You will, if you follow my techniques, be able to oversee the management of sixty-six units or more easily, correctly, in about ten hours a month. And no Excedrin headaches.

You'll want to conduct the management of your property with as much anonymity as possible insofar as your tenants are concerned. At the same time, you want them to be able to contact you if your manager is performing incompetently, or in case of emergency.

I have given each manager a supply of business cards with instructions to distribute them to tenants and tradespeople. They look like this:

RKR Properties

P.O. Box 874
Pacific Palisades,   *Message Phone*
California 90272   *(213) 000-0000*

All apartment house mail goes to my post office box—not my home. It does not get mixed up with personal mail. The box costs about $1.50 a month. I pick the mail up two or three times a week, which is sufficient.

The tenants in both buildings make out their checks to "RKR Properties" and give them to my resident managers. The managers deposit the checks at my bank branch in their neighborhood. These deposits are immediately credited to my business checking account.

On my checks is printed the same information as on my business cards, plus my name—Richard K. Rifenbark. I have my name printed on my business stationery too, because I believe it is discourteous to the recipient of a letter for the name of the sender to be undecipherable. My signature's legibility is about on a par with a doctor's prescription.

I have two telephone lines into my home, both unlisted. The message phone is hooked up to a Phone-Mate with a remote answering device. The message phone is never answered personally. Via a recorded message, I ask the caller's name and phone number, and state that I will return the call the following morning between nine and ten or if that is inconvenient, at whatever time the caller requests.

So the tenant or supplier has access to me by either the

message phone or the post office box. This access is guaranteed—while my privacy is preserved.

When a tenant calls the owner of his building with a complaint, the owner should discuss the problem with the resident manager and let the manager resolve it with the tenant. In this way the resident manager retains authority.

My resident managers, of course, have my personal phone number to use in an emergency. They use the message phone for routine calls.

The remote telephone answering device permits me to pick up my recorded calls from any telephone in the country. So I can keep in touch with business without being tied to home base.

I strongly believe that all public areas of an apartment building should look sharp, cared-for and well-maintained. The paint should not be allowed to deteriorate. Obvious repairs should be accomplished right away. Tenants are quick to observe the esteem in which the owner holds the building they call home. Another consideration is that prospective tenants may be put off by a building front that has been allowed to become shabby.

One vital function of bookkeeping is the planning of future events. This applies in the calculation of a "rerent estimate."

Normally, I will raise my tenants' rent only once a year (December 1) and then only in small increments of 5 to 7 percent to counter inflation. I want to keep good, reliable tenants and not force them to look elsewhere for housing because their rental increases are out of step with their normal salary increases. During years when the economy is sagging, I may not increase rental rates at all.

I think it is better for everyone if I keep my tenants

happy and my buildings fully rented. Accordingly, where a tenant has occupied an apartment for a long period of time, his rental rate may be somewhat lower than the going rate. In other words, the apartment is undervalued in relation to the competition. I am perfectly satisfied with this; it seems to me a healthy and ethical way to conduct business. I have no love of squeezing the last dollar out of any tenant; neither am I entranced by vacant apartments.

But when a tenant moves, this undervaluing must be recognized and flagged. And this is where the "rerent estimate" comes in. Your professional property manager can give you the range of going rates for apartments of your quality in your area: i.e., 30 cents to 33 cents per square foot per month. You might obtain this same information from your apartment house owners association or by some detective work on your own.

If your building is of better quality and well-maintained, you would choose the higher figures for your calculations. Multiply this cents-per-square-foot figure by the square footage of the apartment to get its rerent rate. Some landlords charge an extra $5 a month for each floor above street level, as the view is improved or the street noise reduced. If the apartment has problems with elevator-shaft or stairwell noises, the rental rate is dropped lower.

The rerent rate is posted in your Rental Income Ledger. The rerent will go into effect if the apartment becomes vacant during the period. Most tenants realize that if they move out, their apartment will be rerented for more than they are being charged. This knowledge tends to increase their contentment with their current arrangement. Be certain that your resident manager has a complete and up-to-date list of rerental rates and will automatically apply them as apartments become vacant.

Undoubtedly, hundreds of thousands of dollars are sacrificed by apartment house owners each year because they have not kept abreast of their rental units and do not apply a rerent schedule.

Regarding security deposits—many owners will allow tenants to apply these as a last month's rent. I have found this not a good practice. The tenant assumes his last month's rent is already in the owner's hands. If his rent has gone up during his period of tenancy, he will not be inclined to pay the difference. This defeats the purpose of the security deposit—that is, the protection of the owner against excessive damage by the tenant. I prefer to charge a security deposit that is less than the last month's rent—$150 for a one-bedroom and $200 for a two-bedroom apartment, for example—which is not refundable until the tenant has departed and the damage assessed. This also allows a new tenant to move in for a lower initial outlay. In practice, it has worked better than the other method.

It is a common practice in some areas to charge the new tenant an up-front nonrefundable cleaning fee for preparing his apartment for occupancy. Make certain that these charges reflect current costs of performing the cleaning—$50 for a one-bedroom and $75 for a two-bedroom apartment, for example. Many professional property managers will get stuck in an old rut and assess these charges at rates lower than their true costs. It is your money that they are being careless with.

A laundromat room in your apartment is more of a nuisance than a source of income—but it is desirable in most large buildings as a tenant convenience. The laundromat company installs the machines and services them at no cost to the owner. The quarters are collected by the company and the income is divided between company and owner. These revenues are just about enough to cover the cost of power and hot water used (owner costs).

HOW TO KEEP YOUR BOOKS
FOR PROPERTY MANAGEMENT

The biggest error an owner can make if he decides to manage his own building is to keep careless records.

My first apartment house, I owned and managed many years ago. I kept a correct journal of rental receipts, security deposits, cleaning fees, pet deposits, etc.; however, I grouped most of the expense items in catch-all categories, such as: maintenance, publicity, utilities and such. Now I see that this is not enough. Somewhat more detailed records must be maintained to aid in budgeting and decision-making.

From my retail background, I have developed some record-keeping concepts which provide the owner–property manager a degree of sophistication even professional property managers have not yet attained.

Professional property managers use computerized statements listing each item of expense for the month and year to date, but they do not show comparisons with the prior year. This means you must dig out last year's records and locate the comparable month and item before you can evaluate differences—an awkward, cumbersome procedure.

The bookkeeping systems I show you may at first seem complicated. Once you set them up and work with them, you will find them actually quite simple and automatic. Most important, you will have the specific information you need to run a high-performance operation.

These bookkeeping procedures will help you and your resident managers perform like true professionals.

Your accountant should review my suggestions. Very

likely, he will introduce some of his own ideas and improvements, since he is familiar with your specific needs.

Your Checkbook (Exhibits 10 & 11)

I use my business checkbook for three purposes: for
paying bills, recording deposits, and as a cash journal. My
checkbook is the sort that contains three checks per page
with a check register on the left. The register has space for
420 checks (30 to a page). On the back of each check register
page is a deposit register. With this checkbook system it is
completely unnecessary to keep an additional cash journal,
as all disbursements are made by check. The name of this
checkbook is "The Executive Deluxe" (serial number R8F),
available through your bank through Deluxe Check Printers,
Inc.

The key to tying all the parts of the accounting system
together is the use of General Ledger Account Numbers
(which are described in the next section). Each business cost
is assigned its own three-digit number. In the Utilities section, for example, "222" stands for water service, "223" for
gas, and "224" for telephone.

When a bill comes in, it is marked with its proper account number. If you have more than one property, you may
give each a letter code—"A" for your first building, "B" for
your second, etc. This letter next to your account number
tells which building incurred the expense. When you pay
the bill, you'll draw a line under this coding and write the
number of the paying check beneath it.

It looks like this:

(Building A)   <u>A315</u> (Account #315—gardener)
                #1376 (Check #1376 paid the invoice)

You write "A315" on the face of the check, and then again in the check register. This knits the parts together. If you must research a payment, you can locate it from either direction.

Deposits are also recorded by building and source. While most deposits will come from rentals, there are other sources of income, too—laundromat, key and security deposits, cleaning fees, etc.

At the end of each month I draw a line across my checkbook register and total expenses and deposits by building, and arrive at a balance which should match the checkbook balance.

When I disburse funds to myself, I pay myself by check and assign the disbursement from one building or the other. So, each building maintains its own balance of deposits and payments within one checking account.

I have modified the deposit register so that I can use the bottom portion to draw up a monthly statement of deposits, expenses, disbursements and loan service (Exhibit 11).

To aid my bookkeeper in posting the detailed expense ledger and income ledger pages, which I will show you a little later, I have Xeroxed a list of my General Ledger Account Numbers with space to the right of them for gathering monthly costs by category by building. I mark Building "A" expenses in black, and Building "B" expenses in red. The bookkeeper just runs down the items in the check register and posts the amounts next to their proper account number on the Xeroxed pages. Later it becomes a very easy task to post the General Ledger pages because all the organization has been done.

The total amount of time required each month between my bookkeeper and myself for all the bill-paying, depositing and record-keeping is about ten hours. It is the simplest format I can conceive of that does its job and gives me all the information I need for both records and planning.

Exhibit 10: Business Check Register — Payments

CHECK NO.	DATE	CHECK ISSUED TO	IN PAYMENT OF		AMOUNT OF CHECK	✓	DATE OF DEPOSIT	AMOUNT OF DEPOSIT	BALANCE
							BALANCE BROUGHT FORWARD →		8622 35
1331	1/3/77	RKR (DISTRIBUTION TO OWNER)		662 A	2130 74	B	1/5/77	7260 —	
2	"	" " " "		662 B	2650 19	A	1/4	5845 —	
3	1/7	Dept. Water & Power	152.35 / 212.57	221 B / 221 B	664 92	A	1/4	2575 —	
4	"	So. Calif. Gas		223 A	227 71	A	1/10	868 —	
5	"	R.U. Rubbish Co.		314 B	44 06	B	1/11	810 —	
6	"	So. Calif. Gas		223 B	197 80				
7	"	Perfect Exterminator Co.		313 A	12 00				
8	"	" " " "		313 B	9 50				
9	"	City of Culver City		314 A	55 50				
1340	"	Dept. Water & Power	430.52 / 198.61	221 A / 222 A	629 13				
1	"	Pacific Tel & Tel.		224 B	12 60				
2	"	2nd Federal S&L.	1086.45 / 2662.55	521 A / 522 A	3749 00				
3	"	General Tel.		224 A	15 45				
4	"	K. Suzuki		315 B	75 00				
5	"	Apt. Assoc. of L.A. County		239 A	27 60				
6	"	" " " "		239 B	27 00				
7	"	S.C. State S&L.	780.67 / 2697.33	521 B / 522 B	3478 00				
8	"	A. Mantilla		315 A	75 00				
9	"	W. Data Processing		239 A	5 50				
1350	"	R. Kendrich		233 B	28 24				
1	"	E. Elevator Co.		311 A	23 65				
2	"	" " " "		311 B	126 00				
3	"	K. Stationers		224 A	14 99				
4	"	S.C. Fire Extinguisher Serv.		333 A	140 07				
5	"	M. Kneit		324 A	135 00				
6	1/11	D. Selzer		211 A	395 00				
7	"	R. Lasher		211 B	363 00				
8	"	C & C Cleaners		242 B	67 50				
9	"	Z. Knopf		316 A	75 00				
1360	"	S.S. Service		316 B	65 00				

EXPENSE A - 7710.74   DEPOSIT A-9288   BALA 1577.26
  "   B - 7808.75   "   B-8070   Bal.B 261.25
TOTAL - 15,519.49   TOTAL - 17,358   TOTAL 10,460.86

Exhibit 11: Business Check Register – Deposits & Consolidation

DEPOSIT REGISTER

DATE	DEPOSIT & SOURCE		BLDG.	AMOUNT	
1/5/77	RENT		B	7260	—
1/6	"		A	5845	—
1/6	"		A	2575	—
1/10	"		A	868	—
1/14	"		B	810	—

	CONSOLIDATION — JANUARY '77		BLDG. A		BLDG B		TOTAL	
Ⓐ	BEGINNING BALANCE (BOOK) — SEE LAST MONTH Ⓔ		5166.11		3456	24	8622	35
Ⓑ	DEPOSITS — NET		9288.—		8070	—	17358	—
Ⓒ	TOTAL Ⓐ + Ⓑ		14,454.11		11,526	24	25980	35
Ⓓ	EXPENDITURES		7710.74		7808	75	15519	49
Ⓔ	ENDING BALANCE (BOOK) FOR DISTRIBUTION NOT ENTRY Ⓒ-Ⓓ		6743.37		3717	49	10460	86
Ⓕ	DISTRIBUTION TO OWNERS — JAN '77		2130.74		2650	19	4780	93
Ⓖ	EXPENSES LESS DISTRIBUTION TO OWNERS		5580.00		5158	56	10738	56
Ⓗ	✓ LESS LOAN SERVICE ✓		1831.00		1680	56	3511	56

When the books have been posted for the month, it is quite simple to compare this year's performance with last year's—and to spot any developing problems. I can keep my finger on the pulse of my business without a great deal of effort.

Your General Ledger

For your General Ledger, you will need to set up two books—an Expense Ledger and an Income Ledger.

For your Expense Ledger, I suggest you purchase an 18-column double-page figuring book, such as Boorum & Pease's No. 1602 1/2 Figuring Book. The 150-page book is ample.

For your Income Ledger, I suggest Boorum & Pease's No. 1602 1/2 Figuring Book with 20 columns double-page. You'll need 300 pages here.

There may be other figuring books that work just as well. I'm familiar with these and know they work. I suggest you refer to Exhibits 12 through 14, as I describe how they are to be set up. It can be difficult in the abstract.

General Ledger Account Numbers

There's a risk in telling you to set up your General Ledger Account Numbers in the detail I will give you. It is a rather sophisticated system. It is certainly permissible to tailor it down by combining account numbers under one listing if you do not wish this degree of refinement. In any event, I urge you to give full consideration to the budgeting techniques I show. This is the trick that ensures success. Once it is set up, it works like magic.

Each of the following General Ledger Account Numbers, together with a word description of the account, becomes a double-matching page heading.

GENERAL LEDGER ACCOUNT NUMBERS
EXPENSE LEDGER
(18 columns across)

210   PAYROLL   Total
     211   Resident Manager
     212   Assistant Manager
     213   Maid—Houseman
     214   Maintenance
     219   Miscellaneous

220   UTILITIES   Total
     221   Power
     222   Water
     223   Gas
     224   Telephone

230   MISCELLANEOUS   Total
     231   Advertising
     232   Refunds
     233   Petty Cash
     234   Legal Service
     239   Miscellaneous

240   LAUNDRY AND CLEANING   Total
     241   Apartment Cleaning
     242   Carpet Cleaning
     243   Linens
     244   Curtains
     245   Draperies
     249   Miscellaneous

250   MANAGEMENT FEE   Total
     251   Management Fee

GENERAL LEDGER ACCOUNT NUMBERS (Continued)

310   CONTRACTS Total
- 311   Elevator
- 312   Refrigeration/Air Conditioning
- 313   Pest Control
- 314   Rubbish
- 315   Gardener
- 316   Janitor
- 317   Pool
- 318   Sweeping Service/Window Cleaning
- 319   Miscellaneous

320   SUPPLIES Total
- 321   Electrical
- 322   Cleaning
- 323   Hardware
- 324   Office Supplies
- 329   Miscellaneous

330   REPAIRS Total
- 331   Furniture
- 332   Building
- 333   Maintenance
- 334   Painting
- 335   Plastering
- 336   Plumbing
- 337   Electrical
- 338   Equipment
- 339   Miscellaneous

410   INSURANCE AND TAXES Total
- 411   Insurance
- 412   Payroll Taxes
- 413   Property Taxes

500   CAPITAL EXPENDITURES Total
- 511   Furniture
- 512   Equipment

GENERAL LEDGER ACCOUNT NUMBERS (Continued)

513 Building
521 First Mortgage Principal
522 First Mortgage Interest
523 First Mortgage Impound
531 Second Mortgage Principal
532 Second Mortgage Interest

INCOME LEDGER
(20 columns across)

600 REMITTANCE TO OWNERS Total
661 John and Mary Smith
662 Mark and Martha Jones
663 John Smith (His Separate Property)

700 ADVANCED BY OWNERS Total
771 John and Mary Smith
772 Mark and Martha Jones
773 John Smith (From His Separate Property)

800 OVERAGES AND SHORTAGES
Over/(short)

Your Expense Ledger

You should set up each of the pages in your Expense Ledger as in Exhibit 12.

First, head the top of the righthand page with the account number and the word description. Your first double-matching pages will be headed "EXPENSE SUMMARY." The following sets of pages are headed:
"210—PAYROLL, TOTAL"
"211—PAYROLL, RESIDENT MANAGER"
"212—PAYROLL, ASSISTANT MANAGER"
Etc.

Exhibit 12: Expense Ledger – Total Payroll

(LEFT HAND PAGE)

1. YEAR/ BLDG.	2. SPRING BUDGET	3. JAN.	4. FEB.	5. MAR.	6. APR.	7. MAY	8. JUN.	9. SPRING ACTUAL
1976/A	475⁰⁰	78²¹	78²¹	78²¹	78²¹	78²⁴	76²⁹	469⁹⁹
1976/B	475⁰⁰	76²⁴	78²⁴	78²⁴	78²⁴	78²⁹	101⁹⁹	492⁸ᵈ
1977/A	575⁰⁰	98⁹ᵈ	97⁷⁸	97⁷⁸	97⁷⁸	97⁷⁸	97⁷⁸	576⁹ᵈ
1977/B	575⁰⁰	111²ᵈ	97⁷⁸	97⁷⁸	97⁷⁸	97⁷⁸	97⁷⁸	600²ᵈ

Exhibit 13: Income Ledger – Rental Income

(LEFT HAND PAGE)

1. APT. #	2. F/U	3. RERENT/EST. SPRING RENT	4. JAN.	5. FEB.	6. MAR.	7. APR.	8. MAY	9. JUN.	10. SPRING TOTAL
101	U	/ 330	330	330	330	330	330	330	1980
102	U	/ MGR	MGR	MGR	MGR	MGR	MGR	MGR	MGR
103	U	/ 310	310	310	310	310	310	310	1860
104	U	/ 240	235	235	235 ④ 4/5	117 ⑤²	245 ①	189	1256 ⑤²
105	U	/ 235	235	235	235 ①	235	235	235	1410
106	U	/ 230	230	230	235	235	230	230	1395
107	U	/ 305	305	305	305	305	305	305	1830
108	U	/ 235	235	235	235	235 ①	235	235	1410
109	U	/ 235	235	235	235	235	235	275	1410
110	U	/ 235	235	235	235	235	235	235	1410
111	U	/ 310	310	310	310	310	310	310	1860
201	U	/ 360	360	360	360	360	360 ⑤⁸	360	2160 ⑤⁸
202	U	/ 310	310	310	310	310	310	310	1860
203	U	/ 360	①	260 ①	360	360	360	365	1705
ETC.									
TOTAL	RENTAL	INCOME	8520	8785	8703	8790	8691	8666	52355 ⁴ᵈ
SECURITY	DEPOSITS		100 ①	200 ⑩		200 ⑭	200 ③		900 ⁰⁰
KEY	DEPOSITS				25 ⑥				25 ⁰⁰
CLEANING	CHARGES			50 ⑩	50 ⑥	50 ②	50 ⑦		200 ⁰⁰
LAUNDROMAT	INCOME		35 ⁴ᵍ	33 ⁷ᵈ	83 ⁹ᵈ	42 ⁵²	35 ⁰⁹	42 ²⁹	222 ²ᵈ
MISC	INCOME		26 ⁷ᵈ	10 ²⁵	13 ⁸² ① / 9 ⑧	9. ⁵⁶ ⑥ / 13 ⑥	7 ⁴⁹	10	55 ⁸² / 74 ⁸⁸
TOTAL	INCOME		8682 ²ᵈ	9078 ⁶²	9251 ⁹ᵈ	9118 ⁵²	8983 ⁵⁹	8718 ⁹⁶	53833 ⁶²

(RIGHT HAND PAGE)

#210 - TOTAL PAYROLL

1. FALL BUDGET	2. JUL.	3. AUG.	4. SEP.	5. OCT.	6. NOV.	7. DEC.	8. FALL ACTUAL	9. YEAR ACTUAL
475.00	78.29	78.21	78.21	78.21	78.21	78.21	469.41	938.89
475.00	126.41	89.21	78.21	101.61	78.21	78.21	551.41	1049.81
675.00	97.21	97.21	97.21	97.21	97.21	97.21	586.69	1163.83
575.00	97.21	97.21	97.21	97.21	97.21	97.21	586.69	1186.81

(RIGHT HAND PAGE)

RENTAL INCOME - BLDG. "A" - 300 S. OXFORD - 1977

1. rerent/est. Fall rent	2. JUL.	3. AUG.	4. SEP.	5. OCT.	6. NOV.	7. DEC.	8. FALL TOTAL	9. YEAR TOTAL	10. TOTAL VACANCIES
330/335	330 ①	330	330	330	330	335 ①	1985	3965	
355/355	MGR	MGR	MGR	MGR	MGR	MGR	MGR		
350/325	310	310	310	310	310	325	1875	3735	
255/250	245	245	245	245	245	245	1470	2726 ⑤	
255/245	235	235	235	235	235	245	1420	2830	
250/240	230	230	230 ①	141 240 ⑥ w/o 115	—	240	1285	2690	30
350/315	305	305	305	305	305	315	1840	3670	
255/245	235	235	235	235	235	245	1420	2830	
255/250	235	30	w/o 250 ①	255	116 ⑥	250	1186 ⑥	2596 ⑦	
255/245	235	235	235	235	235	245	1420	2830	
350/325	310	310	310	310	310	325	1875	3735	
400/375	360	360 ②	360	360	360	375	2175	4335 ⑤	
350/320	310	310	310	310	310	320	1870	3730	
395/380	365	365	365	365 ③	365	375	2200	3905	415
ETC.									
									940
	8905	8577 ②	8920	9080	8306 ①	9112 ②	52801 ②		
	200 ⑥ 200 ⑥		200 ①	200 ⑥ 200 ⑥	200 ①		1600		
	25 ⑥	25 ①	25 ①	25 ①		25 ①	125		
	50 ⑥ 50 ⑥		50 ①	50 ⑥ 50 ⑥	75 ①		325		
	41 ②	32 ⑥	54 ③	33 ⑧	33 ⑥	34 ②	230 ⑥		
	2 ⑥	13 ②	4 ⑤	15 ⑧	7 ⑤	23 ⑥ 15 ⑥	46 ⑧ 76		
			15 ⑥ 15 ⑥	5 ⑥ 15 ⑧	15 ①		93		
	9474 ②	8684 ⑨	9278 ⑥	9471 ⑥	8622 ⑫	9245 ⑥	54678 ⑥		

Although you will probably not need all these pages at the start, you may want to set them up now for future use.

Here are the column headings that you will use for every set of pages.

(Lefthand page)
Column 1—YEAR/BLDG. (This column is split—the left half shows the year of operation, the right half gives the building code.)

(Note: As you eventually may have a number of buildings, you will want to establish a code now—"A" for your first building, "B" for the next, etc. On your fly cover or first page, designate your code, such as: "A" = 300 S. Oxford St., "B" = 2608 Campus Dr., etc.)

Column 2—SPRING BUDGET (This will be a total six-months' budget for each item of expense for the January-through-June period. It is taken from last year's actual figures and estimated by you and your resident manager.)

Column 3—JANUARY
Column 4—FEBRUARY
Column 5—MARCH
Column 6—APRIL
Column 7—MAY
Column 8—JUNE
Column 9—SPRING ACTUAL (This will be posted as a total of the first six months' expenses.)

(Righthand page)
Column 1—FALL BUDGET
Column 2—JULY
Column 3—AUGUST
Column 4—SEPTEMBER

Column 5—OCTOBER
Column 6—NOVEMBER
Column 7—DECEMBER
Column 8—FALL ACTUAL
Column 9—YEAR ACTUAL

After your last year's figures are posted in the spring and fall budget columns for each account number and the summary, you should make an appointment with your resident manager to review the previous year's expenses item by item. You will want to discuss expense-saving techniques as you review each item of expense. While you are reviewing the electricity expense (221), for example, you can discuss turning out the garage lights during the day, when they are not needed. While reviewing gas expense (223), you might decide to turn off the pool heat during the winter, when tenants rarely use it.

You will be encouraging your manager to think as a partner in trying to achieve satisfactory expense figures. Since your resident manager has the primary responsibility for the building's day-to-day operations, he is in the best position to implement your budgetary objectives.

As you gain expertise in budget-planning, you will get to know your buildings intimately and profit from your knowledge.

Your Income Ledger

This ledger has two functions. The opening double-matching pages are an accounting of rent received, by apartment, by month. The second group of double-matching pages records income received by category and disbursement to owner(s).

Exhibit 13 is a sample of the first function. This is concerned with rental income by apartment by month in 1978 for Building "A" only.

Exhibit 14 is a sample of the second function. This is a grand total—a summary—of all the income category pages in the section.

Exhibit 13 (pages 266–267) illustrates how you set up your Rental Income section, which occupies the opening pages of your Income Ledger. Beyond the function of recording events, these pages are useful for both planning and diagnosis—anticipating what may happen or should happen, and then seeing how it worked out.

Column 3 on the lefthand page and Column 1 on the righthand page provide the planning function. Their first purpose is to show the estimated monthly rental for each apartment for the upcoming half-year period. The other useful purpose is the rerent estimate.

When preparing your Rental Income Ledger, Column 3, lefthand page (Estimated Spring Rent), and Column 1, right-hand page (Estimated Fall Rent), become split columns—the right figure becoming the current monthly rental rate and the left figure becoming the rerent rate.

Your first set of matching pages might be headed: "RENTAL INCOME—BUILDING 'A'—300 S. Oxford—1978."

(Lefthand page, reading left to right)
Column 1—APARTMENT NUMBER.
Column 2—F OR U. (Furnished or unfurnished. This of course may change from time to time if you have a partially furnished building; you may wish to move the furnishings from one apartment to another or add furnished apartments.)

Column 3—SPRING RERENT RATE & ESTIMATED RENT. (We have already discussed this item. Your resident manager must get your approval for any changes from the rates posted here.)

Column 4—JANUARY. (The rent collected for each apartment during the month of January is posted here by your bookkeeper. If any amount is for less than a full month, a note, such as "to 1/15" should be posted next to the amount.)

Column 5—FEBRUARY.

Column 6—MARCH.

Column 7—APRIL.

Column 8—MAY.

Column 9—JUNE.

Column 10—SPRING TOTAL. (This is the total of all rents received by the apartment January through June.)

(Righthand page)

Column 1—FALL RERENT RATE & ESTIMATED RENT. (Following a discussion with your resident manager, post any changes in apartment rental status here for the Fall season.)

Column 2—JULY.

Column 3—AUGUST.

Column 4—SEPTEMBER.

Column 5—OCTOBER.

Column 6—NOVEMBER.

Column 7—DECEMBER.

Column 8—FALL TOTAL.

Column 9—YEAR TOTAL.

Column 10—TOTAL VACANCIES. (This gives you insight into a possible vacancy problem by apartment. As your records accumulate, you will find some apartments do not retain their tenants as well as others. Perhaps they are noisy, dark, next to an elevator shaft or stairway.

Your job is to correct the problem by redecorating, lowering the rent, insulating against noise, or whatever other adjustment will make the apartment more productive.)

When your headings are complete, you will list the apartments, one to each line, in Column 1. At the bottom of the apartments listing, reserve one line for "TOTAL." Below this, write the following, one to each line:

SECURITY DEPOSITS
KEY DEPOSITS
CLEANING CHARGES
LAUNDROMAT INCOME
MISC. INCOME
TOTAL INCOME

Your Rental Income form is complete.

In practice, as apartments change residents, new security deposits, key deposits, etc. will be made. These deposits and charges are coded by a circled number (1, 2, 3, etc.) and posted in the proper space for apartment number and month. These amounts are also recorded elsewhere, as I will describe later.

Deposits and charges are kept separate from the direct income from rentals—otherwise they would distort the true picture.

This is how you set up your Gross Income Summary section, which occupies the back pages of your Income Ledger. I call for seventeen double-matched pages here, but you may want to reserve as many as thirty if you feel the need to expand the categories.

Your Ledger headings for each set of pages are as follows (refer to Exhibit 14, an example of Gross Income Summary pages):

1. GROSS INCOME SUMMARY. (This item is a recap of all income received each month by each building. The income figure includes rental income, deposits and fees, laundromat and miscellaneous income. The total figure should be the same as reported in the Rental Income section.)
2. RENT.
3. UTILITIES. (There are some circumstances when you advance the payment of certain utilities and the tenant or manager sends a check for reimbursement.)
4. GARAGE. (Payments made by tenants for additional garage space.)
5. SECURITY DEPOSITS. (These pages show total deposits by month for each of your buildings. The deposits are not identified by apartment here.)
6. KEY DEPOSITS. (Same as above.)
7. PET DEPOSITS. (Same as above.)
8. CLEANING CHARGES.
9. LAUNDROMAT INCOME.
10. EXTRA GUESTS.
11. MISCELLANEOUS INCOME.
12. NET INCOME. (This is gross income less expenses.)
13. GENERAL LEDGER #600—REMITTANCE TO OWNERS—TOTAL. (This account shows monthly disbursements to the owners.)
14. GENERAL LEDGER #661—REMITTANCE TO OWNER #1. (If your building has more than one owner who receives income from it, you will need to break down the total remittances shown in General Ledger #600 to show individual payments. You

Exhibit 14: Income Ledger – Gross Income Summary

(LEFT HAND PAGE)

1. YEAR	2. BLDG.	3. SPRING BUDGET	4. JAN.	5. FEB.	6. MAR.	7. APR.	8. MAY	9. JUN.	10. SPRING ACTUAL
1976	A	48,500	8006⁴⁴	7753⁶¹	8228⁷⁷	8069¹³	7964⁴⁴	8239²⁵	48257⁷⁰
"	B	40,000	7055⁹²	7294⁹⁵	6127⁵²	6358¹⁵	6055⁵¹	6402²²	39294³⁶
1977	A	48,500	7642³¹	7554¹⁰	8409⁷⁸	7612⁸¹	7544⁹²	8321⁵⁷	17080⁴⁴
"	B	41,500	7519⁴⁰	6381⁵⁹	6686⁸¹	6938⁸⁹	7331¹⁵	6655⁴¹	41573⁹⁵

Exhibit 15: Tenant Record Card

BLDG B	APT. # 108
TERM:	6 MOS TO 3/5/77
OCCUPANT:	M/M K. KRAUS
DATE IN:	9/15/76
RENT:	$245
SECURITY DEPOSIT:	150
KEY DEPOSIT:	10
CLEANING CHARGE:	50
MISC. DEPOSITS:	—
REFRIGERATOR:	OURS
DATE OUT:	

(RIGHT HAND PAGE)

| | | | | | GROSS INCOME SUMMARY — BLDGS. A & B | | | | |
1.	2.	3.	4.	5.	6.	7.	8.	9.	10.
FALL BUDGET	JUL.	AUG.	SEP.	OCT.	NOV.	DEC.	FALL ACTUAL	YEAR ACTUAL	
48,500	7499⁸⁵	8431²⁵	8169⁹⁴	7498⁵⁵	6633⁶⁹	8697⁸⁰	47131²¹	95368⁹¹	
40,000	6480⁰²	6778⁵⁷	6355²⁹	7212²⁵	6614⁹⁵	6729⁹¹	40169²³	79463⁸⁵	
44,000	8312¹⁵	8089⁴⁴	9087⁸⁰	8228⁶⁵	8215⁸⁷	8060⁹⁰	49993⁸²	97079⁹¹	
41,500	6136⁹¹	7757⁷¹	5775²²	6798⁷⁰	7610⁸⁵	7352⁰⁰	41500⁹⁰	83094²³	

will set up a spread of pages for each owner as
General Ledger #662, General Ledger #663, to
however many owners there are.)

15. GENERAL LEDGER #700—ADVANCED BY
OWNERS—TOTAL. (This account shows payment
of advances to the building by the owners. This
occurs most frequently with extraordinary bills, such
as twice-yearly taxes or annual insurance premiums.)

16. GENERAL LEDGER #771—ADVANCED BY
OWNER #1. (Serves the same function as the
#660 series. That is, it records payments by indi-
vidual owners.)

17. GENERAL LEDGER #800—OVERAGES AND
SHORTAGES. (This picks up over or under situations which are not recorded on other pages, in
order to balance the books.)

You now have all the main page headings for this Gross
Income Summary section.

For each of these sets of pages, you will head the columns as follows (see Exhibit 14):

(Reading left to right)
Column   1—YEAR.
Column   2—BUILDING. (Coded "A," "B," "C," etc.)
Column   3—SPRING BUDGET. (This is income, not ex-
pense budget.)
Column   4—JANUARY.
Column   5—FEBRUARY.
Column   6—MARCH.
Column   7—APRIL.
Column   8—MAY.
Column   9—JUNE.
Column 10—SPRING ACTUAL.

(Righthand page)
Column 1—FALL BUDGET.
Column 2—JULY.
Column 3—AUGUST.
Column 4—SEPTEMBER.
Column 5—OCTOBER.
Column 6—NOVEMBER.
Column 7—DECEMBER.
Column 8—FALL ACTUAL.
Column 9—YEAR ACTUAL.

Rental Agreements, Deposits and Charges

The rental agreements I use are standardized forms I get from my Apartment House Owners Association. I have found it a good practice to keep the originals of these agreements in my home office file. Should a resident manager leave on short notice, you could be left hunting for these important documents.

It is also necessary that you keep a convenient record of tenant deposits and charges. For this, I use a small file box of 3 by 5 cards (see Exhibit 15). The cards are alphabetically indexed behind each building code. There are also "Building 'A'—Out" and "Building 'B'—Out" sections in the back of the box for cards of tenants who have left. Occasionally you will need to check back on their records.

Across the top of the card is the building code ("A") and the apartment number (#209).

These are the listings down the left side of the card:

TERM. (Starting and ending dates of lease.)
OCCUPANT (Tenant name.)
DATE IN. (Date tenant moved in.)
RENT. (Monthly rental rate.)
S.D. (Security deposit.)

K.D. (Key deposit.)
C.C. (Cleaning charge.)
M.D. (Miscellaneous deposits, pets, etc.)
REFRIG. (Refrigerator—owner's or tenant's.)
D.O. (Date tenant moved out.)

Most of this information is recorded on your Rental Income Ledger pages. Here it is in one place, easy to locate.

When a tenant moves out, you pull his card, note the deposits to be returned, deduct the costs of any unusual damage, and send him a check for the balance. His card is placed in the "Out" section of the box. When a new rental agreement for the apartment is received from the resident manager, a new tenant card is made out.

Some Additional Pointers

Do not permit your resident manager or property manager to give a lease for more than one year—unless you build in a rent escalation figure which you mutually agree on.

Where you do not write all your leases to terminate on one date (December 1), you must go through your 3-by-5 file box monthly and pull cards of all tenants whose leases expire 60 days from that time. A letter is sent, notifying the tenant of a rent increase effective 30 days after his receipt of the letter, and suggesting that he sign a new lease.

The key deposit is refundable with the return of the key. The standard deposit is $5. Where you provide an automatic garage-door opener, the standard charge is $25.

You are asking for trouble if you keep pets in your building. I love pets and so have my own problems with them at home. If you decide to allow pets, set a minimum deposit of no less than $100 to take care of damage to carpets, draperies, etc. This amount is posted under Miscellaneous Deposits.

I have found it easier to include a refrigerator in the apartment rental than to make a separate charge for it. If the new tenant brings his own refrigerator, the owner's refrigerator is taken out and stored with no rent reduction.

I recommend that every owner who manages his own building join a local apartment house owners association. They can offer much useful information—area studies of vacancy percentages, legal advice, lists of potential resident managers, important forms and such. The fees are minimal and the advice and professional assistance are valuable.

The issue of rent control is an ever-present problem in large cities. Whenever an elected official wants to pick up cheap brownie points with his constituency, he will pull rent control out of his bag of tricks. Rent control is an appealing issue to anyone who rents. The present savings are much more impressive than the ultimate damage to the quality of rental housing.

The exception to this occurs, of course, during times of national emergency when all prices and wages are frozen. Rents deserve no more special protection than any other important part of the economy.

One professional property manager I know maintains that under a temporary period of rent control, the buildings he managed "spun-off" more profit than in normal times. He informed the tenants of the owner's dilemma—advancing costs and no additional rental income to pay for them. He simply postponed expensive maintenance. Under the circumstances, the tenants respected the owner's position, and vacancies did not rise. But if this condition had prevailed too long—if necessary maintenance was not just postponed but denied—it would have been an open invitation to a slum.

I realized when I wrote this chapter that it might appear formidable to the novice in real estate. It bears a heavy weight of dry detail which will probably have no immediate application. However, when you become an apartment house owner and decide to manage your property yourself, I think you might find it a blessing. I arrived at it only after a long process of trial and error, with many false starts and costly experiments.

Once established, the system works as if run by a genie. It gives me more control over my properties than many professional management firms have over theirs. It enables me to keep a lid on unnecessary expenses and maximize profits. It occupies less than ten hours a month of my time and saves about $8,000 a year in management fees.

That's not too bad a rate of pay for managing one's own investments.

13

Defensive Techniques

To fear the worst oft cures the worse.
> —WILLIAM SHAKESPEARE (1564–1616)
> *Troilus and Cressida*

Better put a strong fence 'round the top of a cliff,
Than an ambulance down in the valley.
> —JOSEPH MALINS (*Floriut* 1895)
> "A Fence or an Ambulance"

It is a natural tendency for the serious investor to be an optimist. And that's good. Why else would you send your hard cash out of the sanctuary of your possession and into the chancy arenas of financial speculation—unless you are optimistic that good things will happen from it?

Yet the prudent investor, even while he keeps an eye on his star, is using the other eye to check the terrain for potholes. The truth is—the more you venture, the more you risk. The ardent investor must be as conscious of his potential liabilities as he is of his opportunities.

I believe there are certain ways of managing your affairs that will help you fend off adversity. I've told you many of them already. Your Cash Equivalent Reserve and your Liquidity Reserve, as examples, are intended to keep you solvent in troubled times. Put all these techniques together and you can learn to form your own defensive strategy.

In each new situation you must learn to ask yourself two key questions: "If the worst happens, how much can I lose?" and "Can I afford to lose it?" If you decide the risks are more than you can bear, then you must either declare a pass or figure out a way to bring the down-side liabilities within bearable boundaries.

In other words, always know how much you are risking before you commit to it.

Following is a list of suggestions which have been threaded through this book, summarized here for easy reference and as an aid to keeping you out of serious trouble.

1. *Run your personal business life as if you were a business*—because you are! Whether you are a ballerina or a barber, a fireman or a flagpole painter—over your lifetime you could be managing close to a million dollars in income alone. If you become financially successful, it could be a lot more. How will you manage it? Will this fortune disappear like water through a sieve? Or will you develop the business-like practices and attitudes that will help your dollars flourish and grow?

2. *Maintain accurate records.* Record-keeping can be a pain and a bore—but the alternatives are even less appetizing. How can you know where you are—and what you should do about it—if you don't keep score? Show me one professional athlete who is not always aware of what the scoreboard reads and I'll show you a jock who is headed for the minors. You needn't be a slave to a set of books. A few simple records, updated at regular intervals, will give you all you need.

3. *Develop a life-style that will assure surplus investment capital.* It's the easiest thing in the world to find a moral justification for spending money. Of course you de-

serve it. If you're not going to be kind to yourself who will be? But know that this attitude can readily become a cop-out, an easy excuse. If you really want to be good to yourself, you won't allow inflationary pressures to destroy your future. You'll know when to cut back—retrench. Take a hard look at your spending habits. Summon up the courage to do without something you think you ought to have. And above all, don't let next year's expected salary increases be your hope for this year's troubles. It doesn't work that way.

4. *Cushion yourself against unforeseen events.* If you can predict all that's to happen to you in the future, you have your fortune made as a mystic. Life is full of surprises—nice and not-so-nice. If you follow professional football you know that the defensive unit can often account for more touchdowns than the offensive unit. Defend yourself against the unexpected.

5. *Keep abreast of the information you need.* The successful investor is the informed investor. Use your team of experts, but also make it a point to keep yourself informed through the media that apply to your interests.

This list could grow to be a mile long—but there's no point to it. No one knows better than you yourself what particular quirks and foibles of yours can get you into trouble, financial or otherwise.

Practical Management of Your Personal Affairs

Your and your family's personal bills should be paid from a joint commercial checking account. If you are married you should maintain a joint savings account at a savings and loan or bank. Your safe deposit box should be near the place you work. This allows you access to important documents during working hours, when you may be required to set aside a few minutes for personal business.

Security certificates are stored in your safe deposit box in separate envelopes marked with their purpose (e.g., "Liquidity Reserve") or the name of the family member who owns them. Deeds, title insurance policies, loan papers and other insurance policies pertaining to a particular parcel of property should be wrapped together and captioned with the property's name. (Keep together all documents related to a property, rather than keeping all deeds, all insurance policies, together.)

For the benefit of your heirs, each time you open your safe deposit box pretend that you will not live to return to it. This will encourage you to keep current and well-organized.

Keep your checkbook register up-to-date, accurate and informative. If the name of the payee is not sufficient to recall the purpose of the check, note the purpose in the register. (Nothing reveals the frailty of memory more glaringly than last year's checkbook register at income tax time.)

Where your affairs are not encompassed by simple W-2 forms, I urge you to keep a simple account book that indicates the month and day of all income received, and a record in this same account book showing to which account the income is deposited. (You'll recall I use this same account book to record my annual net worth.) The income could be from salary, dividends, rental income, or whatever. As your financial structure grows, your sources of income will multiply, and a checkbook register is not flexible enough to explain where all the money comes from.

Keep your budget records current. Don't depend on an empty checkbook to tell you that your plans have gotten screwed up.

Use time payments only when your considered judgment tells you that this is the best way to achieve your ends. Remember that most department stores, bank cards and oil company cards charge up to 18 percent interest on the unpaid balance. That's a lot of interest. When you think it out, you may decide that paying cash has greater financial wisdom.

Your Inflation Defense

Few investors can beat severe inflation, but some can keep pace with it pretty well. Here are some tips for keeping inflation under control.

1. Curb the impulse to improve your standard of living during a period of high inflation. Recognize that higher living costs are denting your budget and crimping your savings goals. This is the time when you may decide there are things you have promised yourself that you don't really need to have. Replace the expensive vacation with a jaunt closer to home. You might decide to postpone that vacation cottage, the extra car, the boat—even if you have reserved sufficient funds. Enter tempting retail stores with your blinders on. This is not the time to spend; it is the time to conserve, and it will pass. The point is not to eliminate the amenities of life entirely. Only choose the ones you want the most, and let the rest dangle. Put a cover on your expenses until there's a lid on rampant inflation.

2. Trust deeds or mortgages that you have on your home or other property at lower-than-current rates of interest should be retained if at all possible. This may require that you live in your current home longer than you would like— even if you want and can afford a better one. Fix up your home, add to it; but try to keep your favorable loan. This is something you will live with for a long, long time.

3. Regarding investment property, if you have a loan at a favorable rate of interest—and you are taking accelerated depreciation—consider switching to straight-line. Your tax

accountant can make this change for you. Under current regulations you can switch at any time to a lesser depreciation schedule (200 percent to 125 percent, 200 percent to straight-line, for example) without penalty. In reducing your depreciation rate, you will be losing some tax shelter. On the other hand, you will not be forced to sell your building so quickly because your depreciation is running low. By retaining your low interest loan, you win in other ways too. No real estate commissions, escrow fees, possible capital gains and incomes taxes on the proceeds—all problems in high-inflation years, when your salary may not have caught up with your increased cost of living.

4. During periods of rampant inflation, such as we experienced in the fall of 1974, the prudent investor should not commit in the securities market for either stocks or bonds. The directions of market values are most uncertain. What appears to be a cheap buy or a solid investment may be illusory—and obtainable at even lower prices later. One unbreakable rule is "Don't buck a trend." I know—I have tried it, and it can be very humbling.

When the investment climate starts to evidence its sunny side and the trend is clearly up, step back into the market slowly, committing only 10 percent of your funds at a time. Corporate and public utility bonds will increase in market value as interest rates decrease, and common stocks can be acquired whenever there is a sell-off in the market. Place your orders to buy a specific security at a price below the current market. When the security price temporarily dips— as it usually does—you can pick up an extra point or so. You will miss a few purchases with this technique, but not many.

Whenever inflation starts to rule the market again, put your money back into fixed capital return investments (cash equivalents)—savings accounts, treasury bills, banker's acceptances, commercial paper, or liquid assets funds—any of which will return your capital intact plus interest.

5. Antiques, artifacts, porcelains and other works of legitimate art are inflation fighters—their value is enhanced as the dollar cheapens. Meanwhile, you can enjoy their beauty in your home or office.

6. While gold and silver have increased in popularity as inflation hedges, you must be most cautious about investing in either of them. Catch them late in an inflationary period and you can watch their values decline in happier days. Better hedge with investment vehicles that bring you a return.

Wills and Trusts

If you have a net worth in five figures or more, you will surely want to consult an attorney about having a proper will drawn up for both you and your spouse. This goes in your safe deposit box with your other important papers. As your wealth increases, you should check your will every now and then to be sure that it includes all your acquired assets and that it does, in fact, will them as you wish. You can prevent frequent trips to consult your will (and amend it) by bequeathing your assets on a percentage basis. Your assets can change dramatically, but the intents of your percentages will not.

If you have been very successful, you should also consult an attorney about the desirability of setting up a living trust, or a testamentary trust, for the benefit of your heirs.

Where taxable income is a problem to you in spite of your real estate depreciation, you might consider an eleven-year reversionary trust, called a "Clifford Trust," for the benefit of one or more of your children. During the period of the trust, the income from it may be used for the child's welfare: for his college education, as an example. Whatever income the child receives is taxed at a very low rate. A second trust deed is excellent for this purpose—with its return of 10 to 12 percent. At the end of the term of the trust, the principal returns to the parent, perhaps at a time he wishes to retire and the cash would be useful.

The Tax Reform Act of 1976 included sweeping changes in provisions for trusts and the rules governing estates and gifts. If you have not already done so, you would do well to become familiar with these regulations.

When you see your attorney about wills and trusts, the question will arise as to who will act as trustee for your estate. Banks have trust departments which generally manage funds conservatively and carefully for a continuing fee. An alternative is to have your spouse and any adult heir serve as co-trustees. This is only desirable, of course, if you respect the business judgment of the heirs. Since heirs have a vested interest in the health of the estate, if they are knowledgeable, they can do a fine job. You will want to develop a close enough relationship with your attorney that you can discuss alternatives with him frankly.

General Insurance

Select a general insurance agent to handle all fire, casualty and automobile insurance for your personal and for your investment properties. Be certain that you are insured against "shock" loss—that is, a loss which would be difficult for you to fund yourself. For example, if you have a major investment in a piece of income real estate, you will want a fire insurance policy that will cover you against full loss of equity in the building. If you are underinsured and a fire occurs, your leveraged opportunity could turn into a leveraged nightmare.

Later, as your financial capacity grows, you may be willing to assume some of the risks in exchange for savings on insurance premiums. For example, you may want to reduce or eliminate collision insurance on one or more of your automobiles. It may be possible to save 30 percent of your auto insurance premiums—possibly $200 to $500 a year for two cars over a year—by self-insuring the risk of collision.

Personal liability insurance is one item you will never want to be without. Relatively minor cases have been settled in the courts for hundreds of thousands of dollars. I make it a point to cover my net worth totally by liability insurance.

It is wise to make an annual appointment with your general insurance agent to review your policies. As inflation renders replacement costs more expensive, insurance limits should be increased. Check all policies to see if increasing the deductible to within your reasonable risk limits will offer you substantial savings. Most insurance companes like to be relieved of these small loss claims. In many cases, the direct premium saving in shifting from $100 to $500 deductible can be 10 percent of the premium cost.

Life Insurance

Some people regard life insurance as an investment vehicle. If you feel as I do that inflation at some varying rate is here to stay, insurance as an investment does not qualify. Yes, ordinary life insurance does pay dividends and you can use it as collateral for a loan. But you pay insurance premiums in this year's "hard" dollars to get back softer, more inflated dollars which will purchase a great deal less than your premium dollars could have bought.

For all that, I must say that life insurance has a place in any investor's portfolio.

A life insurance policy can be kept out of the estate of the investor by having it owned by his spouse, his children or a trust. This is an important consideration. The insured should be certain that the policy is properly written so that there is no possibility of the policy reverting to him should the owner predecease him.

As his real estate investments grow, the investor has new need for life insurance: liquid cash to pay estate taxes. In community property states, at the death of either spouse, one-half of the community property will be subject to income taxes if the value of the deceased's community interest is over $250,000. Under the new Tax Act of 1976, the first $500,000 of community property of an estate can be passed to the spouse without tax liability. Above this amount, the tax increases rapidly.

It is easy to understand that with substantial estates, life insurance is an absolute necessity to provide liquid discounted dollars to pay estate tax liabilities.

Where an estate consists largely of nonliquid investments such as real estate, or if it consists mostly of securities, and death occurs at a time of adverse economic conditions—huge losses in the value of the estate might be incurred if the heirs were forced to sell at inopportune times to raise cash for death taxes.

Keep in mind that if all the property is community property and the wife should die first, the same liabilities exist. In non–community property states, a marital deduction is available to reduce the tax liability, which makes the resultant tax roughly the same as in community property states.

If the investor is young, with limited funds, he can buy term insurance for a very low cost. As he grows older, this cost will increase and eventually he will want to convert this term to ordinary life or permanent insurance.

One new factor of the 1976 Tax Act is of special significance. Until 1977, if an investor died, his estate assumed a new cost basis so that no long-term capital gains tax was incurred on the decendent's property after his death. That is, if the investor had bought a stock for $10,000 and held on to it for a number of years (generally not a practice I advocate) and it was worth $100,000 at death—formerly there was only a death tax on that $100,000, and capital gains liabilities were forgiven. Not any more. Now, in addition to the death tax, the estate must pay a capital gains tax on the difference between the buying price and the value at death. (This applies to capital gains earned after September, 1976.) This regulation creates extreme tax liabilities on larger estates.

With real estate, the situation is somewhat different. The long-term capital gains and the depreciation liabilities do not come due on death of the owner. But neither are they forgiven. They are carried forward as potential tax liabilities against the property. If the property is not sold by the heirs —or if it is traded for an equal or more expensive property— no tax liabilities are incurred, other than death taxes on the value of the property.

If the property must be sold to settle the estate, then all these tax liabilities fall in at one time. It's more than a bit scary.

An investor may choose to incorporate his properties and draw a salary. When he does this he becomes eligible for tax-deductible pension plans, health insurance and other goodies which are available to an employee of a corporation.

The investor should also avail himself of all the long-term disability insurance he can purchase to provide continuing income should he become seriously disabled. In this, he should be most selective and purchase only the best contracts of guaranteed-renewable, noncancelable disability insurance. Most people can survive for ninety days without fresh income (especially if they have maintained a correct Cash Equivalent Reserve), so purchase a contract with a ninety-day waiting period, which will reduce the premium cost. With disability insurance, the best will cost a little more, but the cheaper policy, if it fails you when you need it, is of no value at all to you.

This discussion of insurance varieties and purposes barely skims the surface. It would take shelves of books to cover all the possibilities of this complicated subject. Know the kinds of goals you are hoping to achieve through life insurance and get the help of your insurance agent.

Will Rogers once said, "The man who doesn't believe in life insurance ought to try dying once without it." Whether you buy it or not, someone pays for insurance on your life. If you don't, and you die too soon, your wife and family may pay the price of it in the end.

Separate and Community Property

It is an unfortunate but statistical fact that the divorce rate in the United States approaches 50 percent. I cannot author a volume which deals in investment advice without at least touching on this subject. When you consider it, you can decide what you want to do about it.

An ill-conceived marriage can be a financial disaster. This is nothing new. Rich men and rich women alike, kings and queens, princes and princesses, and commoners too, throughout history have been uniquely dismayed at the costly fripperies and follies of their spouses.

Divorce today can be a very expensive business. It can wreak more havoc on an estate than anything else but death. It would be careless not to consider its possibilities.

If you or your spouse had any separate property before your marriage, you should consider each having a separate checking account and a separate savings account. These would be in addition, of course, to your joint checking and savings accounts. (If you don't have something joint going for you from the outset, you are off to a very bad start.)

If one of you receives a separate bequest or income from separate property, it should be deposited to the account under the recipient's name. Future investments in securities and real estate should be made generally in your own name alone. In this, better consult an attorney, as there may be overiding considerations.

I suggest you keep a simple account book showing the date and amount of all income received and whether the income is joint or separate, and into which account it is deposited. Separate funds cannot be commingled without sacrificing their integrity.

All this is protection for both husband and wife. Both partners should recognize that individual funds are as personal as birth certificates. One partner may decide to use separate funds for some common purpose—a trip, a new sofa, a refrigerator, or whatever—but it should be understood that this is a transfer from separate to joint ownership.

Certainly the exact arrangements concerning separate funds are a matter between husband and wife. There are loving and civilized ways to handle it.

The only caution I give is this—when the ardor cools is no time to begin sorting things out.

I think most of us have a tendency to feel we are managing our affairs pretty well for ourselves. Only when some unexpected event arises do we find that there are chinks in our defensive armor. Fiscal responsibility—the investment mentality—includes being prepared for the unexpected. Anticipate the bad when the going is good.

14

Looking toward Retirement

Grow old along with me!
The best is yet to be,
The last of life for which the first was made.
—ROBERT BROWNING (1812–1889)
"Rabbi Ben Ezra"

There are two things to aim at in life: first, to get what you want; and
after that, to enjoy it. Only the wisest of mankind achieve the second.
—LOGAN PEARSALL SMITH (1865–1946)
Afterthoughts

If you are quite young and your blood runs hot and you have great deeds yet to accomplish and wonderful sights to see; and if the world is new and fresh and exciting, and there's not time enough between sunup and moondown to get done all you want to get done—undoubtedly retirement is the farthest thing from your mind.

You have a rich, full life ahead of you—and who's to say what will happen between now and then, between double vodka martinis and prune juice, between sweat socks and support hose?

As you grow older, retirement looms larger among your concerns. What's to happen when you no longer have a salary to depend on? Will your retirement income be enough to keep you off the welfare roles? Will your family be cared for if you die? Is your estate in a condition that will provide your sons and daughters with the benefits you want them to have?

As a salaried employee, you are already asked to make decisions that will affect your life many years from now. Whether you are youthful or middle-aged, full of beans or pooping out, retirement is something you must come to grips with sooner or later. Better sooner than later.

Here are some things for you to consider in planning for retirement.

Yield on Net Worth

Whereas net worth is one measure of financial success, the income generated by this net worth is the key concern of the person who anticipates retiring.

The salaried employee should think of it this way:

when your investment income exceeds your annual expenses, you have arrived at reasonable financial security.

This assumes, of course, that you are doing all the other things you should be doing right.

If this point of financial security does not occur until you are sixty-two to sixty-five years of age, you have social security to help. But social security is only a help, not a total solution to a financially worry-free retirement, especially if you favor three meals a day. Social security may provide the difference between your investment income and your annual expenses, or it may merely contribute an added safety factor, enabling you to continue your investment capital build-up even in retirement. Then too, if your investment income exceeds your personal annual expenses by an earlier age, you may choose to retire—knowing that social security benefits will help make up for inflation erosion when you reach the proper age.

You must be aware that inflation is the prime devil of retired people living on fixed incomes.

If you have a home or income property which is mortgaged, you will enjoy extra income (or lower expenses) as your mortgages are amortized to zero. When your children grow up and leave home, you may choose to sell or lease your home to gain the freedom you want.

Keep in mind this financial triptych:

1. Net worth must yield . . .
2. Total investment income . . .
3. Which exceeds annual personal expenses.

Although net worth is a measure of your wealth, it is not necessarily a gauge of your financial freedom. It is the relationship between your investment income and your annual expenses that provides the criterion for affordable retirement.

Retirement Plans and Social Security

At this writing, company retirement plans are coming under greater federal control. This will cause a number of important changes.

In the past, when an employee left one company to join another, he often sacrificed his nonvested interest in his previous company's profit-sharing or retirement program. Now the vesting period will be much shorter, giving the employee more freedom to change jobs without loss of valuable assets.

Under the old system, employees who stayed with the

company enjoyed a greater share of the fund as employees who left abandoned their assets. Now, as a fund includes more participants, the prorata share of the company's contribution to the fund may be smaller—one more good reason to take the reins of your financial independence into your own hands.

As the social security law now reads, each salaried person who has contributed the maximum social security deductions for forty quarters or for ten years may begin to receive the maximum social security check allowable at age sixty-two or sixty-five. It matters not if you have retired at fifty or fifty-five or any earlier age so long as you have contributed the maximum amount for ten years.

Specific information may be obtained by calling your local social security office. Often they can answer your question right over the phone.

I think it is important that you recognize fully the realities of both retirement plans and social security as they actually work out in retirement. A retirement program which appears generous and more than enough to meet your needs before you retire, may fall far short of your needs after you retire. Retirement programs (most of them) provide for a fixed rate of income—this when everything else in the world is becoming more expensive through currency inflation. The longer you live with a fixed retirement income, the less substantial it will seem to you.

Social security benefit rates seem to lag permanently behind inflation rates. They never catch up. So if you depend on your company retirement plan and social security without any self-help, your retirement can become less and less financially secure.

What can you do about it? You can go out and get a job to supplement your paltry payments. That can not only shatter your dreams of idle retirement, but if you earn too much, the government will take some of your social security benefits away. They want you to retire and to stay retired so you won't compete for jobs with the younger population.

So you're in a box. Dissatisfied with your retirement income, and with no reasonable way to supplement it. This has given rise to an activist organization calling themselves the "Gray Panthers"—retired people who feel that they are not getting their fair shake out of life. And they are right. I hope they can bring about some changes that make earned financial security in retirement something more than a vague promise.

On the other hand, if your retirement income is derived from investment (and not salary)—interest, dividends, rents, royalties and such—you can take in as much as you're able and not get short-changed on your social security benefits.

Can you conceive of a stronger argument than that for taking the responsibility for your retirement planning into your own hands? It can literally mean the difference between the "golden years" that retirement was meant to be and years of helpless desperation. It is either do for yourself or get done in by the system.

I.R.A. and Keogh

In recent years, the government has approved two tax-sheltered retirement programs which could be of great benefit to you. They are the Individual Retirement Account (I.R.A.) and HR-10, the Keogh Retirement Plan.

The I.R.A. was created under the Employee Retirement Income Security Act of 1974. This act allows any person not covered under a qualified deferred compensation (retirement program) or similar government plan to establish such an account for himself.

The maximum you can put into an I.R.A. account each year is 15 percent of your income or $1,500, whichever is less. This amount is not subject to tax in the year earned or in any later year until it is actually removed from the account. During the years this money is in an approved I.R.A. account, it is earning money for you which is also not taxed until it is withdrawn.

The legal age at which you can withdraw your money from an I.R.A. account is fifty-nine and a half. If you withdraw before then, you'll pay both an income tax on the amount and a 12.5 percent penalty tax.

When you have reached the stipulated age for withdrawal, you can take money from your account at whatever rate you wish, paying straight income tax, which will be far lower than in your working years.

So you have the benefits of an untaxed capital investment earning more untaxed money—and paying only a reduced tax rate at the time when you want to make use of your money. It is an excellent idea.

An employee who leaves a company offering a profit-sharing or pension plan and moves to a company which doesn't have such a plan, has the opportunity to "roll over" his former plan into an I.R.A. (Check your accountant or lawyer for details.)

Another important condition—for married persons, each spouse's income may be treated separately. If, for example, your wife has a part-time job, she can set up her own I.R.A. and so build additional tax-free retirement funds for herself.

If you become permanently disabled, you may begin withdrawing immediately from your I.R.A. account without penalty. In the event of your death, your beneficiaries could receive the funds in a lump sum or over a period of years, however you will it.

The Keogh Plan (HR-10) is similar to I.R.A., with the same kinds of benefits and restrictions. However, the amounts set aside may be larger—up to 15 percent of your annual income or $7,500 per year, whichever is less. This plan is available only to self-employed individuals or to employees of a firm where the Keogh Plan has been installed.

An I.R.A. or Keogh Plan may be set up by any of the following:

1. Bank
2. Savings and loan
3. Credit Union
4. Other organizations which can prove that they will administer this trust properly.

These "other organizations" make for some interesting opportunities.

If you maintain your retirement fund at a bank, savings and loan, or credit union, your fund should be earning the highest interest rate—which currently would be 8 to 10 percent a year. This is fine, but it is not so much as your money could be earning in other investment vehicles.

Some large brokerage houses have installed plans which have been approved by the government that permit you to manage your fund in much the same manner as you would a regular securities investment fund. This means you have a legal, government-approved method of buying and selling securities in which you can totally disregard the long-term capital gains holding period. Since the funds are not taxed during their period of trusteeship, the government doesn't care how often you trade within the framework of your retirement plan.

This is a gigantic advantage to the trading-minded investor who is looking toward retirement with security. He doesn't have to wait the twelve-month interval required for the long-term capital gain. All the money in the fund will be treated alike—subject to the expected lower rate of income tax as it is withdrawn in retirement.

Investments may be switched from stocks to bonds and

back again, depending on market opportunities. In periods of market distress, you can switch to defensive issues. In a rising market, you can move into securities with a greater appreciation potential.

In other words, you can be the master of your retirement fund and not be at the mercy of some placid trust department who will be satisfied with a much smaller return since the money (and thus the motivation) is not theirs.

There are trustee fees involved in setting up these funds with any institution. With the more conventional places, the fees are quite small, usually less than $10 a year. With a brokerage firm, the minimum fee is higher—probably not practical for accounts of $10,000 or less. However, when the fund in the conventional institution has reached sufficient size, it can be "rolled over" into a brokerage program.

This is the kind of program tailored to the equities investor who is sophisticated enough about market activities to know how to make his profits and reinvest. I would not recommend it for the novice.

The full development of an adequate retirement program is much more intricate than I have outlined here. It is a combination of social security, your company's retirement program or your own, plus the results of your own personal wealth-enhancing program. I have made a few suggestions and pointed to a few opportunities. The actual execution of your retirement program should come only after thorough examination of your circumstances and opportunities by you, your accountant and your attorney.

15

Investor's Forum

I kept six honest serving men,
(They taught me all I knew);
Their names are What and Why and When,
And How and Where and Who.

—RUDYARD KIPLING (1865–1936)
"The Elephant's Child"

Curiosity is one of the permanent and certain characteristics of the vigorous mind.

—SAMUEL JOHNSON (1709–1784) *The Rambler*

People who know me and are aware of how I made my way frequently ask me questions about the processes of accumulating wealth. What? When? Where? How fast? Many of these questions I have answered in previous pages of this book. Here are some others.

QUESTION: I have heard that there is a lot more money to be made by investment in foreign countries than there is in the United States—what do you think about that?

ANSWER: Several years ago when my wife and I were in Mexico, in every hotel and every shop there were pamphlets designed to tell the tourist how strong the Mexican currency was. They called it the hardest, finest currency in the Western Hemisphere. They recommended investment on the part of foreigners—particularly United States citizens—in Mexico.

The fact that Mexico expropriated many American investors' property thirty years ago naturally was not mentioned.

The propaganda headlined the fact that one could receive 10 or 12 or even 15 percent return on his money and it was easily convertible to dollars.

Many Americans took advantage of this. It looked virtually foolproof.

Then, as the result of economic pressures, Mexico allowed its peso to float against other world currencies. The value of the peso dropped in relation to the dollar by close to 50 percent almost overnight. American investors who had been talked into buying pesos for their dollars had their capital investment cut in half—a most serious financial consequence.

Many Americans who had retired in Mexico to enjoy the benefits of a lower cost of living could not contend with this 50-percent inflation and the lost value of their converted dollars, and were forced to return home to be supported by their children—their hoped-for independence lost.

It was a tragic example of the hazards of foreign investment.

The United States is a large and diverse country. It offers tremendous investment opportunities. Western Europeans, Arabs and Japanese have invested billions of dollars in American industry and real estate—chosen from among all the world's opportunities. I think that tells us something.

I believe it is the height of folly for individual investors to ignore these at-home opportunities in favor of foreign investment.

Large multinational companies who feel that they

have skimmed the best market potential from this country will venture abroad. They carefully calculate the merits of expanded markets against the inherent risks of alien shores. They always plan a much higher return on their investment because they know that any country's social and political situation can change radically and without warning, and they may have to abandon their assets.

It is a game for the big boys only—too risky for the small investor who would be wiser to find less hazardous recreations.

QUESTION: I have a favorite charity that I want to contribute to. Is there any one way better than another to make this contribution?

ANSWER: When you want to make a charitable contribution to some worthy institution—church, medical center, university, or whatever—you should consider a security you own that has greatly appreciated in value. This has great advantages over straight cash.

The security is tax-deductible at its current market value, regardless of what you paid for it. There is no capital gain liability. In essence, part of your contribution is made in tax-free dollars—which are then tax-deductible.

Where a gift has been made in cash, it has already been diminished by taxes. By giving an appreciated security, both you and your charity can benefit.

QUESTION: My stockbroker has been recommending stocks to me that have very high price/earnings ratios. What do you think about these high-multiples stocks?

ANSWER: The past few years have taught us that it is not worth paying the price of stocks with excessive multiples. You know by now that a stock with a price/ earnings multiple of 6 means that it is priced at about six times its expected earnings for the year. If the company paid out half its earnings in dividends, a stock with a P/E ratio of 6 should yield 8 percent in dividends.

For instance, a stock selling at 60 which produces earnings of $10 a share and pays $5 a year in dividends is giving the shareholder an 8 percent return on his investment. To pay this kind of return, a stock with a P/E multiple of 12 would have to double its earnings; a stock with a P/E multiple of 18 would have to triple its earnings.

We are approaching rarefied altitudes. Few companies, except in special situations, can be expected to double or triple their earnings on any regular basis.

The rationale for investment in high-multiple stocks, of course, is their potential for growth, for rapid appreciation of your capital. But we have seen that stocks which have outrun their capacities to produce earnings are the most suspectible to pneumonia at the first chill breeze.

When you are attracted to a stock bearing a high multiple, take a day or two to think it over. Put yourself in the place of a current stockholder who had bought at a lower multiple and wonder if you would not be happy to sell at this price. And wonder how many more stockholders would not be similarly inclined.

It ought to give you pause.

QUESTION: You have advised the use of professional property management firms to take over the day-to-day problems of running your real estate investment. Have you any reservations about them?

ANSWER: Perhaps I have been unusually lucky in the property management companies I dealt with.

I have few complaints about them. They did a good job for me. If there is a problem with them, it is this: they are satisfied to have the buildings they manage fully rented and are not aggressive about raising rents— even when this is obviously called for.

An owner can't depend on a property manager to tell him when a new rent structure is due. The owner must initiate it. At least once a year you should take your property manager on a tour of your buildings, inspecting all public areas for maintenance and needed repairs; look at one or two competitive buildings in the neighborhood to see what they are doing; and discuss the percentage of increase you wish to apply to your rent schedule. If you warn him in advance, he can have a new tentative rent schedule prepared for you. Consult with your resident manager about these proposed increases. For, while you and your property manager know rental rates in terms of numbers, your resident manager knows tenants as people—input that can be quite useful.

Even though you have delegated management responsibility to a professional property manager, it takes three—you, your property manager and your resident manager—to make a successful operating team.

QUESTION: You have commented frequently on the need to tax-shelter income from investments. Aren't tax-free municipal bonds a good way to accomplish this?

ANSWER: No and yes. Generally their low yields make them unattractive to the young, aggressive investor who has not yet encountered taxation's higher levels. Long-term capital gains and depreciation on real estate are more effective ways to shelter income and usually give you a better ride for your investment dollar.

However, for older, wealthier people, not interested in the responsibilities of investment real estate or in other kinds of tax-sheltering programs, tax-free municipals offer useful benefits. Current yields of 5 to 6 percent make these municipals worth considering. For the person in the 50 percent tax bracket, these yields are equivalent to a 10 to 12 percent return on taxable income.

These bonds are issued in "bearer" form, which means that they are not generally issued or registered in the owner's name. Whoever has possession of them may "clip the coupon" and submit it to his bank or broker and receive cash in return.

If the bonds are of your municipality or state, probably their income will not have to be reported on either the federal or state income tax return. Often these bonds are kept locked up in the safe deposit boxes of sophisticated investors. When the investor dies and his safe deposit box is opened, these bonds, along with his other securities, must be included in the estate. The difference is that, since their income has not been reported on income tax statements, the Internal Revenue Service first learns of their ownership when the executor and the county treasurer's representative open the box.

For practical purposes, most salaried people on their way up will do better to shelter their income with real estate depreciation—and look for higher yields and appreciation in other kinds of securities.

QUESTION: If inflation continues to increase at a rapid rate, shouldn't I buy the things I want now, before the prices go up?

ANSWER: This is the kind of thinking prevalent in many "banana republics" in South America. It is a sure way of staying on life's treadmill. It is giving up the fight. During inflationary periods, *not* buying is the key attitude. To beat inflation, you must budget expenses, refrain from buying nonessentials, make regular deposits in a savings account. In fact, if everyone were price-resistant, more prices would be forced down to more reasonable levels.

QUESTION: Do you really believe that a single, salaried woman can be successful at wealth-building? Isn't it a man's game?

ANSWER: I not only believe, I *know* that the intelligent, ambitious woman can be successful at personal wealth-building. It is not an exclusive sport. While I am no great admirer of the trappings of the women's lib movement, I stand by many of their objectives for the equality of women—especially financial equality. There is nothing in personal wealth-building that a woman cannot do as well as (or better than) a man. And perhaps the motives are even stronger. The days of the all-male financial community are retreating quickly. Where the few barriers still exist, the woman can call on her team of experts to carry her past the rough spots. The main obstacle is a mental one—not believing you can accomplish it. Believe me. Try it. You may be surprised at how well you can do with your own personal wealth-building program—and even find yourself enjoying it.

I'll be the first to carry the banner, "Financial Freedom for Women."

QUESTION: Aren't there any quicker ways to get rich than the steps you have outlined?

ANSWER: Sure there are—hundreds of them, thousands of them. Check the shelves of your local bookstore and you'll find a selection of volumes about how to get rich quick. How many people actually got rich quick by reading them, I am not certain. Great wealth-building opportunities change from day to day. When too many people climb aboard any one get-rich bandwagon, some are bound to fall off. I have plotted a conservative middle course—one that I consider the most failure-proof, with the greatest chance for success, with the least amount of hassle and strain for the salaried person. If you want to get rich quicker, take bigger chances, go to it. It's your money and your life. I have only tried to point out to you what I see to be the opportunities and hazards of personal wealth-building. How you apply this information is really up to your personal tastes and ambitions. I suppose my overriding message is this: If you are dissatisfied with your present life and finances, don't just sit there and take it. Your prison is of your own making. Get up and get moving. Once you're into it, the ways to wealth are limitless.

16

A Summing Up

That book is good,
Which puts me in a working mood.
   —RALPH WALDO EMERSON (1803–1882) "The Poet"

I thought there might be a need for this book, for during my salaried years I met hundreds of fellow workers who handled their financial affairs poorly, without direction—living from paycheck to paycheck, never getting much ahead or far behind. I've seen good people, bright people, caught up on this treadmill to nowhere. Frequently the very people who do brilliant jobs for their employers will shed their business acumen when they set foot on their own doorsteps. This is an unnecessary, self-defeating waste of talent and ability.

I hope I've struck a responsive chord in you—that I've helped you find a way out of the salary trap. All you need is a plan—and a commitment to it. The plan is now in your hands.

I've tried to present a balanced, conservative, virtually fail-safe financial viewpoint—not from the pedestal of the professional speculator, but from the perspective of one who has been down there with you, struggling and sweating. I've earned my paychecks; I've scrimped to save; I've agonized over financial decisions; I've lost and I've won. But overall, through my commitment to a judicious financial plan, I have gained my freedom—and made an enormous amount of money in the bargain.

There is nothing to prevent you from doing as well, or better, than I have. Nothing but yourself.

The plan is simple—eight steps—with ample room for you to perfect your own, more sophisticated techniques. These basic steps are only a launching device: a way to start you on your way to financial independence and wealth. As you develop your wealth-building mentality—your investment style—undoubtedly you'll plot your own individual road map of wealth-enhancement, an expression of your unique ambitions, tastes and pleasures. That's as it should be.

Clearly, your main goal must be to achieve financial independence. As you make progress in working toward this goal, many of your secondary goals will fall naturally into place. However far you venture into the fields of financial investing, you must never stray too far from the verities— those historically validated truths which are so unchanging they could be engraved in stone. I've given you some of them.

Recognize that you have within you the power of financial success—the power of developing a winning investment mentality. Learn to appreciate the rules of the game—the realities of the economic world.

Measure your success with the annual computation of your net worth as your yardstick.

Anticipate and control your expenses. An annual budget is mandatory. In times of inflation, preserve, but do not raise, your standard of living. From every paycheck, in good times and bad, set aside the savings that will become the seeds of your prosperity.

Define attainable goals. With your eye on some specific object off in the distance, your way becomes clearer—the obstacles between, less fearsome.

Call on experts for guidance. There is not time enough

in your full life to become universally authoritative. Certainly as you reach out farther, your proficiency will grow. But when the need occurs, you will not hesitate to call in the professional.

Develop lines of financial defense through reserve funds. As with every successful business, you will create a Cash Equivalent Reserve for short-term contingencies and a Liquidity Reserve for long-term ones. These are inviolate.

Invest as an individual—not as a sheep caught up in a flock. Avoid funds, collectives and other ingenious investment devices which impinge on your financial mobility. Start your own investment fund so you don't have to pay additional commissions. Develop an investment sense and give yourself credit for being able to watch your money better than anyone else could.

Do not become an active trader—you don't have time to do it expertly. Commit to the securities markets only as vehicles for appreciation. When the clouds gather on Dow Jones peaks—run for shelter.

Recognize the values of income property as a tax shelter for today and as a wealth-builder for tomorrow.

Execute a defensive strategy to protect your family, your home, your financial well-being. Take care of business.

Anticipate realistically your retirement years—taking prudent steps now to satisfy the needs of later.

In the beginning I told you that you can beat the salary trap. I promised you that financial independence and wealth were within your reach as a salaried person—that all it required was your decision to grasp them.

The time to make that decision is now—one way or the other. Make it. The clock is ticking.

Glossary

Aggressive (investment): Where the investor assumes greater-than-average risks in the hope of greater-than-average profits on his investment.

Alienation clause: A condition included in a trust deed or mortgage which provides that if the mortgaged property is sold or transferred, the remainder of the loan (trust deed or mortgage) must be immediately paid off in full.

American Stock Exchange (AMEX): The second largest U.S. securities exchange (after the New York Stock Exchange).

Amortize: To liquidate a loan by installment payments. When a loan is fully amortized, it is paid in full.

Assets: All that you own that has a cash worth. This may include real property, obligations to you by others, and on occasions, intangibles of potential worth, such as patents, trademarks, or business goodwill. Your net worth is obtained by subtracting your liabilities (cash obligations) from your assets.

Balloon payment: Where monthly loan payments—interest plus principal—are not sufficient to amortize a loan in full by the end of its term, a final cash reconciliation is required: a lump sum payment which will fully amortize the loan.

Banker's acceptance: A draft, drawn on and accepted by a bank. A time draft (bill of exchange) on the face of which the drawee has written the word "Accepted" over his signature. The date and place payable are also indicated. The person accepting the draft is known as the "acceptor."

Bear market: When unfavorable economic conditions (or the *anticipation* of such conditions) suggest to securities traders that corporate earnings and dividends will be reduced, traders become pessimistic and the trading prices of securities, in general, drop. Thus securities investors see the prices of their securities moving lower and some of their equity being lost (at least temporarily). (The "Bull" market is the opposite condition.)

Blue chip stock: High-grade, investment-grade issue of a major, long-established company with a lengthy history of earnings growth and payment of dividends through good times and bad.

Bonds: A form of corporate borrowing in which a company offers to pay a fixed rate of interest (based on the face value of the bond), over a fixed period of time, or until called. Most corporate bonds are "debentures"—that is, they are secured by the full credit of the issuing corporation and stand first in line to be paid off, after any claims against the real property of the corporation are satisfied. Public utilities bonds are "mortgage bonds" and are secured by a lien on the real property of the utility. Thus the investor is reasonably assured that his equity will be returned to him even in case of the issuer's reorganization or bankruptcy. Bonds are usually issued in units of $1,000, but may be purchased for more or less (at a premium or a discount) depending on the interest rate offered and the financial reputation of the bond issuer.

Bonds—convertible: These offer fixed rates of interest over fixed time periods, just like any other type of bond. However, the issuer attempts to make the bond more attractive by offering a second option—that of converting the bond into a certain number of shares of the issuer's stock. This gives the investor twin benefits—the security of the bond, plus the possible appreciation of his capital should the issuer's stock price rise above the conversion ratio.

Bonds—municipal: These are issued by towns, cities, states and their various political subdivisions, and are secured by the taxing power of these entities. Their main attraction is that interest paid is free of federal taxation, and state taxation within the state where issued. Becaue of relatively low rates of interest paid, municipal bonds are purchased mainly by persons in high tax brackets where the real cash return is multiplied.

Bonds—"trash" or "junk": Where a company's financial credibility is in doubt, the trading value of their bonds may be considerably lower than their face values. Conservative investors regard these as risk investments; more aggressive investors see them as opportunities for greater appreciation and interest yield.

Broker: A middleman between the buyer and the seller. A stockbroker manages the sale and purchase of securities; a real estate broker, of real estate.

Bull market: As securities traders see favorable economic conditions for business (or *anticipate* such conditions), they become optimistic about future corporate earnings and dividends, and are willing to pay higher prices for corporate securities. This increases securities' trading worth—and the investor sees his equity in his securities appreciate. (The opposite condition is the "Bear" market.)

Capital: Any form of wealth that is capable of being used to create further wealth.

Capital gain or loss: The realized cash increase or decrease of a capital investment.

Short-term capital gain or loss: Investment capital returned to cash within less than one year (under present tax laws). Such gain is taxed as straight income; such loss may be used to reduce income tax liabilities. Short-term capital gains are taxable in the year incurred. Short-term capital losses may be carried forward indefinitely until applied to offset taxes on either short-term capital gains or any other gains subject to income tax.

Long-term capital gain or loss: The result of an investment returned to cash after more than one year (under current tax laws). For taxation purposes, long-term capital gains are divided in two and each half is subjected to a different tax rate structure. One half is treated as ordinary income. One half is subject to a "preference" tax. Under current tax law, $10,000 of the gain subject to preference tax (or one-half of regular income tax paid, whichever is greater) is tax-free.

Gains beyond this are taxed at 15 percent. Long-term capital gains or losses may be used to offset each other on a one-to-one basis. Long-term capital losses may be used to offset ordinary income on a two-to-one basis—$2 of long-term capital loss offsetting $1 of income.

Capitalization rate: Cash return on an investment, calculated as
. a percentage of the total investment. For example: if your investment is $100 and your annual return is $12, your capitalization rate is 12 percent.

Cash: Ready money in coin or paper form. A check is a form of cash transaction and may be used in lieu of cash but must be supported by cash. Credit cards may be used like cash but are not cash, they are a form of borrowing. Cash is considered the most liquid of assets. Its main frailty is that, over time, its value diminishes through inflation—that is, the same cash unit will buy fewer goods or services. This is why money-smart people keep only enough cash ready to handle immediate needs, and invest any surplus in vehicles that will offset or overcome the corrosive effects of inflation.

Cash equivalent: Any investment vehicle that guarantees the return of capital plus interest earned intact, and which is readily convertible into currency.

Cash Equivalent Reserve: A key step in any fail-safe wealth-building program. The establishment of a reserve equal to three months' expenses in a savings account, and a total equal to six months' expenses in savings accounts and cash equivalents.

Cash flow: This refers to income (cash) generated—whether by job (salary, wage, fee), or from an investment—at a certain rate. In investment, cash flow differs from appreciation in that appreciation turns into cash only when the investment is sold.

Charting: In the world of securities investment, this is the process of graphing a company's, industry's, security market's, or national economy's historical performance in the hope of gaining insight into future performance.

Collateral: A valuable asset pledged against a loan, which will be forfeited if the loan is not repaid, or which will be returned intact upon loan repayment.

Commercial paper: Notes and acceptances originating from commercial transactions (the transfer and movement of goods). These are usually notes or acceptances with a definite maturity date, which are received by a business enterprise for goods sold or services rendered.

Commodities (futures trading in): So far as futures trading is concerned, commodities are any real basic agricultural or mineral products whose prices may fluctuate over periods of time. The commodities trader buys "futures contracts" to buy or sell a commodity at some future time at a specified price. He will rarely take ownership of the commodity he has contracted for. He will "close out" (sell) the contract prior to its maturation. Usually he will margin his contract—buy it for only 10 to 20 percent cash down. Thus, any price fluctuations in the commodity will give him leveraged gains (or losses). These price fluctuations are inscrutable to all but those close to the market—so commodities trading is too risky for the average investor.

Compounding: The process whereby the profits of the investment are returned to the investment in order to earn even greater profits. While at lower levels and over brief periods of time, the results of compounding may appear insignificant, with larger amounts of investment over longer periods of time, the results can be quite spectacular.

Cyclical stocks: Issued by companies whose earnings tend to fluctuate sharply with the business cycle. They rise or fall in concert with the general economy. Machine tool and automobile manufacturers are examples.

Death taxes (estate taxes): Taxes incurred upon the estate (assets) of an individual following his death. Estates are subject to both federal and state taxation. The person who desires to pass on the maximum amount of his estate to his heirs should consult with his accountant and attorney long before his expected demise.

Debenture: A bond which is secured only by the credit of the issuer.

Defensive stocks: Issued by companies with relative stability even during adverse economic periods. The stocks of banks, utilities and food companies are included here.

Depreciation: For tax purposes, depreciation is the ability to claim the loss of value of a property through use or deterioration and to use this loss (real or assumed) as an offset to income tax liability. Depreciation is a tax postponement and remains an obligation on the property to the limit of the gain, when it is sold, and then must be settled. Tax law allows several forms and rates of depreciation. Depreciation is only allowed on improvements to property and not on the land itself.

Accelerated depreciation: Any form of depreciation that takes tax credits at a faster rate than would be realized by "straight-line" depreciation. The depreciation credits are thus higher in the early years of ownership and lower in later years.

Component depreciation: Assigning different rates of depreciation to various parts of a property, in line with their expected use-lives.

Straight-line depreciation: Depreciation calculated in equal units over the life-span of the property.

Sum-of-years-digits depreciation: A form of accelerated depreciation.

Discretionary cash: For our purposes, any amount of money from income which remains after fixed expenses have been paid.

Diversification: In investment, the spreading of investment capital across a number of investment vehicles so that the loss of any one of them will not result in catastrophic damage to the investment program. Regarding real estate, diversification applies to selecting properties in different neighborhoods for similar investment protection.

Dollars (hard and soft): In real estate, *hard dollars* are those investment dollars upon which a return is expected and measured. *Soft dollars* are those which are tax-deductible in the current year, such as dollars paid out for prepaid taxes, property rehabilitation, etc.

Dollar averaging: A technique for getting into (or out of) the securities markets without committing your investment capital too deeply all at one time.

Dollar cost averaging: A system for buying stock in which the investor decides on a fixed dollar amount he will invest in one stock each month. When the stock price is low, the amount buys more shares; when the price is high, the amount buys fewer shares. Thus, the average cost per share is reduced.

Down payment: The amount of cash required to obtain possession of a property, the remainder being borrowed.

Earnings per share: One measure of a stock's relative value. The total company earnings for the year are divided by the total number of shares in force. (Also see price/earnings ratio.)

Energy-motivated: A stock that shows a tendency to increase in price at a satisfactory rate over a period of time is said to be energy-motivated.

Equities: Common stocks.

Equity: The value of a property less any mortgage or loan or other liability against it—this is the owner's equity in the property.

Escrow: A written agreement (in certain states) in the form of a bond or a deed which is placed in the hands of a third party until the conditions of the agreement are met. A common practice in the sale and purchase of real estate.

Estate: The net worth of an individual; his various assets less his liabilities.

First trust deed (first mortgage): The terms "trust deed" and "mortgage" are nearly interchangeable, one or the other being used in different sections of the country. The "first" is the original obligation on the property. A second trust deed or mortgage must wait until the obligations of the "first" have been repaid (in the case of loan default) before any chance of recovery. Trust deeds and mortgages are secured by the property itself and the down payment (and any subsequent payments) by the borrower.

Fixed expenses: These are items of expense over which the person has relatively little control, such as rent, ultilities, car payments, taxes, etc. These are opposed to discretionary expenses. The line between the two is not always clear.

Good 'til canceled. An instruction given to your stockbroker for the purchase or sale of a stock which will remain in effect until the transaction has been accomplished or you issue another instruction to cancel the first.

Gross income: The sum of all sources of income before deductions of any kind.

Gross multiplier: A real estate term applied as a measure of the value of a property with an eye to its purchase. The asking price of the property is divided by its gross rental income for the prior year to achieve its gross multiplier.

Improvements (to land): For investment purposes, any structures built upon land which are income-producing are considered improvements and so may be depreciated to reduce income tax liability.

Inflation: An increase in the money supply which tends to increase prices with the result that a unit of money will buy less real goods than it could at a prior time. This historic trend of currency is that its value will continue to decrease in relation to real goods. Inflation is a permanent fact of money.

Interest: The charge made for borrowing a sum of money, usually stated as a percentage of the sum, per year.

Invest: To commit money or capital to some enterprise in which there is hopes for the return of a profit (as well as the original capital).

Investment grade (securities): The securities of companies which have earned a favorable financial reputation over an extended period of time and therefore are considered to be less risky than other, similar securities. Stocks are regarded as "investment grade" when they are rated by Standard & Poor's at A— or better. Bonds rated BBB or better are "investment grade."

Investor: A person who commits his capital to some venture which he expects will yield him a profit.

I.R.A. (Individual Retirement Account): A tax-favored retirement program for persons not covered by qualified company or government retirement programs.

Keogh Act (HR-10 plans): Tax-sheltered retirement plans for self-employed individuals.

Leverage: An investment technique for using borrowed money to make a lesser amount of capital accomplish the purposes of more. This strategy is used in real estate investments and in buying stocks or bonds on margin, for two examples.

Liabilities: In money matters, these are financial obligations, whether actual or potential.

Liquid asset funds: See "Money market funds."

Liquidity: The ability of an asset to be turned quickly into cash without undue penalty. Also describes the ratio of liquid assets to nonliquid assets.

Liquidity Reserve: The second-stage reserve (after your Cash Equivalent Reserve) in your wealth-building program. It is made up of investment-grade stocks and bonds, neither margined nor pledged for loans. It should equal 5 percent of your net worth, minimum.

Margin (buying on): A technique of gaining leverage for your investment capital by borrowing. The margin is the amount of equity in the margin account. A margin call occurs when the ratio of equity to borrowed money falls below minimum margin requirements—the investor must either add equity or cash out the investment.

Money market funds (liquid asset funds): Mutual funds that limit their investments to cash equivalents, which makes them quite safe although their potential for appreciation is less than with other types of mutual funds.

Mortgage: Similar to trust deed.

Mortgage broker: The middleman between an aspiring borrower and a lending institution.

Multiples (stock): The selling price of a stock divided by its earnings per share. The stocks with lower multiples have a higher ratio of earnings to price.

Municipal bonds: See "Bonds."

Mutual funds: The collective pooling of investment capital by a number of investors into a fund which is under the management of a group of investment specialists.

N.A.S.D.: National Association of Securities Dealers—a semi-formalized organization for securities trading. Also called the "over-the-counter" exchange. The requirements for trading on this exchange are less strict than for the other two.

Net asset value per share: One measure of a stock's worth. The number is derived by dividing the net assets of the company by the total number of shares outstanding.

Net worth: A measure of wealth. Obtained by subtracting total liabilities from total assets.

New York Stock Exchange: Also called "The Big Board." The largest and oldest stock exchange.

Odd lot: Shares of stock that are purchased in other than batches of 100 shares. (Also see Round lot.)

Optional Investment Fund: Step 7 in your personal wealth-building progarm. A self-developed fund in which you are allowed a fairly wide latitude in selecting investment opportunities.

Options: Agreements to buy or sell stocks at fixed prices within fixed time limits. It is another form of leveraged investing with wide swings between potential profit and loss.

Over-the-counter: See "N.A.S.D."

Paper profit: A profit that is only apparent on paper and will not be realized (turned into an actual profit) until the investment is cashed in.

Pledging: When valuable items (stocks or bonds, for example) are turned over to a lending institution as collateral for a loan, they are said to be "pledged" against the loan.

Points: It is the current practice of lending institutions, when making a loan for real estate purchase, to charge "points," or percentage points of the total amount borrowed, as an up-front, one-time charge for agreeing to give the loan. For example: if you are asking for a mortgage loan of $100,000, it would not be unusual to be charged 3 "points" (3 percent of $100,000, or $3,000) at the outset in order to obtain the loan. Points are exclusive of, and in addition to, the declared loan interest. A form of prepaid interest. Once points were tax-deductible in the year incurred. Since the Tax Reform Act of 1976, tax deductions for points must be spread out over a period of years. Consult your tax account for exact conditions.

Preference income: For our purposes, this consists mainly of one-half of long-term capital gains income. The tax exemption for preference income is currently $10,000 or one half the taxpayer's regular income tax, whichever is greater. Amounts beyond this are taxed at 15 percent. Preference tax must be paid and cannot be sheltered.

Price/earnings ratio: This is one measure of stock value, probably the one most used. The figure is derived by dividing the price of the stock by its most recent annual earnings per share.

Principal: The capital of a financial holding as distinguished from the interest paid or the earnings derived from it. Usually a loan is repaid in even payments with part assigned to interest and part assigned to principal repayment. As you pay down on a loan, your principal grows because a portion of your loan is being repaid.

Real Estate Investment Trusts (REITs): Similar to closed-end mutual funds in that the organization is professionally managed and capital is derived from a pool of investors; profits are shared by the investors, but not the liabilities. However, the investor enjoys no tax-sheltering as in individual or partner ownership. So some of the main benefits of owning real estate are lost.

Realized profit: A profit is realized (becomes an actuality) when the investment is sold and the paper profit is converted into cash.

Recession: A period of business decline caused by adverse economic conditions. Generally a poor time for speculative investing.

Rent control: A limit a municipality places on the amount of rent an apartment house owner can charge his tenants; often imposed without regard for the economic necessities of the marketplace.

Rerent rate: The technique of deciding in advance the rate at which a given apartment unit should be rented should the current tenant vacate.

Residential income property: Real property which offers living accommodations for rent on a continuing basis—apartment units, for example.

Return (on investment): The sum of all profits derived from an investment. May include interest, cash payments, increase of equity, tax benefits, etc.

Risk: The potential loss of capital in an investment.

Round lot (of stocks): 100 shares of stock.

Second trust deed (second mortgage): See "First trust deed."

Securities: Stocks and bonds.

Security deposits: A charge to new tenants, held until they vacate the rental unit, as security against excess damage to the premises which the tenant might cause. Where the tenant leaves the apartment units in reasonable condition, the deposit is returned to him.

Share (of stock): A single unit of a company's stock issue.

Shelter: See "Tax Shelter."

Speculative grade (securities): Stocks or bonds issued by companies whose financial performance is in doubt, whether because the company is new and has no record of financial integrity or because of a history (or expectation) of financial distress.

Splits (stock): When a company decides that a share of its stock has risen to such a high price that the market for it is reduced, the company may choose to divide the share into lower-priced units. Although the shareholder will now own more shares, their total value will be roughly equivalent to his previous holdings.

Stocks: These are ownership equities in a corporation, allowing you to enjoy some of the profits and share some of the risks. Stocks are traded on exchanges and so their prices may vary from day to day, depending on their desirability and economic conditions. A stock may or may not pay a dividend. Generally a stock is purchased for its appreciation potential—that is, the hope that it will increase in price and so create a profit when it is sold.

Common stock: The vast majority of all stock issued is common. It is secured by no real assets of the corporation, but it does include certain voting rights on corporate matters.

Preferred stock: These stocks occupy a kind of middle ground between bonds and common stocks. They offer no voting rights. Usually they promise a fixed rate of dividend, although the dividend may not be paid. However, no dividends may be issued to common stockholders until the requirements of the preferred stockholders have been satisfied.

Syndication (real estate): See "Real estate investment trusts."

Tax shelter: An investment which provides tax protection for ordinary income. A tax shelter is usually desirable only if it is also a sound investment on its own merit.

Time certificates of deposit: A bank deposit that pays a fixed rate of interest but is not withdrawable until its termination date.

Trader: In securities markets, any person who trades in stocks or bonds. Also applied specifically to the person who trades frequently to gain a few dollars per share in the spread between his buying price and his selling price.

Trade up or even: A real estate transaction which is not deemed an outright sale even though property ownership changes hands—thus postponing tax liabilites on capital gains or depreciation taken.

Treasury bills: The Treasury offers two issues of bills each week, one to mature in three months and one to mature in six months. Minimum denominations are $10,000. These bills are bought at discount through bidding and are redeemed at full face value upon maturation. Each month the Treasury also markets series of bills with nine-month and one-year maturation dates. These are purchased and redeemed in the same manner as the shorter-term bills.

Treasury bonds: The government's major form of borrowing. These bonds mature in more than seven years, although because there is an active market for them, they can be sold (but not redeemed) prior to maturation.

Treasury notes: These have maturities of from one to seven years. Interest is paid semiannually.

Trust: A fiduciary arrangement involving three parties: the grantor or creator of the trust, who supplies the cash or assets; the trustee, who assumes legal title to the assets and manages them until the trust has fulfilled its purpose and is dissolved; and the beneficiary, who is to benefit from the trust. A trust may offer tax advantages, the benefits of professional management, or the protection of the beneficiary. A trust is frequently used as a method of transfer of assets to heirs.

Unimproved property: Any piece of real estate which contains no structures that may be depreciated. A farm with no buildings on it is considered unimproved even though it may create a profit for the owner.

Vacancy factor: The percentage that the gross scheduled rental of an apartment house might be reduced due to vacancy.

Wash transaction: When an investor sells a property and buys it back again within thirty days, it is considered by the Internal Revenue Service to be a "wash"—that is, no sale has taken place. Thus, if an investor sells a property near the end of a tax year to incur a capital loss (and so shelter a capital gain), and buys it back too quickly the next year (because he believes it a good investment), the IRS will not allow the capital loss.

Will: A legal document in which a person declares how he wishes his estate to be disposed of following his death.

Wraparound financing: The purpose of this method of financing is to purchase a property while retaining the original loan, with its favorable rate of interest. A second loan is obtained to "wrap around" the first. Payments on both loans are made to the second lender, who takes his share and makes a payment to the first lender. The new owner pays a lower rate of interest overall.

Yield: The annual rate of return from an investment.

Index